Contextualizing English for Academic Purposes in Higher Education

New Perspectives for English for Academic Purposes

Series editors
Alex Ding, Ian Bruce and Melinda Whong

This series sets the agenda for studies in English for Academic Purposes (EAP) by opening up research and scholarship to new domains, ideas and perspectives as well as giving a platform to emerging and established practitioners and researchers in the field.

The volumes in this series are innovative in that they broaden the scope of theoretical and practical interests in EAP by focusing on neglected or new areas of interest, to provide the EAP community with a deeper understanding of some of the key issues in teaching EAP across the world and in diverse contexts.

Also available in this series
What is Good Academic Writing?, edited by Melinda Whong and Jeanne Godfrey
Pedagogies in English for Academic Purposes, edited by Carole MacDiarmid and Jennifer J. MacDonald
Social Theory for English for Academic Purposes, edited by Alex Ding and Michelle Evans

Forthcoming in the series
Practitioner Agency and Identity in English for Academic Purposes, edited by Alex Ding and Laetitia Monbec
Linguistic Approaches in English for Academic Purposes, edited by Milada Walková

Contextualizing English for Academic Purposes in Higher Education

Politics, Policies and Practices

Edited by
Ian Bruce and Bee Bond

BLOOMSBURY ACADEMIC
LONDON · NEW YORK · OXFORD · NEW DELHI · SYDNEY

BLOOMSBURY ACADEMIC
Bloomsbury Publishing Plc
50 Bedford Square, London, WC1B 3DP, UK
1385 Broadway, New York, NY 10018, USA
29 Earlsfort Terrace, Dublin 2, Ireland

BLOOMSBURY, BLOOMSBURY ACADEMIC and the Diana logo are trademarks of Bloomsbury Publishing Plc

First published in Great Britain 2022
Paperback edition published 2024

Copyright © Ian Bruce and Bee Bond and contributors, 2022

Ian Bruce and Bee Bond and contributors have asserted their right under the Copyright, Designs and Patents Act, 1988, to be identified as Authors of this work.

Cover design: Charlotte James
Cover image © Tuomas Lehtinen/ Getty Images

All rights reserved. No part of this publication may be reproduced or transmitted in any form or by any means, electronic or mechanical, including photocopying, recording, or any information storage or retrieval system, without prior permission in writing from the publishers.

Bloomsbury Publishing Plc does not have any control over, or responsibility for, any third-party websites referred to or in this book. All internet addresses given in this book were correct at the time of going to press. The author and publisher regret any inconvenience caused if addresses have changed or sites have ceased to exist, but can accept no responsibility for any such changes.

A catalogue record for this book is available from the British Library.

A catalog record for this book is available from the Library of Congress.

ISBN: HB: 978-1-3502-3045-3
PB: 978-1-3502-3049-1
ePDF: 978-1-3502-3046-0
eBook: 978-1-3502-3047-7

Series: New Perspectives for English for Academic Purposes

Typeset by Newgen KnowledgeWorks Pvt. Ltd., Chennai, India

To find out more about our authors and books visit www.bloomsbury.com and sign up for our newsletters.

For all the EAP students and practitioners who are studying, working and living under precarious conditions.

Contents

List of Illustrations ix
List of Contributors x
Preface xii
Series Editors' Foreword xiv

Introduction 1

Part I Larger Contextual Influences on Contemporary Higher Education

1 Universities in the Twenty-First Century: Structures, Funding, Management and Governance 9
   Ian Bruce
2 The Ideologies and Practices of Internationalization within Universities 27
   Jenna Mittelmeier and Bowen Zhang
3 The Economics, Ethics and Discourse of Recruiting International Students 45
   Sylvie Lomer and Ying Yang

Part II Issues Relating to International Students and English Language

4 International Students, Gatekeeping Tests and a Model of EAP Provision 71
   Neil Murray
5 Proofreading in a UK University Writing Centre: Perspectives and Practices 87
   Chang Liu and Nigel Harwood
6 The Positioning and Purpose of EAP across the University Curriculum: Highlighting Language in Curriculum Policies 109
   Bee Bond

Part III EAP Programmes: Conceptualization, Organization and Delivery

7 The Differing Discursive Constructions of EAP within the University: Contrasting Institutional and Language Centre Perspectives   131
   Jennifer J. MacDonald

8 Perspectives on Directing an EAP Centre   149
   Richard Simpson

9 The Predicament of PEAPPs: Practitioners of EAP in Precarity   165
   Michèle le Roux

Part IV Collective Organization and Positioning of EAP and the Future

10 Association: Power, Politics and Policy   183
   Alex Ding and Ian Bruce

11 Final Reflections: Key Themes and Future Landscapes   203
   Ian Bruce and Bee Bond

Index   215

Illustrations

Figures

5.1   Excerpt from Cici's writing   96
6.1   The 5Cs principles for an EAP curriculum   116

Table

8.1   Pre-sessional Programme Durations   154

Contributors

Bee Bond is Associate Professor of EAP at the University of Leeds, UK. She is the author of *Making Language Visible in the University: English for Academic Purposes and Internationalisation* (2020).

Ian Bruce is Senior Lecturer in Applied Linguistics at the University of Waikato, Hamilton, New Zealand. His research involves the application of genre theory to the teaching of academic writing, and his most recent book is *Expressing Critical Thinking through Disciplinary Texts* (2020).

Alex Ding is Director of Scholarship in the School of Languages, Cultures and Societies and Associate Professor of EAP at the University of Leeds, UK. He is currently co-editing a volume entitled *Social Theory for English for Academic Purposes: Foundations and Perspectives* and co-authored with Ian Bruce *The English for Academic Purposes Practitioner: Operating on the Edge of Academia* (2017).

Nigel Harwood is Professor of Applied Linguistics at the University of Sheffield, UK. He has published articles on EAP, ESP and academic writing in various journals, including *Journal of Second Language Writing*, *Written Communication*, *Journal of Pragmatics*, *Studies in Higher Education* and *Journal of English for Academic Purposes*.

Chang Liu has recently completed her PhD at the University of Sheffield, UK. She is now Lecturer and Executive Director of the writing centre at the School of Foreign Studies, Capital University of Economics and Business, China. Her research interests include writing centres, Chinese international students and academic writing and tutoring.

Sylvie Lomer is Senior Lecturer in Policy and Practice at the University of Manchester, Institute of Education, UK. Her research interests focus on international higher education, specifically the policies, pedagogies and recruitment practices relating to international students in the UK.

Jennifer J. MacDonald is Director of the Department of English Language Studies at Dalhousie University, Canada, where she leads a variety of programs in EAP, professional development in language education and internationalization of the curriculum. She researches, publishes and presents on topics at the intersection between critical applied linguistics, internationalization of higher education and EAP. Her most recent research tackles the challenges of language policies, politics and pedagogy in the linguistically diverse context of internationalized Canadian higher education.

Jenna Mittelmeier is Lecturer in International Education at the University of Manchester, UK. Her research focuses on the internationalization of higher education, particularly the ways that pedagogies and curricula are shaped by teaching international students. She is also Research-in-Context Editor for *Journal of International Students*.

Neil Murray is Professor of Applied Linguistics and Director of Short Courses at the University of Warwick, UK. His research interests include English language policy in higher education, academic literacy, EMI and language assessment. He has published widely and is author of *Standards of English in Higher Education* (2015) and co-editor, with Angela Scarino, of *Dynamic Ecologies: A Relational Perspective on Languages Education in the Asia Pacific Region* (2014).

Michèle le Roux is Course Leader at the University of Bath, UK, and teaches on EAP and MATESOL programmes. She is also a practitioner of circles of trust, spiritual accompaniment and non-violent communication. She seeks to position herself with integrity at the interface of these professional identities and to build bridges, resilience and community.

Richard Simpson gained a BEd in Northampton, UK and spent a sabbatical year there as president of the students union. He taught English in Italy and Japan before taking an MA and teaching at the University of Newcastle, UK. Richard joined the English Language Teaching Centre (ELTC) at the University of Sheffield, UK, in 1995 and has been Director of ELTC since 2007. He is also a part-time doctoral student in the School of Education.

Ying Yang is a doctoral researcher in the Manchester Institute of Education at the University of Manchester, UK. Her research interests focus on internationalization of higher education, international students' motivations, mobilities and experiences, as well as international student recruitment.

Bowen Zhang is a PhD candidate in Education at the University of Manchester, UK. Her research is broadly situated in transnational higher education in China, with a particular focus on the epistemological exchange between Chinese and Western universities through forming educational partnerships throughout history.

Preface

As editors of this volume in the series, neither of us claims to be an expert on all aspects of the politics, policies and practices that shape EAP. However, it is precisely this lacuna across research and scholarship in EAP that we hope that this volume will begin to address. We chose to work on this book because we believe that there is a need for those of us working in EAP within universities and other contexts to have a better understanding of the influences and decisions made by others that shape our working lives. Bringing together our collective knowledge and experiences – of research, scholarship, practice and leadership – we hope that we are making a contribution to the field and to our understandings in this area.

In recent years, the books by Greg Hadley and by Alex Ding and Ian Bruce have begun to highlight the larger social and political issues that surround our work. In this volume, we explore these issues further, but, rather than focusing specifically on the practitioner, we want to address issues that affect the practitioner and their wider working environment. We feel that it is time for EAP to explore far more explicitly the politics and policies that have an impact on and influence over its practices. We also need to become more overtly political in our own practices and work to understand where we can begin to exert an influence over policies that impact us and the students we teach.

The book has been developed over an eighteen-month period, from contacting our contributors and working on a proposal through to submitting the final manuscript. The challenges in getting the book together have been the normal ones of deadlines and coordinating with our chapter contributors, whilst continuing to teach, fulfil administrative roles and adapt to the shifting sands of our governments' and institutions' responses to the global pandemic. Collaborating across the time zones of New Zealand and the UK has not felt as difficult to manage as the envy on both sides as one of us moved into and the other out of some form of lockdown! Given the extra stresses that this period of world history has entailed, we are delighted that we were able to keep within our initial deadlines. This is largely due to the diligence, responsiveness and professionalism of those who have contributed to this volume, for which we are extremely grateful.

In putting the book together, we made a deliberate plan to start with chapters that have a broad focus on the larger forces around EAP and then move to the chapters that examine the issues more closely within the context of EAP. As a result, the process was a little more planned and deliberate than is often the case with edited books. To implement our plan, we approached specific writers who have previously researched and written about the areas that we wanted to cover. In that way, our hope is that the chapters dovetail together and help build up a clear picture drawn from the range of expertise that this volume represents.

However, we also acknowledge that this picture remains a sketch or an outline. A number of the chapters draw on the personal experience and reflections of the author and are context specific. We accept, therefore, that this may not be representative of the experience or context of others in a similar position. We also accept that there are many other political issues that are either underexplored or fully absent from the volume. In that sense, we hope that this book is the beginning of a deeper, wider and ongoing exploration of the politics, policies and practices that inform and impact on EAP. This is the beginning of the conversation.

Series Editors' Foreword

The main purpose of this series is to provide new perspectives on English for Academic Purposes for the field and its practitioners and researchers. We were motivated to extend and deepen the knowledge-base of EAP for practitioners and researchers because we felt that key facets of EAP remained under-represented, neglected or marginalized to the detriment of the field and of practitioners being able to discuss or investigate the full complexity of EAP. The traditional focus on language, text and discourse in EAP has not been accompanied by an equivalent interest in the material, worldly, enmeshed and complex roles, enactments and challenges that practitioners face in their professional lives. In short, politics and policies, the focus of this volume, impact the lives of practitioners and their students and, as such, deserve our attention not only to better understand the impact of politics and policies but also, as is argued by the editors, to become more political to exert better influence over the policies that shape our practices and the education of our students.

In a way, this volume is a paradox; as you read through the table of contents you will notice familiar themes, including internationalization, proofreading, assessment, directing a centre, precarity and so on. All of these and other themes in this volume are part of the everyday discussions of many practitioners in meetings, conference breaks, staff rooms and other fora. They are part of the everyday interests and concerns of those enmeshed in the everyday politics of EAP. Yet these and other political issues generally only receive fragmented attention in the field. The strength of this volume is bringing together in a coherent structure many of the central political and policy related strands that impact practice. This volume enables us, practitioners and researchers, for the first time in one volume to have a clear overview of what is of concern and what is at stake in the field of EAP.

This volume, rather than signalling a definitive answer to the many ways that policy and politics shape EAP, should, as with all the other volumes in this series, be seen as a beginning, a starting point for further development and extension by others in the field. It is a motivation to open up rather than close down neglected areas of concern to EAP that has driven us to develop this series. We welcome critique and questioning of the chapters here and elsewhere if it drives readers to contribute their own scholarship to developing or extending or providing fresh perspectives on ideas discussed here and elsewhere.

Underpinning this volume, throughout either explicitly or implicitly, is a search or desire for a more ethical EAP. The ethics of EAP remains for the field and its practitioners a source of disquiet and concern, and if this volume can contribute to a more public, more inclusive and more concerted discussion of the ethics of EAP then the volume can be considered a success.

Alex Ding on behalf of the series editors

Introduction

English for Academic Purposes (EAP) courses are taught worldwide within universities and English language centres to meet the demand from students from diverse educational and language backgrounds for academic language and literacy skills courses in order to participate in English-medium higher education, undertake research and advanced technological development. The field of EAP has developed rapidly over approximately four decades as the result of a number of global events that have led to the rise of English as a global lingua franca. This rapid growth of EAP has occurred within the current business-focused, neoliberal context of higher education in anglophone countries and elsewhere. However, within this context, EAP practitioners and their organizations have tended to remain apolitical, and to focus centrally on matters relating to curriculum, pedagogy and students. Theorists who have encouraged EAP practitioners towards taking a more political position in their teaching practice have included, inter alia, Critical EAP, Critical Applied Linguistics, English as a lingua franca and there have been attempts to connect the work of academic literacies with EAP. Most recently, a group of practitioners has been seeking to connect EAP with social justice movements. However, in the main, the activity of the teaching of academic English to international students is still presented as a transparent educational activity, lacking in political, economic or social context, with meaning-making being connected only to academic subject disciplines. Thus, EAP practice is seen by many merely as a neutral, bridging activity, as a means of socializing students into the academic status quo – whatever that may be.

In responding to the mostly apolitical and neutral focus of EAP, the overarching aim of this book is to emphasize the importance of politics and policies as they relate to the positioning and practice of EAP. The contributions of the different writers in the volume are evidence for the position that EAP cannot flourish as a profession or a discipline without an awareness of the macro- and meso-level political shifts that impact the wider university. Their contributions suggest that it is necessary for EAP practitioners to engage fully in the politics and policy-making of higher education institutions (the meso-level) as well as for their associations to engage with and advocate at the more macro-level of governmental policy change. The volume also suggests that the practices of EAP are, in fact, political acts and are, therefore, imbued with, as yet unexplored, power dynamics.

Since the terms 'politics' and 'policies' are used in the title of this volume and relate to concepts that are central to all of its chapters, it is important that we define these framing terms. In outlining what we refer to in this volume as 'politics', we draw on the ideas of Pennycook (2021), who suggests that politics relates to questions of the workings of power, not just in formal political domains, but they also relate to 'power as operating through all domains of life' (44). Pennycook suggests that critical applied linguistics (including EAP) 'needs ways of understanding how power operates on and through people in the ongoing tasks of teaching, learning languages, translating, talking in the workplace' (45). Therefore, when we refer to politics here, we are, like Pennycook 'addressing questions of power' (46) as they relate to the field of EAP at all levels, including the societies and institutions where EAP is taught, the administration and management of EAP, EAP practitioners and, importantly, the admission and teaching of students of EAP.

Power and its outworking influence and shape the *policies* that regulate the day-to-day organization and practice of EAP. In defining this adjunct term of 'policies', we draw on the definition of Shohamy (2003), who, when referring to the field of language policies, states that 'policies' 'refers to the *decisions* that people make about languages and their use in society' (279, emphasis added). Here we suggest that 'policies' refers to the decisions that people make relating to the field of EAP, and that these decisions then translate into formalized procedures and processes that regulate practice in EAP. As the basis for proceduralized ways of thinking and acting in the field, the policies that govern EAP are often left unquestioned or uninterrogated and, in particular, the operations of power behind the policies are largely ignored.

In addressing these issues, the chapters of this volume provide an overview of economic, political and sociological perspectives on the policies and politics that influence the organization and delivery of EAP. The chapters are organized into four parts: the larger contextual influences on contemporary Higher Education (HE), issues relating to students and English language, the organization and delivery of EAP programmes and the collective structuring and positioning of EAP and the future.

Part 1: Larger Contextual Influences on Contemporary Higher Education (Chapters 1–3)

In Part 1, three chapters address the macro-level, economic, political and social policies and practices of governments that have shaped contemporary higher education in the past three decades, including EAP. Chapter 1 by Ian Bruce discusses key external governmental and societal influences on universities, including their governance and management and how these relate to the role and practice of EAP. Specifically, these external influences include neoliberal economic policies, governmental demands for widening participation, globalization, entrepreneurial approaches to higher education and the effects of competitive marketization on staff and student roles. In Chapter 2, Jenna Mittelmeier and Bowen Zhang address the policies pursued by universities relating to the much-vaunted concept of internationalization. They discuss how the concept of internationalization is defined, how it shapes current universities' approaches to international students and to EAP and the role of English in facilitating internationalization. The authors raise four important questions for EAP and EAP practitioners in relation to current internationalization policies and practices within universities. Then, further building on the ideology and rhetoric around internationalization, Sylvie Lomer and Ying Yang, in Chapter 3, address the issue of recruitment of international students as a central element in the financialization of universities. In relation to this commercially driven activity, they address the multiple ethical dilemmas of equity, inclusivity and fairness, and they examine the triangular relationships between universities, their agents and international students

Part 2: Issues Relating to International Students and English Language (Chapters 4–6)

The chapters in Part 2 provide an in-depth discussion of important issues that relate to the development of the academic English language competence of international students. In Chapter 4, Neil Murray uncovers and addresses issues relating to the alignment (or possible misalignment) between the English language standards of tests used to screen and admit international students to universities and the actual academic language needs of the students, which the tests ostensibly operationalize. Subsequent to this discussion of the measurement issues of English entry tests, Neil then outlines a model for academic language and skills preparation and support that appropriately addresses the actual language needs of students in disciplinary contexts. In addressing further the English language struggles of international students, Chang Liu and Nigel Harwood, in Chapter 5, raise issues relating to student assignment writing and writing centre support by reporting an empirical study that exposes the tension faced by writing centre staff of providing support for student writing, but not providing proofreading or actual editing of students' work although they are under constant pressure to do this. Continuing the discussion of the ongoing needs of international students and English language, Bee Bond in Chapter 6 provides a detailed discussion of role of language and international students' language needs across the university and the ways in which EAP courses and support may be empowered and best placed within the university to address the issues. Bee argues for a more visible, activist EAP that engages with university policies and administrative practices and that is involved with student language support well beyond the traditional pre-sessional preparation and in-sessional repair workshops.

Part 3: EAP Programmes: Conceptualization, Organization and Delivery (Chapters 7–9)

The three chapters of Part 3 turn the focus of the volume onto actual EAP language centres, their ambivalent location within universities, their portrayal, management and employment practices. In Chapter 7, Jennifer MacDonald examines the policy document and website framings of the roles of English language centres within Canadian universities. She highlights the institutional portrayal of English language centres that offer EAP courses as primarily contributing to the marketing and recruitment of international students for the university, while the English language centres portray themselves and their language work via their websites as sites for academic preparation, transformative learning and cultural exchange. This chapter is an examination of the contrasts and paradoxes at play within the Canadian higher education under neoliberalism, where the English language, EAP and language work have become both commodified and marginalized practices. In further considering some of the tensions described in Jennifer's chapter, Richard Simpson in Chapter 8 provides a descriptive account of the issues and tensions that arise for those managing a university EAP centre within a university, including the potential conflict between institutional demands for quantity and quality of students through its provision of pre-sessional and in-sessional teaching along with the professional activities of managing teacher training, language assessment, technology enhanced learning, online delivery and continuing professional development. In particular, the challenges of managing these areas of work in the context of marketization and massification will be considered. Finally in Part 3, Chapter 9 by Michèle le Roux will focus on the positioning and identity of those EAP practitioners who actually deliver EAP courses under the conditions of precarious employment – a group that she terms 'practitioners of EAP in precarity' (PEAPPs). Michèle examines this employment issue in EAP in terms of its effects on practitioners both professionally and psychologically, and explores a range of possible responses to the PEAPPs predicament by both practitioners themselves and EAP associations.

Part 4: Collective Organization and Positioning of EAP and the Future (Chapters 10 and 11)

In Part 4, two final chapters outline proposals for how the EAP community may begin to consider and collectively respond to many of the issues raised in the earlier chapters of this volume. In Chapter 10, Alex Ding and Ian Bruce discuss EAP associations, their traditional roles. They make the case for a more self-conscious, reflexive, critical and politically and publicly engaged understanding of association that reflects the values and roles of professional bodies. They advocate widening the scope of the concerns of EAP associations to include policy positions and engagement with issues such as the governance and management of EAP units, university policies relating to international students, the privatization and outsourcing of EAP units and a more holistic approach to ethical and social concerns relating to practice. Finally, in Chapter 11, the editors draw together many of the thoughts and arguments of the preceding chapters as they consider the future direction and form of EAP in the context of the contemporary social, economic, political and epidemiological challenges that currently impact on higher education and on EAP within higher education.

References

Pennycook, A. (2021), *Critical Applied Linguistics: A Critical Re-introduction* (2nd edn), New York: Routledge. https://doi.org/10.4324/9781003090571.

Shohamy, E. (2003). 'Implications of Language Education Policies for Language Study in Schools and Universities', *Modern Language Journal*, 87 (2): 278–86.

Part 1

Larger Contextual Influences on Contemporary Higher Education

1

Universities in the Twenty-First Century: Structures, Funding, Management and Governance

Ian Bruce

Motivation for This Chapter

During the last decades of the twentieth century and the first two decades of the twenty-first century, English for Academic Purposes (EAP) emerged as probably the most academically and economically important development in global language teaching, this development being a consequence of the rise of English as the world lingua franca over a fifty-year period. Much of the rise of English can be attributed to the push factors of the emergence of the United States as the sole world superpower during much of this period, the demise of the Soviet Union (and its hegemony over Eastern European and Central Asian states) along with the rising use of English within the European Union. Also during this time, English has increasingly become the language of international business, research publication, transportation and logistics. However, without diminishing the importance of these push factors, almost as important for this rise of English have been the 'pull' factors of the rapid economic development of the BRICS countries (Brazil, Russia, India, China and South Africa) and of the MINT countries (Mexico, Indonesia, Nigeria and Turkey). Within these states, the arrival of rapid economic development, technology and mobility have led to the emergence of a middle class that places a high premium on university education, usually a university education in the dominant world language – undertaken in English as a medium of instruction (EMI) institutions. Students from these states either travel abroad to undertake this type of education in the UK, North America or Australasia, or undertake it in an English-medium university in their own country.

Supported by these economic, linguistic and educational developments during this time period, EAP has developed in order to facilitate entry into, and passage through, English-medium university education for large numbers of students around the world. EAP has been defined as 'the teaching of English with the specific aim of helping learners to study, conduct research or teach in that language' (Flowerdew and Peacock, 2001: 8). EAP has become a globalized subfield of language education with its own journals, conferences, professional organizations and a rapid growth in research and academic publication to support the field. EAP practitioners have often trained as teachers of general English language and tend to be employed within universities on teaching-only contracts, although this is changing with increasing numbers engaged in the scholarship of teaching and learning (SoTL) and research activities. The scholarship and research of EAP largely focuses on the pedagogic and curricular needs of the field and particularly on the academic literacy requirements of specific disciplines that EAP students are preparing to enter or are already trying to navigate their way through.

In the *Competency Framework for Teachers of English for Academic Purposes* (CFTEAP), developed by the UK EAP practitioners' organization BALEAP, the first competency states that 'an EAP teacher will have a reasonable knowledge of the organizational, educational and communicative policies, practices values and conventions of universities' (BALEAP, 2008: 4). While the CFTEAP document mainly focuses on the curricular and pedagogic elements of these policies, practices and values, the chapters of this volume examine aspects of the broader context of higher education within which EAP occurs.

To begin this exploration, this chapter briefly traces the origins of the modern Western university. It then provides a macro-level overview of the political, economic and institutional influences on universities in the twenty-first century, aiming to make explicit how these influences shape their organizational structures, funding models, management and governance, primarily focusing on universities in the English-speaking world. Following this, the chapter then considers how these elements influence teaching, research processes, employment practices and staff–student relationships. EAP units and their practitioners are a central element in the recruitment, preparation and orientation of international students in universities. It is, therefore, the goal of the chapter to make explicit the larger forces that endow EAP with these central roles.

The Changing Idea of a University

Within the past two decades, a considerable literature has developed charting and often decrying what is seen as the transformation of universities in many contexts from ostensibly liberal humanist institutions dedicated to the advancement of knowledge and its dissemination into commodified, business enterprises (see e.g. Connell, 2019; Fleming, 2021; Giroux, 2014). As a basis for considering this ongoing concern, I briefly review the traditional roles and ethos of Western universities and consider the changes that have occurred over historical periods and in the more recent past.

Universities were first established in Europe during the later middle ages (1100–1500) and were oriented towards teaching and the learned professions of priest, lawyer, physician, administrator and clerk. According to Chaplin (1977), the major philosophical goal of the medieval university was 'the pursuit of [divine] truth and learning' (3208). The methods of enquiry of scholars of this period have been often described (sometimes pejoratively) as *scholasticism*, which de Wulf (2003) describes as 'arriving at ... verbal or real definitions' (11) through the applications of certain types of logic or dialectic. Universities were organized like medieval guilds, whose members were both teachers and students. They had legal charters from the church to grant degrees, and were semi-autonomous and self-governing. However, during the period of the development of the modern nation state (1500–1800), 'the relative autonomy of universities was eroded' (Scott, 2006: 10). During that era, they came more under the authority of more powerful national governments, which were in most cases absolute monarchies, and were co-opted into the nation-building projects of the monarchs of this era. Yet, as Ridder-Symoens (1996) notes, despite the growing power of the nation state, universities still retained a measure of independence because of the logistical limitations around state power at the time and the traditional rights and privileges that many retained as a hangover from the medieval period. During this period, humanism replaced medieval scholasticism, leading to the *Scientific Revolution* and the *Enlightenment* of the seventeenth and eighteenth centuries respectively.

Building on the long history of European universities through the medieval and Enlightenment eras, the institution of the modern university as we know it emerged during the past two centuries. The ideas and values attached to conceptualizing universities during this era have been often closely identified with the plans of von Humboldt for the University of Berlin, founded in 1809, and the ideas in Cardinal John Newman's (2008) 1856 book *The Idea of a University*. Newman saw universities as places that provided a rounded humanist education, with knowledge as an end in itself and learning a lifelong process. Newman's idea was that of a student's personal growth and development through becoming immersed in knowledge. In outlining the primary mission of a university, Newman stated that 'its function is intellectual culture ... it educates the intellect to reason well in all matters, to reach out to truth and grasp it' (Newman and Svaglic, 1982: 95). This idea of the cultivation or development of the individual through interacting with knowledge was similar to Immanuel Kant's notion of *bildung* (self-formation) as a basis for enlightenment (Kant, 2009). It was this concept that shaped the type of education offered by the University of Berlin, founded in 1809 by Wilhelm von Humboldt, the Prussian Minister of Education. Central to von Humboldt's vision of a university were the values of *lernfreiheit* (freedom to learn) and *lehrfreiheit* (freedom to teach), fostered within the university as an institution that would serve the needs of the state, but would still remain relatively autonomous.

The nineteenth and twentieth centuries saw considerable growth in the number and distribution of universities worldwide. The ideas from Newman, von Humboldt and others about universities' role in promoting the development of society through individual agency, critical reason and interacting with knowledge were highly influential during this period and especially in the United States. For many, universities' personal educative and developmental roles became a default view of their primary functions for much of this period. However, others (Collini, 2012; Martin, 2012) point out that universities established at this time also had to link their roles to the economic and developmental needs of societies, with the liberal humanist view of the purpose of higher education coexisting alongside more pragmatic roles in many contexts. For example, in England in the 1870s and 1880s, universities were established in the industrial cities of Birmingham, Manchester, Sheffield and Leeds, which taught the more practical subjects of commerce and engineering alongside the traditional curriculum. Similarly the 'land grant' universities in the United States were established in the later nineteenth century to teach practical agriculture, science, military science and engineering, as well as the more traditional subjects. Therefore, it seems that as universities proliferated during the past two centuries, the traditional ideas of Newman and von Humboldt remained influential, but many universities were also required to service the economic and social needs of society. As universities developed during the twentieth century, the nature of their multifaceted roles was reflected in the concept of the *multiversity*, proposed in lectures given at Harvard in 1963 by Clark Kerr, president of the University of California. In explaining the concept, he claimed that a university 'is not one community, but several' (Kerr, 2001: 18). Under the name of a single institutional entity are different communities, including: undergraduates, graduates, humanists, scientists, social scientists, professional schools, administrators and alumni.

It is probably fair to say that for most of the twentieth century, universities emerged as pluralistic, relatively decentralized institutions that still reflected many of the values and characteristics of their medieval and humanist predecessors, but included a greater range of disciplines and were required to perform a wider range of social and economic roles. Universities still retained a degree of autonomy, and academic staff largely exercised self-governance and self-regulation. However, the last three decades of the twentieth century saw a gradual transformation of the organizational structures and ethos of universities through the adoption by national governments of policies proposed by the supranational agencies of the World Bank and the Organisation for Economic Cooperation and Development (OECD). A landmark publication foreshadowing the types of fundamental change to the sector that was about to take place was the document 'Universities Under Scrutiny', an OECD-commissioned report by Taylor and OECD (1987), which emphasized the economic role of universities and argued for a greater focus on applied subjects, vocationalism, efficiency, productivity and accountability to external stakeholders. Another OECD report, 'The Knowledge-Based Economy' (1996), continued to argue for greater linkages between university activities and economic output, proposing that it 'may be necessary to modify or reject the idea that science is a public good' (22). Similarly, a 1994 World Bank report 'Higher Education: The Lessons of Experience' also emphasized the role of knowledge in national economic development. As Ward (2012: 144) notes, reports in the 1980s and 1990s by the supranational agencies of the World Bank, OECD and UNESCO all argued for the role of knowledge in the development of national economies and markets.

The call by these agencies to reconfigure higher education coincided with an era of governments pursuing economic policies more recently termed *neoliberal*, which, according to Boas and Gans-Morse (2009), focus on the centrality of the free market and are based on the theories of Hayek (1978) and Friedman and Friedman (1962). The effects of these economic policies and the types of change promoted by the supranational agencies, such as the OECD, saw the gradual transformation of universities in many countries over the past three to four decades. As a result, the control of universities moved from a degree of self-governance by academics to control by business managers. The primary functions of teaching and research, and values around the roles of universities within wider society gradually changed to align with the more economic and developmental roles called for by the supranational agencies and required by governments following neoliberal, free-market policy agendas. These change processes radically affected the structures and roles of universities, and their outcomes can be described in terms of three trends: *financialization*, *marketization* and *managerialism*. In the next section of the chapter, I will reflect on the types of changes and reconfiguration of universities that have resulted from these three trends.

The Corporate University

Financialization is defined by Epstein (2005) as 'the increasing role of financial motives, financial markets, financial actors and financial institutions in the operation of the domestic and international economies' (3). For universities, the single commodity that they could financialize and bring to the market as a business was that of knowledge. The management theorist Drucker (1993) argues that, in the information economy, knowledge is the most powerful resource, and along with other theorists, he argues that the management of intellectual capital is the principal source of competitive advantage. This trend towards the financialization of knowledge has resulted in universities commercializing their external relations, such as to begin charging fees to students or escalating pre-existing fee structures (especially to international students) and positioning all students as clients. The justificatory narrative constructed around this process, as Haiven (2020) notes, is that it enables the increased empowerment and agency of students to 'invest' in their own academic development so that they can compete in an increasingly globalized and cut-throat job market. However, Haiven also points out that 'the introduction of, or escalation in tuition fees has been accompanied by a state-backed expansion of access to credit' with students accumulating 'post-graduation financial obligations that typically constitute several times the average annual income' (250). For universities, the financialization of knowledge also has involved monetizing other externally related activities, such as commercializing research findings, setting up spin-off companies and contracting research units and other areas of expertise to large corporations.

Financialization and the associated self-perception of universities as business enterprises has also fundamentally influenced the internal relations and *modus operandi* of universities, including their organizational and power structures, the nature of staff–student relationships as well as their approaches to curricular and research activities. In both the human domain and the domain of disciplines, financialization has introduced and reinforced hierarchies that were previously less prominent within universities. Specifically, the hierarchical structures and governance of universities have evolved to resemble those of commercial companies, with a highly paid executive branch absorbing an ever-larger share of budgets and institutional power. Part of the financialized realignment of the internal structures of universities has resulted from the influence of the ideas of *new public management* (NPM) in British contexts (Rhodes, 1994) or *responsibility-center management* (RCM) in North America (Strauss and Curry, 2002). As a result, each department or school becomes a self-funding *cost centre* and any proposal for change or innovation can only be approved if it aligns with the financial parameters and the corporate vision of the institution. The effect of the 'cost centre' approach to funding has also led to a hierarchy of disciplines that did not exist under previous, more uniform funding models. As Newfield (2011) notes, 'accounting gave programs that attracted outside funds – materials science, mathematical finance – a natural advantage over those that provided services, required public sector involvement, criticized policy, developed human capabilities, or rested on self-sponsored research that lacked external markets (anthropology, classics)' (170).

The financialization of the external relations of the university is also closely related to the idea of *marketization*, a concept also drawn from the theories of the economists Hayek (1978) and Friedman and Friedman (1962). The idea of marketization, when applied to universities, suggests that students, as consumers of the services provided by the university, in search of quality and value for money will seek to attend the best universities, obliging all institutions to raise their standards to meet the demands of the market. With students positioned as clients, the manifestations of the marketization of universities are evident in the ballooning of universities' PR departments and their efforts to 'sell' the institutions to prospective students through print, digital and (increasingly) social media communications (Wedlin, 2008). Also integral to the marketization of universities has been the increasing influence of the international university rankings organizations, whose league tables provide a basis for prospective students (as consumers) to choose the best university on the basis of how the rankings organizations perceive and rate quality. Universities see rankings as particularly important for attracting international students, which are an important source of revenue for them.

A major consequence of the marketization of universities and the activities of the rankings organizations has been the development of hierarchies among universities themselves that were not previously seen. For example, De Vries and Slowey (2012) point out that marketization policies in many countries have resulted in 'a growing stratification (of university systems) … many systems now have first, second and third "classes" of institutions, even when in most cases all institutions prepare in the same way for the same professions' (220). In relation to the idea of rankings leading to a hierarchy of universities, Marginson (2011) sees the scramble for positive rankings (resulting from the marketization process) as what he terms 'the status incentive trap' which 'confirms the dominance of the comprehensive Anglo-American science university' but *'narrows the diversity of knowledge* that secures global value, through which public goods are created' (429, emphasis added).

Reflecting this narrowing diversity of knowledge and subject offerings (driven by perceptions of market demand), universities have moved to offer more vocational courses at the expense of the more traditional humanities, social sciences and physical sciences degree programmes. In their marketing, this is reflected in claims about employability. Also, other researchers note that the marketization trend has resulted in a uniformity in the types of courses and education that universities offer rather than the distinctiveness that they often claim in their marketing materials. Evidence for this narrowing trend is seen in six case studies of UK universities by Durazzi (2021), which indicate that 'the array of choices that organisations can resort to is rather limited, to the extent that organisations are subject to the same coercive mechanisms (e.g. rankings and performance indicators) and depend upon the same resources (e.g. student fees)' (402).

In order to implement regimes that support policies and processes related to financialization and marketization, universities have imported systems of organization and control from the business world, systems collectively termed *managerialism*. Managerialism is defined by Deem (1998) as 'the adoption by public sector organisations of organisational forms, technologies, management practices and values more commonly found in the private business sector' (47). According to Hyde, Clarke and Drennan (2013), managerialism encompasses 'discourses and practices established in the private market such as corporate modes of speech, professional administrators, line management, and competition for resources' (42). Effectively universities have moved from the old, idealized, self-regulating community of scholars to control by corporatized line-managers, responsible for cost centres. According to Kolsaker (2008), managerialism in universities means that organizational goals assume primacy over individual research interests, goals that are enforced by surveillance and monitoring under entrepreneurial governance structures. Goals are expressed in terms of corporate-style mission statements, the top-down imposition of research policies and development plans, the establishment and monitoring of key performance objectives and personal professional development reviews.

Over a three-decade period, it seems that many universities have implemented managerial means of control and monitoring of their institutions and their staff, which contrasts with the looser types of collegial self-regulation that universities traditionally followed previously. In investigating how this type of change has affected the identity and modus operandi of academics, the previously mentioned study by Kolsaker (2008), although now more than a decade old, found that in the UK context, 'academics are reasonably comfortable working within managerialist regimes, and that they are instrumental in sustaining them' (522). However, she does suggest that 'because managerialism is embedded in discourses across the political spectrum and all sectors of society, academics may simply be attuned to its axioms' (522). However, a more recent US study by Vican, Friedman and Andreasen (2020) suggests that, over time, the embedding of managerialism within universities along with increasing managerial control over decision-making has led to, what they term, *competing logics*. Academic managers' corporate logics involve 'the primacy of certain disciplines, research and external funding, success quantified by metrics, hierarchical administrative control, revenue and rankings and a focus on enrolment and tuition income' (158). On the other hand, the logics of academic faculty identified in their study involve 'expert knowledge, research, teaching, service, autonomy, shared governance (collegiality), knowledge creation, education via teaching, advising and mentoring students' (158). It seems that the earlier rationalization and accommodation towards managerialism that Kolsaker identified may have moved to a more obvious and identifiable rift between the logics both of the corporate managers of universities and of academics as creative professionals. This sense of disarticulation in the contemporary university between the logics and values of the more recently imposed business management structure and those of the existing academic community has also been identified in the studies of a number of other researchers (e.g. Kenny, 2018; Shams, 2019; Tapanila, Siivonen and Filander, 2020).

Students and Staff in the Corporate University

This section considers the triple effects of financialization, marketization and managerialism on students and staff working within the increasingly corporatized university of recent decades. These influences are predicated on notions of the university as a business providing a service to paying customers, university staff as service providers and students as rational consumers and active choice-makers as they avail themselves of the 'services' of a university. Universities, their staff and students are cast in these roles by means of a number of policy levers pursued by governments and by the leadership of universities themselves. However, the 'student as a consumer' role is also underpinned and reinforced by the acceptance by wider society of an ideology that promotes the right of the individual to exercise their own economic freedom and personal autonomy to purchase education as a personal good that aligns with the customer's terms and preferences.

Students are positioned as consumers through the imposition or escalation of tuition fees and supported by government or private loan schemes. They are encouraged to exercise their choice as a consumer by evaluating universities' publication of data about their performance on a number of student-related matters, such as teaching satisfaction, student assessment outcomes, student contact hours and graduate employment rates. This notion of student consumerism is inherent in official government policy discourses around higher education, and it is reinforced at the level of institutions, with practices and concepts borrowed from the corporate world, such as 'the student experience' and 'the student voice'. However, this is a trend that Tomlinson (2017) suggests puts universities 'at risk of imitating the customer sovereignty ethos of service hospitality industries' (465).

Early during the emergence of this trend, McMillan and Cheney (1996) expressed concerns that the positioning of students as consumers within a marketized university environment obscures important aspects of a university education. Specifically, they suggest that it creates distance between the student and the learning processes of tertiary education. Rather than intellectually engaging with their studies and actively co-constructing their learning as novice academics, they are likely to be more passive, based on the expectation that education is a service that will be delivered to them in the same way as any other service for which they have paid. Along with a number of other writers concerned about this changed student role, Williams (2012) suggests that when universities position students as clients, the role of the university is to provide a satisfactory service 'flattering and appeasing students rather than intellectually challenging them through the pursuit of new knowledge' (58). This student-as-a-client view was starkly expressed by the editor of a New Zealand university student magazine, who stated: 'Lecturers need to realize that they are in a service industry. Make your product engaging – sure – but don't try and limit my access to it or define how I use the service' (Buchanan, 2018: 1). In researching the extent to which students in the UK context see themselves as consumers, Tomlinson (2017) found that 'consumerist discourses have certainly become more widespread and are increasingly framing students' relationship to higher education' (464), especially given the large amounts of money they have to borrow for tuition fees. However, he also found that attitudes varied across different groups, from those fully identifying with the 'student as a consumer' view through to those that are critical of and emphatically disassociate themselves from it.

While students are being increasingly positioned as consumers within the corporatized university, academic staff has also seen their roles changing. From the 1980s, in response to the urgings of the supranational agencies, such as the OECD and the World Bank, governments have 'reformed' universities so that their organizational and management structures increasingly resemble those of commercial companies. As a result, changes to the roles of academic staff in universities include: a reduced role in academic decision-making, increased workloads (and a wider range of types of work) and subjection to greater surveillance and accountability regimes.

The diminished roles of academic staff in institutional decision-making is a direct result of governmental 'reforms' of universities, now increasingly governed by corporate structures that have appropriated authority from the collegial senates or academic boards. The latter structures traditionally gave academics considerable autonomy and control over their own affairs. However, the corporatization of universities has largely disempowered the majority of the academic staff body although redistributed greater power to the few that form part of the senior management of the institution (Bleiklie and Kogan, 2007). In many cases, this power redistribution also has the effect of distancing of academic staff from the management of the university. Drawing on the Australian context, Connell (2019) suggests that 'the isolation of senior managers from rank-and-file workers is now a key feature of the university scene. Active academic and operations workers can go for years without seeing a member of their SMG [senior management group], except on a podium or website' (130). Along with their separation from the power structures of the university, individual academics have also experienced a distancing from its academic structures. Combined with the more centralized, managerial control of universities, the administrative units themselves have changed, affecting the working relationships of academics. As Gibbons (1994) notes, 'faculties have become organisational rather than intellectual categories; even departments are seen as administrative units rather than intellectual centres' (80). As a result, individual academics form their working relationships and research collaborations through their own personal networks, which may be across units within, or outside of, their own institution. While this has always been the case to some extent, it would be fair to say that with the dissolution of the internal, academic organizational structures of universities, these informal networks have become more important for individual academics.

As well as experiencing diminished participation in the running of the university, academic staff have been subject to increased workloads through the imposition of corporate structures. Kenny (2017) claims that 'administrative compliance requirements, extended teaching periods (e.g. trimesters) and the introduction of technology-based teaching have intensified academic work and "blurred the boundaries" between work and home' (898). In addition, beyond the core tasks of teaching and research, Haddock-Fraser (2020) also suggests that intensification has resulted from the implementation of performance appraisal systems, workload allocation models, administrative processes and the student-as-a-customer ethos adopted by many universities. In relation to the core work of academic staff (teaching and research), intensification has resulted from the systems of surveillance and performance management to which academic staff are subject. *Academic performance management* (APM) requires individual academic staff to negotiate performance goals with a line manager, with outcomes annually reviewed and goals renegotiated for the subsequent year. Morphing from professional development support, it is suggested that APM has become widely entrenched as a means of controlling academics and driving productivity as personal performance objectives are often aligned with larger key performance objectives of the institution (Connell, 2015). Connell also claims that a key function of performance management systems within universities is that of choosing 'underperforming' staff for forced redundancy, and have the especially useful effect of obliging staff to monitor themselves, and report their performance to their managers (2015: 98).

Finally, another aspect of intensification of the work of academic staff in universities has been the casualization of labour, with much academic teaching done by staff employed on part-time or temporary contracts. The trend appears to be that teaching is offloaded onto junior academics or doctoral students on temporary or part-time contracts at low rates of pay so that those permanently employed can pursue lucrative research contracts and funding opportunities for universities. Universities seem to have become increasingly reliant on the fact that there will always be a pool of qualified junior academics that can be drawn upon for short-term teaching or research roles when the need arises. For some time, a growing literature has been documenting this casualization of the work of university staff, especially in Anglophone countries, such as the United States and Canada (Dobbie and Robinson, 2008), the UK (Mason and Megoran, 2021), Australia (Thomas, Forsyth and Bonnell, 2020) and Ireland (Courteois and O'Keefe, 2015). The British University and College Union (UCU) has estimated that between 20 and 30 per cent of academic teaching is now done by part-time or temporary contract academics on low rates of pay (UCU, 2019), while the Australian union for university staff, the National Tertiary Education Union (NTEU), estimates that more than 50 per cent of academic teaching in Australian universities is now done by casual labour (Connell, 2015).

Overall, the changing ethos of universities with a business focus involving financialization, marketization and managerialism has fundamentally affected the roles of the key institutional actors of academic staff and students. This business-focused environment has the potential to influence fundamentally, what is taught, the ways in which students engage with knowledge and the core academic staff roles of teaching and research.

EAP within the Corporate University

The purpose of this chapter is to provide, for those working in the field of EAP, an overview of the social, political and economic forces that have shaped contemporary higher education and also endow EAP with its particular role in universities. It is important for those working in EAP to have a clear understanding of the nature of the corporatized university – its values, processes and constraints – within which EAP is located as a strategic activity. International fee-paying students constitute a vital revenue source, and, for that reason, they are actively sought after and recruited by business-focused universities. As a strategic activity of the university, EAP has the roles of overseeing the successful development of these students in the areas of their academic English language competencies and their acculturation into the university's academic values, practices and processes. EAP practice is, therefore, essential for the success of this type of commercialized activity. However, the academic challenge for EAP (in the environment of the contemporary corporatized university) is to access the resources and create the academic environment necessary to achieve its core roles.

EAP involves the development of discourse competence in academic English, which includes academic literacies development and induction into the processes, practices and values of the university. EAP, therefore, is a complex, multifaceted academic activity drawing upon both theory and research, of which there is a growing body. The danger for EAP within the current business-focused, corporatized environment is that it too, as a result of being subject to commercial forces (like the rest of the university), is seen merely as a commodifiable 'service' activity that is able to be privatized and outsourced to generate even greater profits. In such cases, the academic dimensions of needs analysis, discourse competence and academic skills development become occluded as EAP courses are reduced to Common European Framework of Reference (CEFR)-benchmarked, language proficiency courses, based on commercial TESOL-style materials that have an 'academic' flavour. Staff are employed piecemeal to teach from these materials, but not to engage with the universities as academics actively involved in the scholarship and research of their field.

Awareness, therefore, of the contextual forces that shape universities (and EAP within universities) is essential as a basis for EAP practice, scholarship, research and career planning within the field. This type of awareness enables the practitioner to exercise agency in evaluating specific university contexts and how they configure EAP organizationally and academically. These types of insights then provide a basis for practitioners to chart their own specific career trajectories and to inform the choices that they make when engaging with and undertaking scholarship and research in the field.

References

Bleiklie, I., and M. Kogan (2007), 'Organization and Governance of Universities', *Higher Education Policy*, 20 (4): 477–93.

Boas, T., and J. Gans-Morse (2009), 'Neoliberalism: From New Liberal Philosophy to Anti-Liberal Slogan', *Studies in Comparative International Development*, 44 (2): 137–61.

British Association of Lecturers in English for Academic Purposes (BALEAP) (2008), *Competency Framework for Teachers of English for Academic Purposes*. http://www.baleap.org.uk/teap/teapcompetencyframework.pdf (accessed 24 November 2021).

Buchanan, L. (2018), 'Editorial', *Nexus*, 16: 1.

Chaplin, M. (1977), 'Philosophies of Higher Education, Historical and Contemporary', in *International Encyclopedia of Higher Education*, 7: 3204–20, San Francisco, CA: Jossey-Bass.

Collini, S. (2012), *What Are Universities For?* London: Penguin.
Connell, R. (2015), 'The Knowledge Economy and University Workers', *Australian Universities' Review*, 57 (2): 91–5.
Connell, R. (2019), *The Good University: What Universities Actually Do and Why It's Time for Radical Change*, London: Zed Books.
Courtois, A., and T. O'Keefe (2015), 'Precarity in the Ivory Cage: Neoliberalism and Casualisation of Work in the Irish Higher Education Sector', *Journal for Critical Education Policy Studies*, 13 (1): 43–66.
De Vries, W., and M. Slowey (2012), 'Concluding Reflections. Between Humboldt and Newman: Marketization and Global Contributions in Contemporary Higher Education', in H. G. Schuetze and G. Álvarez Mendiola (eds), *State and Market in Higher Education Reforms*, 213–23, Rotterdam: Sense.
De Wulf, M. (2003), *An Introduction to Scholastic Philosophy: Medieval and Modern: Scholasticism Old and New*, Eugene, OR: Wipf and Stock.
Deem, R. (1998), 'New Managerialism and Higher Education: The Management of Performances and Cultures in Universities in the United Kingdom', *International Studies in Sociology of Education*, 8 (1): 47–70.
Dobbie, D., and I. Robinson (2008), 'Reorganizing Higher Education in the United States and Canada: The Erosion of Tenure and the Unionization of Contingent Faculty', *Labor Studies Journal*, 33 (2): 117–40.
Drucker, P. F. (1993), *Post-Capitalist Society*, New York: Harper Business.
Durazzi, N. (2021), 'Opening Universities' Doors for Business? Marketization, the Search for Differentiation and Employability in England', *Journal of Social Policy*, 50 (2): 386–405.
Epstein, G. A. (2005), *Financialization and the World Economy*, Cheltenham: Edward Elgar.
Fleming, P. (2021), *Dark Academia: Despair in the Neoliberal University*, London: Pluto Press.
Flowerdew, J. A., and M. Peacock eds (2001), *Research Perspectives on English for Academic Purposes*, Cambridge: Cambridge University Press.
Friedman, M., and R. D. Friedman (1962), *Capitalism and Freedom*, Chicago: University of Chicago Press.
Gibbons, M. (1994), *The New Production of Knowledge: The Dynamics of Science and Research in Contemporary Societies*, London: Sage.
Giroux, H. (2014), *Neoliberalism's War on Higher Education*, Chicago: Haymarket Books.
Haddock-Fraser, J. (2020), 'The Unseen Pressures of Academia', in M. Antoniadou and M. Crowder (eds), *Modern Day Challenges in Academia*, 211–25, Cheltenham: Edward Elgar.
Haiven, M. (2020), 'Culture and Financialization: Four Approaches', in P. Mader, D. Mertens and N. van der Zwan (eds), *The Routledge International Handbook of Financialization*, 347–57, London: Routledge.

Hayek, F. A. (1978), *The Constitution of Liberty*, Chicago: University of Chicago Press.
Hyde, A., M. Clarke and J. Drennan (2013), 'The Changing Role of Academics and the Rise of Managerialism', in B. M. Kehm and U. Teichler (eds), *The Academic Profession in Europe: New Tasks and New Challenges*, 39–52, Dordrecht: Springer.
Kant, I. (2009), *An Answer to the Question 'What Is Enlightenment?'*, trans. H. Nisbet, London: Penguin.
Kenny, J. (2017), 'Academic Work and Performativity', *Higher Education*, 74 (5): 897–913.
Kenny, J. (2018), 'Re-empowering Academics in a Corporate Culture: An Exploration of Workload and Performativity in a University', *Higher Education*, 75 (2): 365–80.
Kerr, C. (2001), *The Uses of the University*, Cambridge, MA: Harvard University Press.
Kolsaker, A. (2008), 'Academic Professionalism in the Managerialist Era: A Study of English Universities', *Studies in Higher Education*, 33 (5): 513–25.
Marginson, S. (2011), 'Higher Education and Public Good', *Higher Education Quarterly*, 65 (4): 411–33.
Martin, B. R. (2012), 'Are Universities and University Research under Threat? Towards an Evolutionary Model of University Speciation', *Cambridge Journal of Economics*, 36 (3): 543–65.
Mason, O., and N. Megoran (2021), 'Precarity and Dehumanisation in Higher Education', *Learning and Teaching*, 14 (1): 35–59.
McMillan, J. J., and G. Cheney (1996), 'The Student as Consumer: The Implications and Limitations of a Metaphor', *Communication Education*, 45 (1): 1–15.
Newfield, C. (2011), *Unmaking the Public University: The Forty-Year Assault on the Middle Class*, Cambridge, MA: Harvard University Press.
Newman, J. (2008), *The Idea of a University*, New Haven, CT: Yale University Press.
Newman, J. H., and M. J. Svaglic (1982), *The Idea of a University: Defined and Illustrated in Nine Discourses Delivered to the Catholics of Dublin in Occasional Lectures and Essays Addressed to the Members of the Catholic University*, Notre Dame, IN: University of Notre Dame Press.
Organisation for Economic Cooperation and Development (OECD) (1996), *The Knowledge-Based Economy*, Paris: Organisation for Economic Cooperation and Development.
Rhodes, R. A. W. (1994), 'The Hollowing Out of the State: The Changing Nature of the Public Service in Britain', *Political Quarterly*, 65 (2): 138–51.
Ridder-Symoens, H. de (1996), *A History of the University in Europe*, vol. 2, Cambridge: Cambridge University Press.
Scott, J. C. (2006), 'The Mission of the University: Medieval to Postmodern Transformations', *Journal of Higher Education*, 77 (1): 1–39.
Shams, F. (2019), 'Managing Academic Identity Tensions in a Canadian Public University: The Role of Identity Work in Coping with Managerialism', *Journal of Higher Education Policy and Management*, 41 (6): 619–32.

Strauss, J. C., and J. R. Curry (2002), *Responsibility Center Management: Lessons from 25 Years of Decentralized Management*, Annapolis Junction, MD: National Association of College and University Business Officials.

Tapanila, K., P. Siivonen and K. Filander (2020), 'Academics Social Positioning towards the Restructured Management System in Finnish Universities', *Studies in Higher Education*, 45 (1): 117–28.

Taylor, W., and Organization for Economic Cooperation and Development (OECD) Staff (1987), *Universities under Scrutiny*, Washington, DC: OECD Information and Publication Centre.

Thomas, A., H. Forsyth and A. G. Bonnell (2020), 'The Dice are Loaded: History, Solidarity and Precarity in Australian Universities', *History Australia*, 17 (1): 21–39.

Tomlinson, M. (2017), 'Student Perceptions of Themselves as "Consumers" of Higher Education', *British Journal of Sociology of Education*, 38 (4): 450–67.

University and College Union (UCU) (2019), *Counting the Costs of Casualisation*. https://www.ucu.org.uk/media/10336/Counting-the-costs-of-casualisation-in-higher-education-Jun-19/pdf/ucu_casualisation_in_HE_survey_report_Jun19.pdf (accessed 24 February 2022).

Vican, S., A. Friedman and R. Andreasen (2020), 'Metrics, Money, and Managerialism: Faculty Experiences of Competing Logics in Higher Education', *Journal of Higher Education*, 91 (1): 139–64.

Ward, S. C. (2012), *Neoliberalism and the Global Restructuring of Knowledge and Education*, New York: Routledge.

Wedlin, L. (2008), 'University Marketization: The Process and its Limits', in L. Engwall and D. Weaire (eds), *The University in the Market*, 143–53, London: Portland Press.

Williams, J. (2012), *Consuming Higher Education: Why Learning Can't Be Bought*, London: Bloomsbury Academic.

World Bank (1994), *Higher Education: The Lessons of Experience*. Washington, DC: World Bank.

2

The Ideologies and Practices of Internationalization within Universities

Jenna Mittelmeier and Bowen Zhang

Introduction

Internationalization has been previously outlined as a disrupting force on global higher education practices (Kosmützky and Putty, 2016). Many practices in higher education are now influenced and informed by internationalization, from growing international student numbers (OECD, 2021), to developing internationally relevant curricula (Leask and Carroll, 2011), to increased pressures to demonstrate international relevance through institutional rankings (Hauptman Komotar, 2019), among many others. Although internationalization is a contested term, it is perhaps classically defined as

> the process of integrating an international, intercultural or global dimension into the purpose, functions or delivery of post-secondary education. (Knight, 2004: 11)

This definition is purposefully broad in recognition that internationalization can be highly contextual and the approaches taken by individual institutions can vary widely. However, this means that internationalization is often considered a 'fuzzy' term (Kehm and Teichler, 2007) taking on multiple meanings and perspectives by individual institutions and practitioners (Hudzik, 2015).

Across these approaches, English is often considered a 'symbol' of internationalization (Duong and Chua, 2016). One reason for this is that the global flow of international students has disproportionately favoured movement from the Global South to institutions based in the Global North, predominantly in English-speaking countries such as the UK, the United States or Australia (OECD, 2021). Other considerations relate to the rising use of English in universities through English-medium instruction (EMI), leading to an assumed lingua franca in international education settings (Jenkins, 2013). In this chapter, we reflect on these issues, considering the role of English and, by extension, English for Academic Purposes (EAP) as both drivers and outcomes of internationalization.

In doing so, we take a critical lens, considering how this relationship might be underpinned by issues such as uneven power dynamics and hegemonic privilege, both between countries and between students and staff. We argue that critical considerations should be made about how English might perpetuate commodification, commercialization, 'Westernization' and domination within higher education practices. With this macro-level picture in mind, and in consideration of the contextual nature of EAP in different settings, we close with a set of critical reflection questions for practitioners working within internationalized university learning spaces. We start first, though, with a reflection on the perceived 'fuzziness' of internationalization as a concept and some of the ways it manifests in practice in higher education institutions.

Fuzzy Conceptualizations of Internationalization

Internationalization is a complex and multifaceted concept that has various meanings for different stakeholders; it is perhaps a concept that everyone in the higher education sector is talking about, but without a clear definition of what it means. Scholars have argued that approaches to internationalization are unsystematic across the sector (Kehm and Teichler, 2007), meaning that it is conceptualized and defined in different ways by different institutions and actors. Internationalization is often an umbrella term, intended to encompass a vast array of practices related broadly to the international and the intercultural.

For this reason, definitions of internationalization have purposefully sought not to 'specify rationales, benefits, outcomes, actors, activities, and stakeholders of internationalization' (Knight, 2004: 11). Hudzik (2015) conceptualized this as 'comprehensive internationalization', intending to encompass all international activities across the research, teaching, and service provisions at individual institutions. However, the purposeful broadness of the concept can also lead to uncertainties about its meaning. For example, Knight (2014: 76) reflected that internationalization has become a go-to phrase that is 'used to describe anything and everything remotely linked to the global, intercultural or international dimensions of higher education and is thus losing its way'.

Therefore, internationalization activities might be perceived as unrelated and fragmented, rather than holistic, transformative or uniform across the sector (de Wit, 2017). The wide-reaching nature of internationalization and the multifaceted ways it manifests in practice (as we highlight in the next section) perhaps contributes to the challenges around defining it. After all, as outlined by Buckner and Stein (2020), even the major international higher education institutions – the National Association of Foreign Student Advisers (NAFSA), International Association of Universities (IAU) and European Association for International Education (EAIE) – are inconsistent in their definitions and conceptualizations of what internationalization means. This has led to concerns about internationalization being conceptualized as a measurable goal rather than a process or orientation, with overarching discourses about 'achieving "successful" internationalization, rather than prompting thoughtful engagements and systemic analyses around why or how we should do so' (152). This uncertainty is also present in the scholarly literature, where Mwangi et al. (2018) found that few articles explicitly defined internationalization and that conceptualizations of the topic were persistently uncritical.

While there are uncertainties about what 'counts' as internationalization, both in theory and in practice, the literature on this topic provides insights into the key thematic areas that are of interest in this subfield. Tight (2021), for example, identified several common focus areas in scholarly publications, including: international students' experiences, experiences of academic staff (including teaching international students and experiences of expatriate staff), internationalization of the curriculum and pedagogy and the role of English language as lingua franca. Other scholars have mapped the growing interest in internationalization research over time, mimicking the trajectory of rising numbers of international students (Yemini and Sagie, 2016).

Worth reflecting here is that conceptualizations of internationalization are overwhelmingly influenced by the hegemonic position of academic norms and practices in the Global North. After all, the vast majority of scholarly publications about internationalization are written by Global North scholars and systematic reviews on the topic have outlined missing or silenced voices from the Global South, particularly from countries in Latin America or Africa (Tight, 2021). As a result, there are increasing calls for conceptualizing internationalization beyond Global North perspectives and assumptions. For example, Liu (2021) proposed an alternative definition specifically for the context of Chinese higher education, reflecting that internationalization in this context is a nationally coordinated, institutionally integrated and comprehensive effort to import the Western-led world standards in teaching, research, management and facility development through the exposure of academic staff, students and administrators to Western practices, and to export the Chinese discourse, voice and cultural understanding in the international community through international student education in China and Chinese language/culture promotion overseas. (12)

In summary, internationalization is a complex, contested and fuzzy term that purposefully encompasses a broad range of activities that are simultaneously interrelated and disparate, made meaningful or meaningless depending on its context.

Internationalization in Practice in Relation to EAP

The fuzzy conceptualizations of internationalization match the multifaceted ways that it manifests in practice, encompassing the full range of research, teaching, and service operations within universities. Universities' responses to globalization and approaches to internationalization vary, even within countries, leading scholars to reflect that internationalization is primarily an institutional effort (Buckner and Stein 2020; Hudzik 2015). However, these are often underpinned by national or international policies (see e.g. Lomer, 2017). Examples of internationalization in practice include the recruitment of internationally mobile students and staff, the establishment of transnational higher education institutions (e.g. branch campuses), the internationalization of curriculum content, the building of transborder research collaborations or the development of EMI programmes (Altbach and Knight, 2007), among many others.

In relation to EAP, international student mobility is perhaps one of the most influential aspects of internationalization. International study has become a popular choice, and there are currently over five million international students globally (OECD, 2021). Notably, the student mobility patterns are dominated by Asian countries sending students to countries in the Global North (Kondakci, Bedenlier and Zawacki-Richter, 2018). However, in the past twenty years, international students' destination choices deviated from this pattern into new mobility flows, particularly towards 'regional hubs' which attract international students within a geographic region. Examples of this include South Africa, Turkey, Russia, South Africa or Malaysia, which attract students from neighbouring countries, with students motivated by cultural proximity or ease of visa procedures, among other reasons (Kondakci, Bedenlier and Zawacki-Richter, 2018). The prevalence of regional hubs influences growing provisions for EMI and the dominant position of English, as institutions strategically compete for regional international students by offering EMI courses (Galloway, Numajiri and Rees, 2020).

Relatedly, internationalization is reflected in increased international staff mobility. In the UK, for example, 31 per cent of academic staff hold non-UK citizenship (HESA, 2021); in other countries in Europe, international staff can make up to 50 per cent of academic staff (Leisyte and Rose, 2017). In China, although the percentage of international staff remains low (2.3 per cent) (Cheng, Zhang and Zu , 2014), this has been marked by rapid increases that have nearly doubled in ten years (Liu, Zhong and Hamish, 2019). Staff mobility has further strengthened the position of English as a lingua franca for global science and publications (Liu, 2017), while simultaneously further diversifying the linguistic backgrounds present within higher education classrooms.

The diversification of people in higher education has coincided with rising numbers of transnational higher educational institutions. One prominent example is international branch campuses, whereby institutions may expand their physical presence by opening branches in other countries. In 2020, there were more than 300 international branch campuses worldwide, with most providers originating from predominantly English-speaking countries and countries such as China (n=42) and the United Arab Emirates (n=32) being the top importers (C-BERT, 2021). As branch campuses operate overwhelmingly through EMI, provisions for EAP are commonly developed as student supports (Evans and Morrison, 2011).

This backdrop may help explain the significant global increase in English language teaching. Across Europe, for example, courses taught in English have grown by 1,000 per cent since 2002 (Wächter and Maiworm, 2014), driven partially by the Bologna Agreement, which allows for free movement of students and qualifications between European countries. National and institutional prestige development policies in many Asian countries (particularly in East Asia: China, Japan and South Korea) have also led to record numbers of programmes being taught in English (Fenton-Smith, Humphreys and Walkinshaw, 2017). In other regions, English teaching has been embedded in the development of newer higher education systems; one example is Oman, where the majority of universities opened since the 1980s have programmes taught in English (Al-Mahrooqi and Denman, 2018). Thus, we can see in many areas a shift towards EMI (although, not without critique, as we outline later).

Although internationalization is, of course, wider ranging than these examples, this paints a picture of the prevalence of English as an assumed lingua franca in international higher education. With international students increasingly choosing predominantly English-speaking countries as their study destination, alongside the growing prevalence of EMI, there has been growing interest and awareness in both research and practice on the role of EAP as a support service (Macaro et al., 2018; Tight, 2021).

English as Both a Driver and Outcome of Internationalization

The trends outlined in the previous section demonstrate that English can be thought of as a common denominator behind many internationalization efforts in higher education around the world. Phan (2013), for example, argues:

> The policies and practices of the internationalisation of HE [higher education] in global contexts often assume the importance of English in the production, circulation, and dissemination of academic knowledge. (160)

This links to assumptions about the 'desired linguistic capital' of English (Pauwels, 2014: 310), whereby speaking English has been historically commodified internationally as critical for personal and institutional success or development. For universities, this means implicit (and, at times, explicit) assumptions that to *be international* one needs to also operate in English (Phan, 2013). English, thus, might be seen as a 'symbol' of internationalization (Duong and Chua, 2016), whereby it, alongside EAP, can be conceptualized as both a driver towards internationalization and an outcome of 'becoming international'.

English as a Driver of Internationalization

Although the reasons why individual institutions adopt English are complex and contextual, one reason is a pervasive perception and assumption that English is a pathway to global recognition (Phan, 2013). This is perhaps best seen in the discourses about 'world-class universities' in places such as China (Rose et al., 2020), Japan (Rose and McKinley, 2018) or Vietnam (Duong and Chua, 2016), where ambitious policies for developing globally high-ranked institutions have specifically focused on shifts towards EMI.

This is linked to the broader hegemonic role of English in global academic practices, where more publications are made in English than any other world language (Liu, 2017). There are, thus, discourses that English is a normalized lingua franca or default language for knowledge dissemination (Werther et al., 2014). This is, in part, driven by institutional rankings, which fuel competition between nations and institutions for top positions in hierarchies produced by organizations such as Times Higher Education, Academic Rankings of World Universities or QS World University Rankings. The historical tendency for rankings to demonstrate biases towards universities in English-speaking countries (particularly the United States and the UK) creates pressures for institutions based elsewhere to assimilate to existing hegemonic structures in a global race for prestige (Ordorika and Lloyd, 2015).

Another influential factor is the flow of international student mobility (as described in the previous section and in more detail in Chapter 3). The drive to recruit international students lies in their tendency to pay higher tuition fees compared to home students in many countries (Choudaha, 2017); in England, for example, undergraduate tuition fees for home students are legally capped at £9,250 per year (as of 2021), while international students' fees typically range between £10,000 and £25,000 per year. Considering that neoliberal austerity measures around the world have increased universities' reliance on private contributions through tuition fees in many countries (Slaughter and Cantwell, 2012), this means that there are increased financial incentives and pressures to increase or maintain international student enrolment numbers.

International students are, after all, frequently characterized by institutions to be 'cash cows' who contribute significantly to institutional finances and local economies (Choudaha, 2017). On the one hand, the marketization of higher education drives concerns about losing international student revenue for countries that already recruit high numbers (i.e. in predominantly English-speaking countries). This was made clear in the UK government's briefing on the financial impact of Covid-19 on universities, which plainly stated:

> International students' fees provide a large and increasing share of providers' total income and universities gain a surplus or 'profit' on teaching international students. This surplus helps to fund important 'loss making' activities such as research. (House of Commons Library, 2021)

In countries such as the United States, a 16 per cent decline in international student numbers in 2019–20 led to $1.8 billion lost revenue to the US economy and over 42,000 lost jobs (NAFSA, 2021). Thus, there are economic imperatives to maintaining one's status as a host of international students, upheld by the skewed recruitment towards English-speaking countries.

On the other hand, neoliberalism increases pressures in the global market for countries that do not yet host high numbers of international students (Bamberger, Morris and Yemini, 2019). This might be particularly seen in places where there may be increased reliance on tuition fees for university operations (Goksu and Goksu, 2015) and, thus, a sense of 'missing out' on potential revenue streams from international students. Under such conditions, English has become a symbolic good that drives institutions towards EMI (and, often, greater provisions for EAP) through assumptions of increased opportunity, prestige and revenue (Galloway, Numajiri and Rees, 2020).

Yet, English as a driving factor for internationalization is complex and contextually based. One example is the case of Portugal, where Kerklaan, Moreira and Boersma (2008) highlighted how the Bologna Agreement created pressures to adopt EMI to recruit and support greater numbers of European international students. However, this has simultaneously been underpinned by pressures from local communities to retain the national culture through teaching in Portuguese, supported further by the presence of international students from former Portuguese colonies. Yet, it is within these complex and individual contexts that EAP operates globally, whereby the backdrop of internationalization increases pressures to adopt English, which in turn leads to greater needs for supporting learners through targeted language provisions for academic contexts. This role of EAP as an outcome of internationalization is where we turn our attention next.

EAP as an Outcome of Internationalization

Internationalization potentially increases the linguistic diversity present at higher education institutions through the mobility of international students or increased provisions for EMI. As such, EAP becomes a common outcome of internationalization through the development of support systems to prepare students for undertaking a degree in English (Ding and Bruce, 2017). This is often framed through recognition that additional provisions may be needed to support students in the transition to using academic English in educational contexts (Hadley, 2015). Although there is no systematic data collected around the world about the extent to which EAP provisions are made available to students, the rising focus on EMI and EAP in education research points to its growing prominence in practice (see, e.g. Macaro et al., 2018).

The growth in EAP provisions is driven in part by academic staff members' perceptions of students' language proficiencies, which are consistently described as a key barrier for (international) students (e.g. Jin and Schneider, 2019). Such discourses are often through a deficit lens which portrays students' language skills as insufficient or 'lowering standards' (Haugh, 2016). In situations where international students are perceived to require additional language support, some lecturing staff at universities may see this as outside of their remit or expertise (Skyrme and McGee, 2016), particularly considering the dearth of training opportunities for staff to develop competencies for teaching in linguistically diverse environments. Thus, in many institutions, there are increased pressures for additional support provisions through English language centres or pre-sessional courses to support 'readiness' for learning through EMI alongside academic subjects.

Yet, the growth in EAP is also driven by international students themselves. As higher education is increasingly positioned as a commodity that can be bought (often at a significant price) and sold internationally, EAP becomes part of institutions' marketing packages for competing for international students. For example, Hadley (2015: 38) argues that one 'strategy for undercutting the competition, therefore, is to highlight the quality of support services to allay the fears of students and parents'. After all, international students and their families may want assurance that their significant financial investments in international education will provide the necessary support for success. Language may sit at the forefront here, as deficit discourses about language proficiencies are often self-perpetuated by students, who may 'have internalised a sense of inferiority that their English is not good enough' (Hua and Gao, 2021: 7).

Thus, we see EAP playing a dual role within many institutions. On the one hand, English may be seen as an instrument for internationalization through increased marketability for international student recruitment or as a tool for increasing global scientific collaboration or institutional recognition. On the other hand, EAP can be viewed as an outcome of internationalization through its perceived assimilative function of providing language support for students and staff after arrival. However, both of these roles are underpinned by critical assumptions and ideologies about internationalization as a process, which we now turn our attention towards.

Critical Reflections on the Assumptions and Ideologies of Internationalization

With this background in mind, we raise four critical points about the underlying assumptions and ideologies that link EAP (and English, more broadly) with internationalization. We argue that future directions for EAP should critically reflect on its relationships with the commodification and commercialization of higher education, assumptions about language assimilation, uneven global power flows and tensions between Englishification and localization.

Commodification and Commercialization of Higher Education

The first critical consideration is the extent to which EAP, in relation to internationalization, further perpetuates the commodification and commercialization of global higher education. On the one hand, this relates to increasing trends of limited national funding for higher education in many countries, leading to increased reliance on tuition fee payments for operation (Slaughter and Cantwell, 2012). As previously highlighted, international students tend to pay higher tuition fees than home students in most countries, leading to growing global discourses about their status as financial contributors to the viability of many institutions (Choudaha, 2017). This, coupled with the exponential growth in global interest in international study (OECD, 2021), has led to intensified competition between countries and institutions for recruiting international students, with a growing number of countries vying for entry into the market. Thus, reflections can be made about the ways that internationalization, more broadly, and international students, more specifically, are both a symptom and a driver for marketization. Higher education, after all, is now a global commodity that can be bought, sold and traded across borders.

EAP, in its role as both a driver and outcome of internationalization, plays a prominent role in the increased marketization of higher education. On the one hand, it is positioned as part of the support package provided for international students (Hadley, 2015), contributing to an institution's marketability and competitiveness in the wider education market. The changing narratives of students as customers, thus, bring additional pressures to showcase EAP provisions, often alongside marketized claims of programme effectiveness (Pearson, 2020). The presence of EAP, therefore, contributes to the overall commercialization of higher education and the positioning of a university education as a market good.

On the other hand, EAP is often a money-making endeavour for institutions in and of themselves, as language support might be provided at an additional (often premium) cost in some contexts. One key example is pre-sessional courses, which are often positioned as intensive language readiness programmes that are required or highly suggested for international students, especially those with lower tested English scores. Yet, pre-sessional courses are expensive; at UK universities, for example, a ten-week pre-sessional course generally costs between £2000 and £5000, in addition to programme tuition fees. Therefore, there are questions about the extent to which EAP might perpetuate the commodification of higher education through its function as either an 'add-on' service or an additional financial hurdle for international students.

Assumptions about Language Assimilation

As previously outlined, internationalization leads to increased numbers of international students or students learning through EMI. Under such circumstances, EAP functions as a support provision for developing students' readiness and proficiencies for using English in academic settings (Hadley, 2015). Within this role, there is a normative assimilative function, whereby there is a set standard of English that students are expected to achieve or internalize. Academic English, in this way, is often considered a skill that is passed down or transmitted, rather than co-negotiated or transformed through multilingual environments (e.g. Galante et al., 2019). However, this brings up critical questions about how such standards or skills are developed or decided (and by whom). Within an internationalized learning environment, EAP upholds and reinforces potentially problematic benchmarks for what 'counts' as standard English and whose lexicons are accepted or not accepted in academic settings.

Uneven Global Power Flows

Relatedly, an additional critical consideration is the extent to which EAP contributes to and is a result of uneven global power flows, particularly between the Global North and Global South. One element relates to EAP's assimilative quality (as discussed above), in the sense that EAP assumes a normative standard of English to which students are expected to obtain to succeed in their academic programme. Although EAP can take different forms in different contexts, the prevailing global focus for proficiency testing and teaching provisions hegemonically centre the language of countries such as the UK, the United States, Canada or Australia. This creates a normative standard of language proficiency that potentially fails to recognize other world Englishes, contributing to deficit narratives of international students as lacking language skills necessary for success. For example, China English, the localization of English grammar and lexicon in Chinese contexts, is often viewed as an error or insufficiency for academic writing in contexts elsewhere (Nuske, 2017). Thus, there is a need for EAP to reflect on the extent to which internationalization perpetuates power differentiation between the Global North and Global South, particularly considering the uneven mobility patterns of international students.

Another consideration is the extent to which pivots towards English symbolizes the 'Westernization' of higher education. In some contexts, English is perceived as a desirable linguistic capital or development potential (Spolsky, 2004). However, language is by no means neutral and EMI is often embedded within power structures that favour the cultures, norms and values of the Global North at the expense of students' own backgrounds, cultures and languages (Galloway, Numajiri and Rees, 2020). Thus, discourses about the desirability of English raise concerns that internationalization, and by extension EMI or EAP, further promote the normative valuing of the Global North, thereby risking reproducing academic capitalism and claims to superiority (Phan, 2013). This position means English from the Global North is taken to represent the universal, while other languages and dialects, especially those in the Global South, represent 'cultural specificity' (Choi, 2010: 247).

Tensions between Englishification and Localization

In countries where English is not the predominant language, there are additional critical considerations about how pressures to internationalize (and, therefore, Englishize) impact local cultures and linguistic identities (Cots, Llurda and Garrett, 2014). For example, moves to teach through EMI have met lukewarm reactions in the Netherlands, where students have questioned the relevance and value of learning in English for their future locally based careers (Mittelmeier, Slof and Rienties, 2021). Similarly in Hong Kong, student protests in 2005 centred around the Chinese University of Hong Kong's decision to increase EMI courses at the expense of programmes in Chinese (Choi, 2010). Thus, the pivot towards English, and subsequent pivots towards EAP provisions, has been argued to be a 'neglect of local languages' (Wihlborg and Robson, 2018: 10) that lead to 'eroding national cultural identities' (Knight, 2014: 80). This means there is a need to further reflect on why and how English and EAP are relevant to students' lives within their local contexts and the extent to which EAP may in turn disregard local languages or local socio-linguistic values.

Conclusion and Critical Considerations for EAP

Altogether, the relationship between English, EAP and the internationalization of higher education is complicated. In higher education institutions, English and EAP hold a dual position of both contributing to internationalization efforts, while concurrently being on the receiving end of internationalization as a resource for growing numbers of international students. Considering that English serves as a symbol for the internationalization of higher education (Duong and Chua, 2016), there are critical questions raised about what that symbol might signify, particularly in the uneven global power dynamics of international education. For researchers and practitioners in this area, this brings up several reflection points, including:

- How does EAP contribute to the commodification and marketization of higher education?
- To what extent does EAP assume assimilation to a normative standard of language proficiency?
- How might EAP perpetuate existing power imbalances between the Global North and Global South?
- How might EAP disrupt, disturb or disregard local language practices and students' linguistic identities?
- How can EAP be transformed to better value linguistic diversity and other world Englishes?

Such questions demonstrate an agenda moving forward for reconceptualizing EAP beyond deficit narratives of students' language proficiencies that have perhaps formed a foundation for its existence. After all, it has been argued that EAP represents potential 'laboratories of innovation' (Schaffner, 2020) through developing cutting-edge pedagogies in intercultural settings. However, there is a danger that EAP might instead be positioned as a bandage for internationalization's challenges, rather than a transformative space for intercultural learning, without critical reflection on its relationship with internationalization and positioning in an unequal world.

References

Al-Mahrooqi, R. I., and C. J. Denman (2018), *English Education in Oman: Current Scenarios and Future Trajectories*, London: Springer.

Altbach, P. G., and J. Knight (2007), 'The Internationalization of Higher Education: Motivations and Realities', *Journal of Studies in International Education*, 11 (3–4): 290–305.

Bamberger, A., P. Morris and M. Yemini (2019), 'Neoliberalism, Internationalisation, and Higher Education: Connections, Contradictions, and Alternatives', *Discourse: Studies in the Cultural Politics of Education*, 40 (20): 203–16.

Buckner, E., and S. Stein (2020), 'What Counts as Internationalization? Deconstructing the Internationalization Imperative', *Journal of Studies in International Education*, 24 (2): 151–66.

C-BERT (2021), 'C-BERT Branch Campus Listing. [Data originally collected by Kevin Kinser and Jason E Lane]'. Available online: http://cbert.org/resources-data/ (accessed 24 February 2022).

Cheng, Y., M. Zhang and Y. Zu (2014), 'Statistical Analysis of Indicators of Internationalization for Key Higher Education Institutions in China', *Journal of Higher Education*, 35: 46–54.

Choi, P. K. (2010), 'Weep for Chinese University: A Case Study of English Hegemony and Academic Capitalism in Higher Education in Hong Kong', *Journal of Educational Policy*, 25 (2): 233–52.

Choudaha, R. (2017), 'Are International Students "cash cows"?' *International Higher Education*, 90: 5–6.

Cots, J. M., E. Llurda and P. Garrett (2014), 'Language Policies and Practices in the Internationalisation of Higher Education on the European Margins: An Introduction', *Journal of Multilingual and Multicultural Development*, 35 (4): 311–17.

de Wit, H. (2017), 'The Importance of Internationalization at Home: In a Time of Political Tensions', *TH&MA Hoger Onderwijs*, 5: 25–9.

Ding, A., and I. Bruce (2017), *The English for Academic Purposes Practitioner: Operating on the Edge of Academia*, London: Palgrave Macmillan.

Duong, V. A., and C. S. K. Chua (2016), 'English as a Symbol of Internationalisation of Higher Education: Terminology, Typologies, and Power', *Higher Education Research & Development*, 30 (5): 609–22.

Evans, S., and B. Morrison (2011), 'The First Term at University: Implications for EAP', *ELT Journal*, 65 (4): 387–97.

Fenton-Smith, B., P. Humphreys and I. Walkinshaw (2017), *English Medium Instruction in Higher Education in Asia-Pacific*, Singapore: Springer.

Galante, A., K. Okubo, C. Cole, N. A. Elkader, N. Carozza, C. Wilkinson, C. Wotton and J. Vasic (2019), 'Plurilingualism in Higher Education: A Collaborative Initiative for the Implementation of Plurilingual Pedagogy in an Engilsh for Academic Purposes Program at a Canadian University', *TESL Canada Journal*, 36 (1): 121–33.

Galloway, N., T. Numajiri and N. Rees (2020), 'The "Internationalisation", or "Englishisation", of Higher Education in East Asia', *Higher Education*, 80: 395–414.

Goksu, A., and G. G. Goksu (2015), 'A Comparative Analysis of Higher Education Financing in Different Countries', *Procedia Economics and Finance*, 26: 1152–8.

Hadley, G. (2015), *English for Academic Purposes in Neoliberal Universities: A Critical Grounded Theory*, London: Springer.

Haugh, M. (2016), 'Complaints and Troubles Talk about the English Language Skills of International Students in Australian Universities', *Higher Education Research & Development*, 35 (4): 727–40.

Hauptman Komotar, M. (2019), 'Global University Rankings and Their Impact on the Internationalisation of Higher Education', *European Journal of Education*, 54 (2): 299–310.

HESA (2021), Higher Education Statistics for the UK: 2019/2020. Available online: www.hesa.ac.uk/stats (accessed 24 February 2022).

House of Commons Library (2021), 'Coronavirus: Financial Impacts on Higher Education. Research Briefing'. Available online: https://commonslibrary.parliament.uk/research-briefings/cbp-8954/ (accessd 24 February 2022).

Hua, Z., and X. Gao (2021), 'Language, Culture, and Curriculum: Lived Intercultural Experiences of International Students', *Language, Culture, & Curriculum*, 34 (4): 358–465.

Hudzik, J. K. (2015), *Comprehensive Internationalization: Institutional Pathways to Success*, London: Routledge.

Jenkins, J. (2013), *English as a Lingua Franca in the International University: The Politics of Academic English Language Policy*, London: Routledge.

Jin, L., and J. Schneider (2019), 'Faculty Views on International Students: A Survey Study', *Journal of International Students*, 9 (1): 84–96.

Kehm, B. M., and U. Teichler (2007), 'Research on Internationalisation in Higher Education', *Journal of Studies in International Education*, 11 (3–4): 260–73.

Kerklaan, V., G. Moreira and K. Boersma (2008), 'The Role of Language in the Internationalisation of Higher Education: An Example of Portugal', *European Journal of Education*, 43 (2): 241–55.

Kondakci, Y., S. Bedenlier and O. Zawacki-Richter (2018), 'Social Network Analysis of International Student Mobility: Uncovering the Rise of Regional Hubs', *Higher Education*, 75: 517–35.

Kosmützky, A., and R. Putty (2016), 'Transcending Borders and Traversing Boundaries: A Systematic Review of the Literature on Transnational, Offshore, Cross-Border, and Borderless Higher Education', *Journal of Studies in International Education*, 20 (1): 8–33.

Knight, J. (2004), 'Internationalization Remodeled: Definitions, Approaches, and Rationales', *Journal of Studies in International Education*, 8 (1): 5–31.

Knight, J. (2014), 'Is Internationalisation of Higher Education having an Identity Crisis?', in A. Maldonado-Maldonado and R. M. Bassett (eds), *The Forefront of*

International Higher Education: A Festschrift in Honor of Philip G. Altbach, 75–87, London: Springer.

Leask, B., and J. Carroll. (2011), 'Moving Beyond "Wishing and Hoping": Internationalisation and Student Experiences of Inclusion and Engagement', *Higher Education Research and Development*, 30 (5): 647–59.

Leisyte, L., and A. L. Rose (2017), 'Academic Staff Mobility in the Age of Trump and Brexit?' *International Higher Education*, 89: 5–6.

Liu, L., Z. Zhong and C. Hamish (2019), 'The Realistic Dilemma and Countermeasures of International Talent Governance in Universities under the Background of "Double First-Class" Construction', *Chinese Higher Education Study*, 9: 42–7.

Liu, W. (2017), 'The Changing Role of Non-English Papers in Scholarly Communication: Evidence from Web of Science's Three Journal Citation Indexes', *Learned Publishing*, 30: 115–23.

Liu, W. (2021), 'The Chinese Definition of Internationalisation in Higher Education', *Journal of Higher Education Policy and Management*, 43 (2): 230–45.

Lomer, S. (2017), 'Soft Power as a Policy Rationale for International Education in the UK: A Critical Analysis', *Higher Education*, 74: 581–98.

Macaro, E., S. Curle, J. Pun, J. An and J. Dearden (2018), 'A Systematic Review of English Medium Instruction in Higher Education', *Language Teaching*, 51 (1): 36–76.

Mittelmeier, J., B. Slof and B. Rienties (2021), 'Students' Perspectives on Curriculum Internationalisation Policies in Transition: Insights from a Master's Degree Programme in the Netherlands', *Innovations in Education and Teaching International*, 58 (1): 107–19.

Mwangi, C., S. Latafat, S. Hammond, S. Kommers, H. Thoma, J. Berger and G. Blanco-Ramirez (2018), 'Criticality in International Higher Education Research: A Critical Discourse Analysis of Higher Education Journals', *Higher Education*, 76 (6): 1091–107.

NAFSA (2021), 'International Student Economic Value Tool'. Available online: https://www.nafsa.org/policy-and-advocacy/policy-resources/nafsa-international-student-economic-value-tool-v2 (accessed 24 February 2022).

Nuske, K. (2017), '"I Mean I'm Kind of Discriminating My Own People": A Chinese TESOL Graduate Student's Shifting Perceptions of China English', *TESOL Quarterly*, 52 (2): 360–91.

OECD (2021), 'International Student Mobility'. Available online: https://data.oecd.org/students/international-student-mobility.htm (accessed 24 February 2022).

Ordorika, I., and M. Lloyd (2015), 'International Rankings and the Contest for University Hegemony', *Journal of Education Policy*, 30 (3): 385–405.

Pauwels, A. (2014), 'The Teaching of Languages at University in the Context of Super-Diversity', *International Journal of Multilingualism*, 11 (3): 307–19.

Pearson, W. S. (2020), 'The Effectiveness of Pre-Sessional EAP Programmes in UK Higher Education: A Review of the Evidence', *Review of Education*, 8 (2): 420–47.

Phan, L. H. (2013), 'Issues Surrounding English, the Internationalisation of Higher Education and National Cultural Identity in Asia: A Focus on Japan', *Critical Studies in Education*, 54 (2): 160–75.

Rose, H., and J. McKinley (2018), 'Japan's English-Medium Instruction Initiatives and the Globalization of Higher Education', *Higher Education*, 75: 111–29.

Rose, H., J. McKinley, X. Xu and S. Zhou. (2020), 'Investigating Policy and Implementation of English Medium Instruction in Higher Education', British Council. Available online: https://www.teachingenglish.org.uk/sites/teacheng/files/Investigating_EMI_in_HEIs_China.pdf (accessed 24 February 2022).

Schaffner, S. (2020), 'The Language Centre as a Laboratory of Innovation', *Language Learning in Higher Education*, 10 (2): 317–25.

Skyrme, G., and A. McGee (2016), 'Pulled in Many Directions: Tensions and Complexity for Academic Staff Responding to International Students', *Teaching in Higher Education*, 21 (7): 759–72.

Slaughter, S., and B. Cantwell (2012), 'Transatlantic Moves to the Market: The United States and the European Union', *Higher Education*, 63: 583–606.

Spolsky, B. (2004), *Language Policy*, Cambridge: Cambridge University Press.

Tight, M. (2021), 'Globalization and Internationalization as Frameworks for Higher Education Research', *Research Papers in Education*, 36 (1): 52–74.

Wächter, B., and F. Maiworm (2014), *English-Taught Programmes in European Higher Education: The State of Play in 2014*, Brussels: Lemmens.

Werther, C., L. Denver, C. Jensen and I. M. Mees (2014), 'Using English as a Medium of Instruction at University Level in Denmark: The Lecturer's Perspective', *Journal of Multilingual and Multicultural Development*, 35 (5): 443–62.

Wihlborg, M., and S. Robson (2018), 'Internationalisation of Higher Education: Drivers, Rationales, Priorities, Values, and Impacts', *European Journal of Higher Education*, 8 (1): 8–18.

Yemini, M., and N. Sagie (2016), 'Research on Internationalisation in Higher Education – Exploratory Analysis', *Perspectives: Policy and Practice in Higher Education*, 20 (2–3): 90–8.

3

The Economics, Ethics and Discourse of Recruiting International Students

Sylvie Lomer and Ying Yang

Introduction

More than five million students studied in degree courses outside their home country in 2017, with a projected increase to eight million by 2025 (UNESCO, 2018). Host countries rely on these students for income, specifically to cross subsidize higher education, but also for the broader economic gains, and to a lesser extent, to facilitate internationalization of the curriculum. International student flows are increasingly multidimensional, with students travelling regionally for study as well as to traditional destinations in the West and Global North (Cheng, 2021), generating an increasingly competitive environment. While the Covid-19 pandemic has substantially impacted physical mobility, students have continued to engage in substantial numbers with temporarily distanced learning (ICEF Monitor, 2020). This has created substantial challenges for institutions which have met calls to reduce tuition fees in recognition of the curtailed nature of the pandemic student experience (*The Independent*, 2020; Yang et al., 2020). While these calls may not take full account of the resourcing required and challenges of delivering online learning, they do highlight tensions around tuition fees and the equity and ethics around international student recruitment. These dynamics shape the context where pre-sessional English for Academic Purposes (EAP) programmes catalyse the supply of international higher education and facilitate international student recruitment by bridging the linguistic shortfalls of degree programmes (Pearson, 2020). Pre-sessional programmes enable universities to recruit students who do not meet language entry requirements, thereby significantly expanding potential student numbers. EAP also encompasses in-sessional skills and language support, meaning the provision of workshops, tutorials and resources for students currently studying. Often, this is provided by a centre, but some institutions embed EAP provision within academic departments.

In established host countries, the marketization and internationalization of higher education have become taken for granted. This chapter aims to explore and expose some of the tensions in relation to international student recruitment. Marketization creates ethical tensions for all those involved in international student recruitment, from students, to agents, to universities, to host countries. It generates economic incentives which would not exist (or would be highly attenuated) in a publicly oriented system. The aim of this chapter is to explore some of these tensions, not in the interest of 'resolving' them, but rather to expose the challenges.

We draw on several recent projects for data, and seek to synthesize these with previous policy analyses. In most of these projects, the focus has been on the UK, or on actors with intentions or connections to the UK, and this is reflected throughout the chapter. We have sought to draw parallels and make connections with other countries where possible to highlight the global relevance of these insights. This approach unfortunately continues to centre the UK and therefore fails to undermine the persistent intellectual coloniality inherent to the contemporary field of international student mobility. Instead, we take on Moosavi's (2020a) challenge to 'de-imperialize', rather than seek to decolonize: in this case by destabilizing the imperialist assumptions that configure international higher education in the UK context.

Context

Marketization, distinct from marketing, signifies the process by which previously regarded as public goods become privately owned products (Findlay, McCollum and Packwood, 2017). In the higher education domain, as public support declines, tuition fees become an important source of supplementary income. Using market competition was considered as an effective policy incentive for greater innovation and adaptation as well as low cost delivery (Foskett, 2011). In such a marketized system, three main vectors are involved (Teixeira et al., 2004: 4–5): 'promotion of competition between higher education providers, privatisation of higher education either by emergence of a private higher education sector or by means of privatisation of certain aspects of public institutions, as well as promotion of economic autonomy of their education institutions, enhancing their responsiveness and articulation to supply and demand of factors and products'. In the broader context of globalizing neoliberalism, the discourses of marketization have become dominant in higher education (HE) sectors worldwide. In market terms, customer satisfaction should be the measure of success; therefore student satisfaction has become the key indicator of higher education quality. Yet, scant evidence indicates the benefits of marketization of education apart from the short-term financial benefits for universities (Judson and Taylor, 2014). Specifically, educational outcomes in terms of long-term skills such as critical thinking and complex reasoning are not improving in the process of marketization (Arum and Roksa, 2011). In this regard, some scholars critique that marketization has transformed the nature of higher education from a public to a private good (Newman and Jahdi, 2009), alumni from lifelong learners into professionals, students from critical thinkers into consumers (Judson and Taylor, 2014: 52), and transformed the relationship between researchers and learners into the relationship between a service provider and a consumer (Hall, 2018). Marketization may be a dominant discourse and organizing principle, but it has many critics.

In recent years, the rise of the international higher education market has become significant (Maringe and Foskett, 2010), which is more diverse and dynamic than the home market and offers opportunities for countries to gain export income. Along with the trend of globalization (Varghese, 2013), promoting international higher education and recruiting full-paying international students as an alternative source of income are considered lucrative choices for many universities across the world (Lomer, 2017). In general, as discussed below, international students are charged higher tuition fees than domestic students (Tannock, 2013). As a result, more universities especially in the popular host countries such as the United States, the UK, Australia and Canada, cast their attention to developing markets abroad and seek to secure an advantageous position in competition for international students by employing various recruitment strategies (Foskett, 2011). In the UK, for example, the strategies range from national branding, to targeted recruitment practices depending on the specificity of the geographical markets, to multiple marketing approaches, to brand building of individual universities (Findley, McCollum and Packwood, 2017). Among those, contracting with education agents and agencies from emerging or key markets such as China and India is conceived of as a cost-effective and important way of undertaking international student recruitment (BUILA, 2021). In this sense, the marketization of international higher education is enhanced (Foskett, 2011).

Indeed, the marketization of international higher education has become widely accepted and received little public resistance. This may be tied to the challenges of imagining higher education as a 'global public good', when it has historically been closely linked to the project of nation building (Marginson, 2016). However, some critiques and concerns associated with this special quasi-market still arise. First, marketization of international higher education has shifted to the financial interest that the host countries can achieve, rather than cultivating global talents (Findley, McCollum and Packwood, 2017). Second, international students are over-represented by wealthy or elite groups from particular nationalities given much higher tuition fees charged to them (Bolsmann and Miller, 2008), deviating from the apparent/stated intention of bringing diversity to the campus and classes for its educational benefits. International students are often referred to as offering a 'window on the world' for home students (Lomer, Papatsiba and Naidoo, 2018). This over-representation results in negative stereotyping of international students in general by domestic students and by academic staff. This also implies the potential risk of overdependence on income generation from limited markets. Therefore, marketization of international higher education exacerbates issues of educational inequity (Tannock, 2013), as international higher education is predominantly exploited by wealthy, middle-class and elite families as a channel to get rid of the equity constraint of domestic education systems in their home country and reproduce positional advantages through studying abroad (Waters and Brooks, 2010). It also compromises the potential educational benefits of internationalization and globalization in relation to higher education.

On the grounds that international student recruitment has become a significant revenue source for universities, the discourse of international students as cash cows is prevalent. For example, the most recent UK International Education Strategy (DfIT and DfE, 2019) sets a target of recruiting 600,000 international students by 2030, in the context of the revenue education exports in general to the UK. They specifically justify this ambition by saying that 'international students bring important revenue to the UK higher education sector and to the UK economy' (11). This narrative has been identified on both the national scale in the UK (Lomer, Papatsiba and Naidoo, 2018; Tannock, 2018), Australia (Robertson, 2011) and the United States (Choudaha, 2017). On the institutional level, Cantwell's (2019) research on international undergraduates' tuition revenue among some US colleges and universities indicates that tuition revenues differ within and between those higher education institutions (HEIs) that can attract many international students and those that do not have the visibility to do so. Precisely, not every university in the United States that recruits international students will benefit, which is probably applicable to HEIs in other countries, as discussed further below. Moreover, Choudaha (2017) points that viewing international students as cash cows is unethical and detrimental to the reputation of universities. Yet the economic rationale remains dominant as a legitimation of international student recruitment.

The Economics

International students' tuition fees are a key source of support for the UK higher education sector, and the economy more broadly (DfIT and DfE, 2019; Johnson et al, 2021). The practice of setting differential fee levels for home and overseas students is often taken as unproblematic, particularly in countries where universities are partially subsidized by taxpayers. Where students or their parents have not paid taxes in that country, these additional fees can be considered to reflect the unsubsidized cost (Walker, 2014). After long resistance, countries such as Norway, Finland and Germany (Altbach and de Wit, 2018) are moving towards introducing international student fees, making this a globalized norm (Kauko and Medvedeva, 2016). But it is worth remembering that not so long ago, subsidizing international student fees was considered to be an important political and cultural endeavour (Walker, 2014). Indeed, in the postcolonial period it was seen as a matter of responsibility for imperial powers to support the development of newly independent nations through international higher education, and the framing of international students as 'ambassadors' remains an important rationale (Chankseliani, 2018).

In this section, we draw on the preliminary analysis of data from the Reddin survey[1] on tuition fees to illustrate and challenge the rationalities that underpin international student recruitment (Oliver, 2021).

In contrast to national policies set for home students, British policy has set no cap on international tuition fees (Walker, 2014). Our analysis of the Reddin survey data shows that international postgraduate tuition fees for classroom-based courses (PET) have increased from an average of £8,606 in 2006 to an average of £16,455 in 2020. This represents a nearly 200 per cent increase over this time. The highest fee charged at this level is £29,796 at the London School of Economics and Politics, while the lowest is £9,750 at the Royal Veterinary College. In 2020, international PGT students were charged on average 188 per cent more than home students, or £7,037.

Our analysis suggests that international tuition fee levels correspond negatively to institutional reliance on tuition fee income. The less an institution relies on tuition fees, the higher its international student fees are set. Typically, lower ranked institutions rely more on tuition fee income in the absence of other sources. International higher education can be understood as a status good (Marginson, 2013), valuable to the extent that it is positional – not everyone has it. Pricing international fees highly confers a symbolic value that suggests the degree or course at this university has scarcity value and connotes high quality. This is exemplified by the single highest fee charged in 2020 by the University of Oxford for its MBA: £54,590. In a sense, the MBA can be understood as the least essential degree, most similar to a luxury product (British Council, 2003).

This discussion of tuition fees illustrates several points. First, international tuition fees are increasing rapidly over time in marked contrast to home student fees. This generates an ethical tension, as follows. Second, international student fees are being charged in many cases nearly double the price that home students are paying for precisely the same experience and education. International students are not typically entitled to any additional services or support which might justify this fee differential. Even in-sessional EAP and language support, which is often represented as for overseas students, is available to all, and also supports non-native English speaking students categorized as 'home' students for fee-paying purposes. International fee-paying students, therefore, do not have access to a specialized, targeted range of services that high fees might imply. Third, institutions do not set their prices with reference to the 'product' on offer. Oduoza (2009) suggests that it is often challenging to make an accurate accounting of the costs of an individual school, particularly in terms of central administration, overheads and so on. Unlike more traditional commodities, higher education pricing is not directly tied to the cost of providing the services, and the educational offering at two different price points may not be quantifiably distinct in terms of course content, teaching methods, contact hours, staff expertise and so on. Tuition fee levels rather reflect the relative prestige and potential labour market value of degrees from different universities (Marginson, 2013).

High prices and the construction of international students in general as cash cows for the institution in the nation lead to the presumption that all international students as individuals are wealthy. Xie et al. (2020) identified 'nouveau riche' as a significant negative stereotype experienced by Chinese students in the United States. In this study, several students reported overtly discriminatory behaviours directed towards apparently rich Chinese students. Certainly most Chinese students, the largest group of international students in the UK, self fund – Iannelli and Huang (2014) put this estimate at 82 per cent overall and 90 per cent for undergraduates. However, this does not necessarily mean that they are personally wealthy. Choudaha, Orosz and Chang's (2012) study indicated that many students could be categorized as financially either 'striving' or 'struggling'. There is limited national level data available on international students' funding sources, but our interviews with Chinese students suggest that self-funding is a term that conceals a wide range of financial strategies, including extended family contributions and family savings over several years of preparation. As Forbes-Mewett et al. (2009) highlight, such dependence can create its own challenges and 37 per cent of students in their survey in Australia experienced financial difficulties. The Covid-19 pandemic left many students in the UK without access to part-time work and some became dependent on food banks for survival (Popp, 2021). UK universities' economic dependence on international students is therefore not an unproblematic exchange of luxury services for high prices. The notion of education exports masks complex trade-offs and sacrifices that take place on both a global and an intensely private stage.

Recruitment Practices

Countries that rely heavily on, or are seeking to improve or increase their international student recruitment often engage in national-level activities to enhance their attractiveness on the global stage. What is possible for countries to do depends significantly on governance and policy structures (Geddie, 2015). Countries with more centralized policy regimes such as the UK, Australia and China are able to mobilize a wider range of resources and activities than those with decentralized governance structures such as the United States. China has, for instance, increased scholarship opportunities available to international students (Mulvey and Lo, 2021) in line with its broader ambitions to internationalize the higher education sector and grow its soft power. Like China, the UK aims to attract more international students, and the 2019 International Education Strategy (DfIT and DfE, 2019) set the target of 600,000 international students in higher education by 2030. Framed as part of education exports, this strategy, like others before, sees international students as an opportunity for income generation. This relies on a national-branding campaign which includes higher education (Lomer, Papatsiba and Naidoo, 2018). This comprehensive national brand enables the promotion of the higher education sector overseas, associating British universities with other 'pillars' of the campaign including creativity, innovation, technology and so on. In this initiative, we see the adoption of practices more commonly associated with traditional businesses becoming mainstream in international higher education.

Centralized policy regimes also enable countries such as the UK to introduce initiatives beyond the domain of education which shape its attractiveness, and immigration policy is a key domain. For instance, the recent reintroduction of the post-study work visa scheme has been welcomed by the sector and international students alike, and may remedy the decline in numbers particularly from India observed in the wake of the original removal of this scheme in 2011 (Lomer, Papatsiba and Naidoo, 2018). Chinese student numbers, in contrast, rose dramatically during the same period, suggesting a greater focus on credentials and short-term educational experiences. For many years, at least until the 2020 Covid-19 pandemic, Australia and Canada were for example able to implement a points-based immigration system which became an attractive option for those international students seeking long-term mobility opportunities overseas (Geddie, 2015).

On the institutional level, universities are able to set their own strategies within the structures of the national policy context. In many cases, UK universities make international student recruitment a key part of their institutional strategy or mission statement (Yang et al., 2022). This is sometimes set in the form of specific targets for recruitment, but often framed more broadly within the context of internationalizing and global engagement (Lewis, 2021). Out of the 134 strategy documents identified for inclusion in this project, 59 mentioned increasing or enhancing international student recruitment. While this was often couched in broader terms around increasing the attractiveness of the institution, increasing numbers of international students was a dominant strategy. Lewis (2021) concurs, finding that, of those strategic plans with explicit key performance indicators, the most commonly applied indicator was the recruitment of international students. In our analysis, several specifically cited it as fundamental to institutional survival, while others emphasized the educational and curricular benefits of a more diverse student body. These strategies can be said to be drawing upon the educational rationale for international student recruitment (Lomer, Papatsiba and Naidoo, 2018).

A clear trend in these documents is nuanced awareness of the perceived challenges and problems around international student recruitment in the UK to date. There is an emphasis on 'high quality', 'talented' and 'the best' international students, in addition to an emphasis on diversity. The former focus on 'quality' echoes the discursive shift in national policy from 2006 to 2016 (Lomer, Papatsiba and Naidoo, 2018), implicitly referring to an understanding that there has been a trade-off between the numbers of international students and academic selectivity. This has resulted in a perception held by some academic staff and media (e.g. BBC, 2012) that the 'quality' of international students is not appropriate (Lomer, Mittelmeier and Carmichael-Murphy, 2021), despite apparent equivalence in formal admissions requirements. This narrative intersected with the anti-immigration rhetoric driven by the far right in British politics, in the context of the Brexit debate, generating an emphasis in national policy on getting 'the right students'. 'Diversity' refers implicitly to the shared understanding of international student recruitment as dominated by students from mainland China, who account for 35 per cent of non-EU student admissions in the UK (Johnson et al., 2021). The apparent lack of diversity compromises the potential for international and intercultural exchange in classrooms and on campuses, and teaching staff in a recent interview study (Lomer, Mittelmeier and Carmichael-Murphy, 2021) confirmed that in some student cohorts only a few nationalities were represented. However, this reductive understanding of diversity focuses on an ethno-national understanding of culture and disregards other dimensions of diversity which are given more prominence in domestic widening participation narratives. Not all students from China are the same, in other words. The persistent deficit narrative particularly associated with students from mainland China (Moosavi, 2020b) underpins this strategic emphasis. From a business perspective, this 'over-reliance' also creates a future risk should the 'bubble' of recruitment from China burst (Johnson et al., 2021).

More pragmatically, institutions can develop a range of courses designed to increase international student recruitment. Pre-sessional courses are increasingly common to provide opportunities for students to increase their English language level prior to starting their main degree course. It is challenging to gain a sense of the scale and scope of pre-sessional provision, as this is not reported separately through any of the national UK datasets. However, our subjective impression is that most universities with substantial international student numbers would offer these programs. Many universities also offer articulation or top-up programs in affiliation with international partners, such that international students can complete the final year of study in the UK and receive a degree certificate from the UK institution. Also, many institutions offer international foundation years or pre-Masters courses, creating an additional route of entry where academic qualifications are considered insufficient for direct entry. Increasingly, these programs are delivered by private pathway providers, such as Kaplan, INTO, StudyGroup and Navitas (Universities UK, 2014). Around 40 per cent of non-EU HEI students in 2011 in the UK entered via one of these providers. The latter example indicates how the intensification of market activities shapes contemporary international student recruitment. Finally, some universities may create additional degree programmes that bear substantial similarities to existing provision, for the purposes of generating additional recruitment, as reported in recent student interviews. Taken together, these examples show how UK universities look for multiple opportunities to generate income through international student recruitment.

Education Agents

Education agents are an increasingly important, but often less discussed, actor in the field of international student recruitment. They mediate between international students and recruiting education providers. As private entities, they provide a range of services from counselling students, preparing application documents and supporting institutions with marketing promotion (BUILA, 2021) – and charge commission from institutions and/or fees from students. In this section, we draw on several linked research projects led by Ying Yang which explore the role of education agents in China in shaping the international higher education trajectories of Chinese postgraduate students (Yang et al., 2020; Yang et al., 2022).

BUILA (2021) estimates that 50 per cent of international students in the UK used the services of an education agent to help gain admission and navigate visa processes. Agents are therefore seen as essential to the UK's international student recruitment. Particularly during the uncertainties of the Covid-19 pandemic, agents filtered and interpreted the rapidly changing information coming from institutions and governments to support students in applying and preparing to study (Yang et al., 2022). Our research with prospective Chinese international students who used education agents to apply to UK universities indicates that overall agents' input into the university application process, including both practical and emotional support, is recognized and appreciated by all the participants (Zhang, Yang and Hoh, 2021). Agents also play an important role in supporting student recruitment from India, Nigeria, Malaysia, Vietnam and Pakistan (BUILA, 2021). Not all recruiting countries have historically relied on agents to the same extent, however, and the United States has only recently come to accept their presence (Wang, Wang and Jiang, 2020). Students commented on how much choice they had between agents, highlighting the scale and diversity of the industry. They interpreted this level of activity as signifying recruiting universities' need for international students, and universities' reliance on education agents legitimated them as a whole.

In the Chinese context, education agents support institutions in recruiting international students. They promote international student recruitment overall by disseminating information about studying abroad, facilitating the process and bridging the information gap (Yang et al., 2022). Agents can mediate between the country, university and the student, to make sense of information, regulations and create accurate expectations about prospective student experiences. Operating independently, agents gain a sense of which universities or programmes are 'offer machines', where students are effectively guaranteed an offer regardless of their background because the institution needs international students and which are more selective (Yang et al., in press). Except where they operate in partnership, education agents can be situated as supporting international student recruitment as a whole, rather than for specific institutions. Partnerships between universities and agencies, which take a range of contractual forms (Huang, Raimo and Humfrey, 2016), can offer more targeted promotion and support from delegated offer-making to separate application systems, developed exclusively for students applying through partnerships (BUILA, 2021). However, agents are often less motivated to work with institutions with lower profiles and rankings in international markets (who typically most 'need' students), since their student clients tend to seek access to more elite, famous institutions. This confirms the preliminary analysis of international tuition fee levels in relation to institutional reliance on overall tuition fee income.

While the need for agents' services, both from universities and students, is significant, unregulated business practices with low minimum standards of service raise concerns about ethics, particularly among sole traders (BUILA, 2021). This can compromise students' opportunities to study abroad and cause reputational damage to host institutions misrepresented through over-optimistic counselling or indeed lead to outright forgery and cheating (Wang, Wang and Jiang, 2020). Accurate advice and representation from qualified and well-trained agents is essential for institutions to sustain a long-term approach to international student recruitment. Students in our interviews mentioned concerns such as provision of insufficient information, less effective advice on universities or programmes and grammar mistakes in the essay editing such as verb tense and spelling. Many appear to empathize with education agents and their limitations, which in a way imply development or enhancement of their relationship with agents in the course of application. However, it should be acknowledged that students in the research all achieved ideal application results, which probably results in commenting positively on agents' function in students' application process, but it still effectively reflects the value of agents. Nevertheless, most suggested that they would not use agents again because they found the process less complicated than they originally imagined.

The complexity of education agents' position in the marketized field of international higher education is revealed in the dynamics of payment. Nearly all (97 per cent) of education agents get a commission from universities, often a percentage of the first year's tuition fee (BUILA, 2021). In some cases, agents would not charge students for their core services, which are covered by the commission. In others, smaller companies might link up with a larger agency to obtain a part-share of the commission. Agents also receive other perquisites from some institutions, including expenses-paid visits as training opportunities. Most agencies have a range of ancillary fee-paying services such as language classes, travel services, visa application support, internship placements, help with personal statements, interview preparation, among others (Yang et al., 2020). Paying for these additional services creates an additional financial burden to students. In the case of language support, for example, the expectation is created that students will pay for additional language classes, sometimes multiple expensive exams (the IELTS exam being in itself highly marketized) (Pearson, 2019) to meet the admissions standards set by universities. It can thus be seen that marketization of international higher education engenders more financial barriers to international students. Since universities benefit so greatly from international students' presence, both economically and pedagogically, why is this burden placed on students rather than institutions?

Yet students perceived these fees as reasonable given the average price in the current market, the number of applications they submitted, as well as the level of agents' engagement. Compared with the tuition fee and living expenses abroad, all the participants view the service fee as an affordable and small 'insurance investment'. Students understood themselves as consumers, friends and students in relation to their agents, which makes them able to negotiate their expectations with agents directly.

Taken together, education agents have become a significant part of the marketized international higher education as they fundamentally contribute to generating economic benefits by effectively promoting international student recruitment in different key and emerging markets. For example, 'education agents contribute approximately £11.88 billion (including tuition fees and all the living expenses) to the UK economy each year' (BUILA, 2021: 32). Education agents also facilitate the evolution of international higher education into a positional good in the forms of stimulating competition between universities, accentuating information gaps between students and universities and charging additional fees to students, fostering education inequities in the international higher education market.

Ethical Issues for Education

Having established that recruiting institutions rely heavily on international students for tuition fee income and deploy a range of recruitment strategies to attract and enrol them, we now turn to the ethical dimensions of what happens in the classroom of British universities.

International students tend to get lower marks at undergraduate level than home students. There is a persistent though undramatic gap between the level of degree awarded on graduation for international domiciled students in the UK, compared to UK domiciled or EU students. At undergraduate level (the only level on which national attainment data is published), a smaller proportion of students domiciled outside the EU[2] consistently attain first class degrees (27 per cent) than either British (34 per cent) or EU students (40 per cent). They get proportionally lower second class (21 per cent, vs 14 per cent UK and 11 per cent EU) and third class or pass degree marks (4 per cent, vs 3 per cent UK and 2 per cent EU) (HESA, 2021). These differences are not enormous, but they represent slight improvements over the last several years, suggesting that the awarding gap is entrenched. The data reported above are the only data published on this issue by Higher Education Statistics Authority (HESA), and it is not further disaggregated by institution, subject or more detailed demographic attributes. This is in stark contrast to the Office for Students' recent publication of an interactive data dashboard, which includes data on attainment and widening participation indicators for British domiciled students, building on an increased awareness of awarding gaps for British Black, Asian and Minority Ethic (BAME) students. The epistemic exclusion of international students from equivalent indicators (Hayes, 2019) is superficially pragmatic, since data such as international employability indicators and postcode level information is not available for internationally domiciled students and is highly significant to the British widening participation policy context. However, it also serves to camouflage this persistent difference in awards, as Tannock (2018) has discussed.

Multiple institutions have separately identified an awards gap in relation to international students, including the University of Keele and University College London. However, these are complicated by questions of ethnicity and racism. There is an obvious intersection between groups minoritized in the British context, such as, for example, Black African or East Asian students, and between those racialized as white as the 'default', such as EU students (Madriaga and McCaig, 2019: 2). EU-domiciled students outperform both British students and international students in the first-class degree category, implying a racialized pattern since the vast majority of EU students would be racialized as 'white' in the UK context. Indeed, interviews with lecturers (Lomer, Mittelmeier and Carmichael-Murphy, 2021) frequently differentiated between EU or US students and the implied norm of the 'East Asian' international students. While these statistics cannot disaggregate between ethnic groups or particular domiciles which previous literature has shown to be relevant (Gemmell and Harrison, 2020; Iannelli and Huang, 2014), it does support the interpretation that outcomes gaps may be linked to the racialization of international students.

In particular, Iannelli and Huang (2014) found that Chinese first-degree graduates were persistently awarded lower class degrees than their home and other international counterparts. In contrast, Gemmell and Harrison's (2020) analysis, conducted on a distance learning postgraduate course, found that Black African, Arab and Black Caribbean students had lower GPA than White, Chinese and Asian students, and concluded that ethnicity was the strongest predictor of outcomes. However, as literature on the BAME outcomes gap has highlighted, ethnicity is unlikely to be the 'effective variable' (Gayton, 2020), once a biological model of race in relation to academic achievement has been discounted as structurally and historically racist and empirically unsound. Rather, ethnicity is the most readily collected piece of data that indicates there is a 'pattern of racialised attainment' (Decolonising SOAS Working Group, 2018). Underpinning this pattern may be dynamics of linguistic prejudice and implicit hierarchies that situate 'native speaker Englishes' as 'superior'.

> Because their (non-native speaker international students) use of English differs from 'standard' (i.e. native) English, ... they may find they have marks deducted from their written work and sometimes oral presentations too, because their English is not sufficiently nativelike. They will therefore graduate with lower

grades than their home student peers, purely on account of their English. (Jenkins, 2020: 64)

Moosavi (2021) suggests that East Asian students in particular are often stigmatized in relation to deficit narratives that position them as uncritical thinkers, frequent plagiarists and looking for an easier degree. The construction of both the skills of referencing and critical thinking as indicative of students' 'quality' ignores the extensive literatures that build on Bourdieu's (1977) depiction of acquisition of cultural capital as a social process, as well as the academic literacies framework that propose these skills as situated knowledges embedded in social networks and disciplines (e.g. Lea and Street, 1998).

Recent research with teaching staff in the UK (Lomer, Mittelmeier and Caemichael-Murphy, 2021) engaged with international students suggests that they are superficially positive about the presence of international students. Many were hampered in pedagogic innovation by large student numbers, workload resourcing constraints, limited time and resources for reflection on their own practices. Several described (and others reflected in their tone of voice) the sense of exhaustion compounded but not only caused by the particular demands of a Covid-19 academic year. They described a fairly consistent pedagogic approach, emphasizing opportunities for interaction, discussion, active learning and the structured delivery of content in small chunks. Many used technology-enhanced learning approaches to facilitate engagement across multiple modes. Few emphasized the importance of lecturing. But many explicitly stated that they would not change the teaching approaches with a different group of students such as international students, believing their approach reflected best practice in inclusion. While several teachers commented on their efforts to support international students in acquiring the skills and capabilities required for academic success in a UK university, few reflected on how their own or their department's curriculum, pedagogy and assessment decisions reinforce international students' marginalization. This approach continues to centre UK, and Western, norms as superior approaches to teaching, and therefore does not question the coloniality of such practices or their capacity to accidentally exclude or marginalize those who are Othered.

Further, deficit discourses are challenging to extricate themselves from even where they are committed to inclusivity and internationalization in principle. In particular, concerns about international students' language standards and learning skills including research, writing and referencing, critical thinking and oral participation in discussions and seminars were frequently mentioned.

Staff explained that they tried to teach inclusively and sought to embed or refer students to support to enable them to access the curriculum and engage with the teaching methods. However, few staff evinced a pedagogical approach that capitalized on the epistemic value of international students in the classroom beyond multicultural group work. In a few cases, staff either expressed their own view or reported on the views of others towards international students that were simply racist. It is possible that these enduring stereotypes of international students underpin awarding gaps.

An ethical international higher education should mean equal access to knowledge, learning opportunities, support and the possibility to reach equal standards of academic achievement. A persistent inequality in outcomes implies that there is inequality of access to these opportunities, raising ethical concerns about the state of teaching in the internationalized university classroom in the UK.

Conclusion

EAP as a domain of professional practice takes place within the context of marketization of international higher education. Both marketization and internationalization in the specific form of the recruitment of international students to study physically in a host country have become a norm. International higher education is more commonly understood as a private good that benefits the individual students, which legitimates the charging of tuition fee. Host countries and recruiting institutions invest in a range of recruitment practices aimed at increasing this income including national branding, strategy making, target setting and the development of particular products – courses such as pre-sessional programmes which incorporate EAP. The marketization of international higher education has also allowed the development of a specific profession, the education agent who mediates between aspiring international students and recruiting providers. Supported by commissions from recruiting universities, agents smooth the path of international applications and enable universities to reach wider markets and increase their enrollments. Agents also provide additional services which students may pay for directly, such as language classes, visa application support and travel support. Agents are therefore symbiotic with universities, working to expand the international education market and correspondingly entrenching its discourses.

The narrative that centres the economic benefits of recruiting international students, who pay far larger tuition fee than do home students in most countries, represents the students as cash cows. These fee differentials privilege the already economically privileged and marginalize the experiences of less wealthy or struggling international students. These economic benefits are felt predominantly at the upper end of the sector in the UK, in Russell Group universities at the higher end of the rankings, and only to a very limited extent at the lower end of the rankings in smaller and lesser-known universities. While institutions and countries often contextualize the economic benefits in relation to educational benefits that result from a more diverse classroom, the impact that tuition fees have in shaping this diversity is rarely acknowledged.

Elite universities are therefore able to charge exorbitant tuition fees to international students, who gain access to limited additional resources and services. Unlike nearly any other marketized commodity, a higher price for an international university experience confers no additional privileges (other than visa support). Even access to in-sessional EAP support is rarely dedicated exclusively to international students and nor, from a perspective of equity in widening participation, should it be. Indeed, EAP is frequently under-resourced and positioned as a technical, centralized body, a place to refer international students or speakers of English as a second language when the pedagogic and curricular structures place them in deficit. This devalues EAP centres as secondary to disciplinary teaching, allowing departments to deflect challenges to the way language constructs meaning at the disciplinary level. By ascribing international student deficit to a 'technical' failing in the implementation of skills like academic style or citation practices and referring students out to EAP or in-sessional support, academics avoid the complex task of systematically evaluating established pedagogic practices of assessment and teaching.

International students act as an economic resource for universities but are not themselves resourced. Educational interventions that might help to structure and promote learning through diversity are neither appropriately resourced or conceptualized. Academic staff feel stretched and exhausted, asked to teach large groups of international students with no additional support or teaching assistants. They rely on their best knowledge of inclusive pedagogy, without further training that might help them to organize these principles in relation to an international and globalizing space. Instead, universities draw on dominant deficit discourses with reference to international students, constructing them as academically lacking and in need of further support in the form of EAP or paid-for pre-sessional or pathway courses. This academic marginalization may help to explain the racialized patterns of student outcomes, which see international students systematically underperforming home and EU-domiciled students.

International higher education is marketized in both its practices and its discourses. This is unlikely to change in the near future. What reflexive professionals in this context can achieve is a considered critical awareness of the forces that structure international student recruitment to reflect on the ethical tensions that emerge in our daily practice.

Notes

1 The Reddin survey is an annual survey coordinated by the Complete University guide, with publicly available data from 2006 to the present. It is a voluntary survey.
2 We use the term here of awarding gap to avoid implications of ability on the part of the student. This discussion has emerged in the context of Black, Asia and Minority Ethnic (BAME) student achievement debates, which frame the language of 'achievement' and 'attainment' as connoting individual responsibility. The language of 'awards' or 'outcomes' connote institutional responsibility and it is the latter that we wish to emphasize.

References

Altbach, P., and H. De Wit (2018), 'Are We Facing a Fundamental Challenge to Higher Education Internationalization?', *International Higher Education*, 93 (Spring): 2–4.

Arum, R., and J. Roksa (2011), *Academically Adrift: Limited Learning on College Campuses*, Chicago: University of Chicago Press.

BBC (2012), 'Lecturer Claims Pressure to Accept Substandard Work from Overseas Students', 16 October. Available online: https://www.bbc.co.uk/news/uk-wales-19945919 (accessed 31 May 2021).

Bourdieu, P. (1977), *Outline of a Theory of Practice*, Cambridge: Cambridge University Press. Available online: https://www.cambridge.org/core/books/outline-of-a-theory-of-practice/193A11572779B478F5BAA3E3028827D8 (accessed 15 May 2021).

Bolsmann, C., and H. Miller (2008), 'International Student Recruitment to Universities in England: Discourse, Rationales and Globalisation', *Globalisation, Societies and Education*, 6 (1): 75–88.

British Council (2003), *Education UK: Positioning for Success*, consultation document, London: British Council.

BUILA (2021), *A Route to a UK Quality Framework with Education Agents*. Available online: https://www.ukcisa.org.uk/uploads/files/1/Policy%20and%20lobbying/BUILA%20UKCISA%20Research%20Report%20FINAL.pdf (accessed 31 May 2021).

Cantwell, B. (2019), 'Are International Students Cash Cows? Examining the Relationship between New International Undergraduate Enrollments and Institutional Revenue at Public Colleges and Universities in the US', *Journal of International Students*, 5 (4): 512–25.

Chankseliani, M. (2018), 'Four Rationales of HE Internationalization: Perspectives of UK. Universities on Attracting Students from Former Soviet Countries', *Journal of Studies in International Education*, 22 (1): 53–70.

Cheng, M. (2021), 'Shifting Trends in International Student Mobility: Embracing Diversity and Responding to Change', *NAFSA: Association of International Educators*. Available online: https://www.nafsa.org/professional-resources/research-and-trends/shifting-trends-international-student-mobility-embracing (accessed 31 May 2021).

Choudaha, R. (2017), 'Are International Students "Cash Cows"?', *International Higher Education*, 90 (Summer): 5–6.

Choudaha, R., K. Orosz and L. Chang (2012), 'Not All International Students Are the Same: Understanding Segments, Mapping Behavior', *World Education News & Reviews*, August, 25 (7): 1–21.

Decolonising SOAS Working Group (2018), *Decolonising SOAS Learning and Teaching Toolkit for Programme and Module Convenors*. Available online: https://blogs.soas.ac.uk/decolonisingsoas/files/2018/10/Decolonising-SOAS-Learning-and-Teaching-Toolkit-AB.pdf (accessed 31 May 2021).

Department for International Trade (DfIT) and Department for Education (DfE) (2019), *International Education Strategy: Global Potential, Global Growth*, HM government. Available online: https://www.gov.uk/government/publications/international-education-strategy-global-potential-global-growth (accessed 31 May 2021).

Findlay, A. M., D. McCollum and H. Packwood (2017), 'Marketization, Marketing and the Production of International Student Migration', *International Migration*, 3 (55): 139–55.

Forbes-Mewett, H., S. Marginson, C. Nyland, G. Ramia and E. Sawir (2009), 'Australian University International Student Finances', *Higher Education Policy*, 22 (2):141–61.

Foskett, N. (2011), 'Markets, Government, Funding and the Marketisation of UK Higher Education', in M. Molesworth, R. Scullion and E. Nixon (eds), *The Marketisation of Higher Education and the Student as Consumer*, 39–52. Abingdon: Routledge.

Gayton, A. M. (2020), 'Exploring the Widening Participation-Internationalisation Nexus: Evidence from Current Theory and Practice', *Journal of Further and Higher Education*, 44 (9): 1275–88.

Geddie, K. (2015), 'Policy Mobilities in the Race for Talent: Competitive State Strategies in International Student Mobility', *Transactions of the Institute of British Geographers*, 40 (2): 235–48.

Gemmell, I., and R. Harrison (2020), 'Factors Associated with Differential Attainment among Transnational Students on an Online Distance Learning Programme', *Open Learning: The Journal of Open, Distance and E-Learning*: 1–13.

Hall, H. (2018), 'The Marketisation of Higher Education: Symptoms, Controversies, Trends', *Ekonomia I Prawo. Economics and Law*, 17 (1): 33–42.

Hayes, A. (2019), *Inclusion, Epistemic Democracy and International Students: The Teaching Excellence Framework and Education Policy*, London: Palgrave MacMillan.

Higher Education Statistics Authority (2021), 'What Are HE Students' Progression Rates and Qualifications?', *Higher Education Statistics Authority*. Available online: https://www.hesa.ac.uk/data-and-analysis/students/outcomes (accessed 30 July 2021).

Huang, I. Y., V. Raimo and C. Humfrey (2016), 'Power and Control: Managing Agents for International Student Recruitment in Higher Education', *Studies in Higher Education*, 41 (8): 1333–54.

Iannelli, C., and J. Huang (2014), 'Trends in Participation and Attainment of Chinese Students in UK Higher Education', *Studies in Higher Education*, 39 (5): 805–22. https://doi.org/10.1080/03075079.2012.754863 (accessed 15 July 2021).

ICEF Monitor (2020), 'English Universities in "Relatively Positive" Position Despite COVID-19'. https://monitor.icef.com/2020/12/english-universities-in-relatively-positive-position-despite-covid-19/ (accessed 20 July 2021).

Jenkins, J. (2020), 'Red Herrings and the Case of Language in UK Higher Education', *Nordic Journal of English Studies*, 19 (3): 59–67.

Johnson, J., J. Adams, J. Ilieva, J. Grant, J. Northend, N. Sreenan, V. Moxham-Hall, K. Greene and S. Mishra (2021), *The China Question: Managing Risks and Maximising Benefits from Partnership in Higher Education and Research*, The Policy Institute at King's College London and the Mossavar Rahmani Center for Business and Government (M-RCBG) at the Harvard Kennedy School. Available online: https://www.kcl.ac.uk/policy-institute/assets/china-question.pdf (accessed 15 July 2021).

Judson, K. M., and S. A. Taylor (2014), 'Moving from marketization to marketing of Higher Education: The Co-creation of Value in Higher Education', *Higher Education Studies*, 4 (1): 51–67.

Kauko, J., and A. Medvedeva (2016), 'Internationalisation as Marketisation? Tuition Fees for International Students in Finland', *Research in Comparative and International Education*, 11 (1): 98–114. Available online: https://journals.sagepub.com/doi/full/10.1177/1745499916631061 (accessed 25 June 2021).

Lea, M. R., and B. V. Street (1998), 'Student Writing in Higher Education: An Academic Literacies Approach', *Studies in Higher Education*, 23 (2): 157–72.

Lewis, V. (2021), *UK Universities' Global Engagement Strategies: Time for a Rethink?* Vicky Lewis Consulting. Available online: https://www.vickylewisconsulting.co.uk/global-strategies-report.php (accessed 1 July 2021).

Lomer, S. (2017), *Recruiting International Students in Higher Education: Representations and Rationales in British Policy*, Cham: Springer.

Lomer, S., J. Mittelmeier and P. Carmichael-Murphy (2021), *Cash Cows Or Pedagogic Partners? Mapping Pedagogic Practices For and With International Students*.

Available online: https://srhe.ac.uk/research/completed-award-reports/ (accessed 25 June 2021).

Lomer, S., V. Papatsiba and R. Naidoo (2018), 'Constructing a National Higher Education Brand for the UK: Positional Competition and Promised Capitals', *Studies in Higher Education*, 43 (1): 134–53.

Madriaga, M., and C. McCaig (2019), 'How International Students of Colour Become Black: A Story of Whiteness in English Higher Education', *Teaching in Higher Education*: 1–15.

Marginson, S. (2013), 'The Impossibility of Capitalist Markets in Higher Education', *Journal of Education Policy*, 28 (3): 353–70.

Marginson, S. (2016), *Public/Private in Higher Education: A Synthesis of Economic and Political Approaches*, 1–26, London: Centre for Global and Higher Education, University College London.

Maringe, F., and N. Foskett (eds) (2010), *Globalization and Internationalization in Higher Education: Theoretical, Strategic and Management Perspectives*, London: Bloomsbury.

Moosavi, L. (2020a), 'The Decolonial Bandwagon and the Dangers of Intellectual Decolonisation', *International Review of Sociology*, 30 (2): 332–54.

Moosavi, L. (2020b), '"Can East Asian Students Think?": Orientalism, Critical Thinking, and the Decolonial Project', *Education Sciences*, 10 (10): 286–306.

Moosavi, L. (2021), 'The Myth of Academic Tolerance: The Stigmatisation of East Asian Students in Western Higher Education', *Asian Ethnicity*: 1–20.

Mulvey, B., and W. Y. W. Lo (2021), 'Learning to "Tell China's Story Well": The Constructions of International Students in Chinese Higher Education Policy', *Globalisation, Societies and Education*, 19 (5): 545–57.

Newman, S., and K. Jahdi (2009), 'Marketization of Education: Marketing, Rhetoric, and Reality', *Journal of Further and Higher Education*, 33 (1): 1–11.

Oduoza, C. F. (2009), 'Reflections on Costing, Pricing and Income Measurement at UK Higher Education Institutions', *Journal of Higher Education Policy and Management*, 31 (2): 133–47.

Oliver, C. (2021), 'Reddin Survey of University Tuition Fees', Complete University Guide, 10 August. Available online: https://www.thecompleteuniversityguide.co.uk/sector/insights/reddin-survey-of-university-tuition-fees (accessed 31 May 2021).

Pearson, W. S. (2019), 'Critical Perspectives on the IELTS Test', *ELT Journal*, 73 (2): 197–206.

Pearson, W. S. (2020), 'Mapping English Language Proficiency Cut-off Scores and Pre-Sessional EAP Programmes in UK Higher Education', *Journal of English for Academic Purposes*, 45 (100866): 1–11.

Popp A. (2021), 'The International Students Struggling to Feed Themselves in Lockdown', Channel 4, 29 January. Available online: https://www.channel4.com/news/the-international-students-struggling-to-feed-themselves-in-lockdown (accessed 31 May 2021).

Robertson, S. (2011), 'Cash Cows, Backdoor Migrants, or Activist Citizens? International Students, Citizenship, and Rights in Australia', *Ethnic and Racial Studies*, 34 (12): 2192–211.

Tannock, S. (2013), 'When the Demand for Educational Equality Stops at the Border: Wealthy Students, International Students and the Restructuring of Higher Education in the UK', *Journal of Education Policy*, 28 (4): 449–64.

Tannock, S. (2018), 'Educational Equality and International Students: Justice across Borders?', in *Educational Equality and International Students: Justice across Borders?*, New York: Springer. https://doi.org/10.1007/978-3-319-76381-1 (accessed 2 July 2021).

Teixeira, P., B. Jongbloed, D. Dill and A. Amaral (eds) (2004) *Markets in Higher Education – Rhetoric or Reality?* Amsterdam: Kluwer Academic.

The Independent (2020), 'University Students Call for Tuition Fee Refunds Amid Government Lockdowns'. https://www.independent.co.uk/news/education/education-news/coronavirus-university-tuition-fees-refund-b1724308.html (accessed 16 June 2021).

United Nations Education, Social and Cultural Organization (UNESCO) (2018), *Education: International Student Mobility in Tertiary Education*. https://undatacatalog.org/dataset/education-international-student-mobility-tertiary-education (accessed 2 July 2021).

Universities UK (2014) *One Size Fits All? An Analysis of the International Student's Journey through the UK Higher Education System*, Commission on International Student Destinations, Universities UK. https://www.universitiesuk.ac.uk/policy-and-analysis/reports/Documents/2015/international-student-journey-through-UK-higher-education-system.pdf (accessed 1 July 2021).

Varghese, N. V. (2013), 'Globalization and Higher Education: Changing Trends in Cross Border Education', *Analytical Reports in International Education*, 5 (1): 7–20.

Walker, P. (2014), 'International Student Policies in UK Higher Education from Colonialism to the Coalition: Developments and Consequences', *Journal of Studies in International Education*, 18 (4): 325–44.

Wang, Z., J. Wang and W. Jiang (2020), 'Angel or Demon, the Image of Education Agents in Chinese International Students' Eyes', *International Journal of Innovation and Research in Educational Sciences*, 7 (4): 2349–5219.

Waters, J., and R. Brooks (2010), 'Accidental Achievers: International Higher Education, Class Reproduction and Privilege in the Experiences of UK Students Overseas', *British Journal of Sociology of Education*, 31 (2): 217–28.

Xie, M., D. B. Qin, S. Liu, Y. Duan, M. Sato and C.-F. Tseng (2020), 'Crazy Rich Chinese? A Mixed-Methods Examination of Perceived Stereotypes and Associated Psychosocial Adaptation Challenges among Chinese International Students in the United States', *Applied Psychology: Health and Well-Being*, 13 (3): 653–76.

Yang, Y., J. Mittelmeier, M. A. Lim and S. Lomer (2020), *Chinese International Student Recruitment During the COVID-19 Crisis: Education Agents' Practices and*

Reflections. Available online: https://www.research.manchester.ac.uk/portal/en/publications/chinese-international-student-recruitment-during-the-covid19-crisis(be489a37-107c-480e-82c4-4583bc3dfeeb).html (accessed 20 June 2021).

Yang, Y., S. Lomer, M. A. Lim and J. Mittelmeier (2022), 'A Study of Chinese Students' Application to UK Universities in Uncertain Times: From the Perspective of Education Agents', *Journal of International Students*, 12 (3), online first.

Zhang, C., Y. Yang and L. Hoh (2021), *A Dialogue on International Student Recruitment within China, UK, and Malaysia* [Conference presentation], the 33rd Annual CHER Conference 2021, Online, September 1–3.

Part 2

Issues Relating to International Students and English Language

4

International Students, Gatekeeping Tests and a Model of EAP Provision

Neil Murray

Introduction

There has been a good deal of debate in recent years focused on the efficacy of so-called gatekeeping tests, such as IELTS and TOEFL, used by universities to assess the linguistic readiness of prospective students to engage in degree-level study (Coley, 1999; O'Loughlin, 2015; Ransom, 2009; Trenkic, 2018). Much of this has been driven by concerns over students meeting institutional language entry criteria but subsequently struggling to cope with the language demands of their studies. Meanwhile, evidence confirming or otherwise the validity of these tests has remained somewhat elusive with the many predictive validity studies that have been undertaken showing mixed results (Daller and Phelan, 2013; Dooey and Oliver, 2002; Ingram and Bayliss, 2007; Kerstjens and Nery, 2000; Schoepp, 2018) and offering little in the way of reassurance to test users. Within the context of unprecedented growth in international student numbers as a result of increased social mobility and the consequential globalization of higher education, questions concerning the suitability of these tests have taken on increased significance. Students who meet language entry requirements and then discover that they lack the language skills needed to successfully engage with their coursework can suffer stress, anxiety and failure; furthermore, they represent a risk to the reputations of their universities. This is especially so in cases where, due to weak language skills, students struggle in professional placements that form part of their degree programmes, or where they successfully graduate only to find themselves unable to communicate sufficiently well in their workplace contexts. In certain professions such as nursing and pharmacy, a lack of relevant language skills can result in a failure to secure professional registration (Allan and Westwood, 2016; Arkoudis et al., 2014).

For some, knowingly setting entry requirements too low or without due diligence is unethical and cause for disquiet not only because it is seen as accepting students under false pretenses but also because in what is an increasingly competitive higher education environment there is a suggestion that financial imperatives and the fee income generated by international students may be compromising standards and forcing academic staff to simplify or 'dumb down' the curriculum, thus calling into question the rigour and quality of the degrees awarded by universities (Alderman, 2010; Baty, 2004; Pearson, 2021; Quality Assurance Agency [UK], 2009).

Academic Literacy and Its Misalignment with University Gatekeeping Tests

However, while it may be the case that some institutions – intentionally or otherwise – set their language entry requirements too low, raising them is unlikely to improve the situation significantly. This is because gatekeeping tests assess students' proficiency in a generic variety of academic English but fail to assess their working knowledge of the particular literacy practices of their future disciplines. There are, of course, good reasons for this, not least of which is the cost to testing organizations of developing a suite of discipline-specific tests and having a sufficient number of appropriately qualified examiners familiar with those practices and, therefore, able to assess meaningfully students' exam scripts. Added to this is the fact that the existing testing regime is now deeply embedded in the sector, and while the gatekeeping tests that universities depend on may be imperfect and somewhat blunt instruments, they are generally seen as broadly fit for purpose. Whether, in reality, this is the case is difficult to determine in the absence of incontrovertible evidence to the contrary in terms of educational standards and the academic fortunes of the students themselves who enroll in degree programmes.

This partial misalignment of the language focus of gatekeeping tests with the particular 'varieties' of language – or discourses – that students need to master as they engage with their disciplines is reflected in a distinction, increasingly invoked in the applied linguistics literature, between English for General Academic Purposes (EGAP) and English for Specific Academic Purposes (ESAP) (Bruce, 2011; Jordan, 1997; Murray and Muller, 2019). As its name suggests, EGAP refers to the teaching and learning of academic English that is generic in nature, having 'a cross-disciplinary focus designed to provide students with a broad understanding of the principles of language use that apply to most, if not all, academic disciplines', and typically prioritizing the arts and humanities and social science disciplines over the pure sciences (Murray and Muller 2019: 258). ESAP, in contrast, essentially reflects an academic literacies perspective that recognizes 'the requirement to switch practices between one setting [one discipline] and another, to deploy a repertoire of linguistic practices appropriate to each setting, and to handle the social meanings and identities that each evokes' (Lea and Street 1998: 159; my parenthetic insert). These practices are captured in the nature of disciplinary discourses and the genres embedded within them, through which subject matter is expressed, explored, analyzed and contested (Henderson and Hirst, 2006; Nesi and Gardner, 2012). They collectively help define a discipline, and through acquiring and appropriately deploying them and thereby becoming socialized into that discipline, an individual effectively secures membership of its community of practice (Lave and Wenger, 1991 Wenger, 2010). This disciplinary variation in the way in which language incorporates linguistic, social and cognitive elements embodies Halliday's idea, central to Systemic Functional Linguistics, that language develops to serve the particular purposes for which its users choose to employ it (Halliday, 1978); that is, economists, for example, have developed and employ a shared set of practices that express the meanings and communicative purposes germane to their field, just as mathematicians, nurses and so on have to theirs.

If conversancy in the literacy practices of a given discipline is a necessary condition of the individual's ability to effectively and appropriately communicate within that discipline, then it is something that needs to be acquired by *all* students, and the fact that applicants' familiarity with those practices is not assessed at point of application is significant. Firstly, as I have indicated, it reflects a belief that current gatekeeping tests are seen as fulfilling their role sufficiently well as indicators of students' proficiency in EGAP, as evidenced by 'acceptable' dropout rates among non-native speaker students, and this militates against any inclination on the part of testing organizations to provide a suite of discipline-specific language gatekeeping tests that would be costly to develop yet would still likely have limited functionality given the necessarily selective nature of their content. Secondly, there are subjects taught at tertiary level, such as accounting, law, global sustainable development, astronomy and linguistics, that are generally not available in secondary school curricula, whether in English-speaking countries or elsewhere; as such there would be little point in assessing applicants' facility with the literacy practices of these disciplines. This could lead to an inequitable situation where those applicants looking to study subjects available in the secondary school curriculum would have their academic literacy assessed, while those applying to study subjects not featured in the secondary curriculum would not. Finally, the fact that universities do not assess students' conversancy in the literacy practices of their future disciplines reflects an historically held belief that regardless of their status as native or non-native speakers of English, they will acquire those practices under their own steam, through exposure to them during the course of their studies. Today's diverse student demographic is a reason to call this belief into serious question, however.

Traditionally, university students have acquired the literacy practices of their disciplines through their engagement with reading texts, classroom discourse and feedback received on written assignments. While such an inductive process that is widely seen as obviating the need for direct pedagogical intervention may not be the most efficient way to develop conversancy in those practices, it is notable that students in the 1970s and 1980s accounted for between 8 and 19 per cent of young British school-leavers (Lambert, 2019). As such they could be seen as having constituted an academic elite who were arguably relatively well-equipped to 'pick up' the practices of their disciplines, coming as they did to higher education with a significant measure of the required cultural capital (Bourdieu, 1986; Ryan and Hellmundt, 2005) and the ability to adjust quickly to what Thomas (2002) and Sheridan (2011) have referred to as the institutional habitus. However, today's considerably higher levels of domestic student participation (50 per cent) and the increase in the overall linguistic, cultural, socio-economic and educational diversity of the student demographic mean that we can make fewer assumptions regarding the knowledge and skills with which students – both local and international – come to their studies and their ability to pick up the academic literacies of their disciplines (Dunworth et al., 2014; Wingate and Tribble, 2012). This fact amounts to a compelling argument for embedding the teaching of academic literacy within students' degree curricula in a manner that ensures equal opportunity for all students, while simultaneously removing the potential for extra-curricular language development activity to stigmatize those students for whom English is not a first language. As Arkoudis and Kelly (2016) have noted, 'the literature is unequivocal that high impact student learning occurs when communication skills are integrated within disciplinary learning and assessment' (4). Such integration, however, brings with it considerable logistical and cultural challenges and represents a significant departure from the traditional, service-based model of academic literacy support that typically sees it delivered centrally by English for Academic Purposes (EAP) teachers as an extra-curricular, non-credit bearing activity.

The Challenges with Embedding Academic Literacy in the Curriculum

There has of late been a notable surge in the number of articles reporting on efforts to embed academic literacy in the curriculum – an indication of a general shift in the field away from EGAP and towards ESAP (see, e.g. Baik and Greig, 2009; Bohemia et al., 2007; Curnow and Liddicoat, 2008; Edwards et al., 2021; McKay, 2013; Macnaught et al., 2022; Murray and Nallaya, 2016; Gunn, Hearne and Sibthorpe, 2011; Wingate, Andon and Cogo, 2011). Three features emerge as particularly salient in that literature and indicate some of the key challenges embedding presents. The first is the variation in the way in which the notion of embedding is understood and/or applied. The second is that very few cases report on embedding initiatives where academic content lecturers (ACLs) assume primary responsibility for imparting knowledge of their respective disciplines' literacy practices to their students, despite the fact that they would appear to be best placed to do so. Indeed, given that those practices are fundamental and specific to each and every discipline, it is a matter of some curiosity that ACLs have traditionally assumed responsibility for imparting knowledge of discipline subject matter but *not* the means through which that knowledge is expressed, explored, analyzed and contested. The third feature that emerges is that, in almost every case, authors report on only small-scale initiatives (often one course) rather than anything more ambitious. It seems that these initiatives are often locally based and/or serve to trial the approach, with a view to possible larger-scale implementation; yet evidence of such expansion is notable by its absence. As I hope to demonstrate, these three features are causally connected.

Importantly, the nature of the challenges faced during the process of embedding academic literacies will depend in large part on how embedding is conceived and whether what might be termed the 'hard form' or 'soft form' of embedding is being adopted. I use the hard form of embedding to refer to the case where space is created in degree curricula for academic literacy development and where primary responsibility for imparting the relevant practices lies with ACLs rather than EAP teachers. The soft form of embedding, in contrast, refers to the teaching of disciplinary academic literacy practices by EAP teachers outside of the regular curriculum but in such a way that input is designed and timed to support the delivery of degree course content and any associated tasks in which students are expected to engage. In this way, and as with the hard form of embedding, pedagogical interventions respond to the particular academic literacy needs of the moment and thereby assume immediate relevance. In so doing, they promote student motivation, engagement and thus learning.

Whichever form of embedding is adopted, one initial task that needs to be completed is the specification of those particular literacies and associated practices integral to a given discipline and which students are expected to master. This presents its own challenges as there is evidence that ACLs struggle to identify the literacies and associated practices of their particular disciplines despite demonstrating a working knowledge of them in their daily professional lives (Jacobs, 2005; Lea and Street 1998, 1999; Murray and Nallaya, 2016). While they have what Jacobs refers to as 'tacit' knowledge of their disciplines' discourse conventions (2005: 447), they have difficulty articulating that knowledge. There is, it seems, a problem converting procedural to declarative knowledge and making what is implicit explicit, and this is where EAP teachers and academic developers can usefully work with ACLs to tease out the relevant literacies and their associated practices (Curnow and Liddicoat, 2008; Thies, 2012; Wingate, 2018). If the hard form of embedding is to be adopted, those literacies, once identified, then need to be strategically located in the curriculum – a process described in some detail by Curnow and Liddicoat (2008) in relation to an undergraduate Applied Linguistics degree programme. Having identified the academic literacies in which students would be expected to demonstrate competence upon completion of the programme, they describe how these were then distributed across the different assessment items for those core courses where they arose most naturally in the sense of being a prerequisite to engaging effectively with course content. In order to ensure that all students had the necessary exposure to these literacies and the opportunity to develop the associated discourse practices, they were embedded in core modules on the understanding that students would, in most cases, get additional exposure to them in other, optional modules.

The hard form of embedding is certainly a hard road to travel, and it is perhaps unsurprising, therefore, that there are few reports in the literature on attempts to implement it. One potential obstacle to implementation is the existing curriculum and whether there is sufficient space to enable the embedding process to take place. This can be a particular issue for curricula prescribed in part or in full by external professional bodies or that have been subject to other embedding initiatives that may be perceived as more 'of the moment', and thus a higher priority such as sustainability, experiential learning and equality, diversity and inclusion. Another likely obstacle to the hard form of embedding is that of its reception by ACL's tasked with teaching the literacies of their disciplines. Evidence suggests that there is likely to be considerable resistance here, with ACLs feeling that it is not part of their job and that they have neither the time nor the necessary skills set to undertake this role (Dunworth et al., 2014; Murray and Nallaya, 2016) – something captured in the following quote from a study by Jenkins and Wingate (2015):

> I am a Law lecturer ... I am quite happy to help as far as I can ... but you know I am not an English support teacher. I'm not trained to help people who really need specific targeted support, nor are any of my colleagues.

Personal experience suggests that ACLs tend to think of academic language and literacy rather narrowly in terms of grammar and syntax, resulting in this belief that they are unqualified to teach it. While this misperception can be addressed as part of the collaborative process of identifying and embedding academic literacies, it is nonetheless the case that ACLs will, in most cases, need to undergo professional development if they are to facilitate students' acquisition of the literacy practices of their disciplines, and this can be an unsavoury prospect for many, and particularly for those who do not, anyway, see it as part of their role. This is not helped by the fact that academic staff are frequently at the sharp end of curricular and other initiatives many of which are quite disruptive, only to fizzle out leaving little or no evidence of any tangible and lasting outcomes. This is likely to breed scepticism and a reluctance to engage with any new curricular initiatives regardless of their apparent merits (Dunworth et al., 2014). The securing of compliance can become difficult as a result, leading to a reluctance on the part of university senior management to put their weight behind the idea of embedding academic literacy in the curriculum, particularly if there are no individuals within their ranks who feel qualified and moved to champion the idea and who remain in post long enough for it to take root, gain traction and bring about the change of culture ultimately required.

Given these challenges, the soft form of embedding would appear to offer a more workable alternative; yet even this would appear to be far from straightforward as the costs associated with resourcing it can be considerable and would likely be seen as prohibitive by most, if not all, institutions. If it is to be comparable to the hard form of embedding and ensure that all students receive support with academic literacy, it would require a team of EAP teachers large enough to service the needs of every discipline and its constituent degree programmes. Furthermore, it would present almost insurmountable scheduling difficulties: just as finding space in the curriculum to embed academic literacies would be problematic, the same would be true of finding sufficient space outside of the curriculum, given students' variable timetables, social lives and such, and their ability and willingness, therefore, to commit to academic literacy programmes. As a result of these constraints, what typically happens is that, in place of a comprehensive and thus equitable institution-wide scheme, ESAP tuition is either (1) centralized but with a faculty focus (e.g. English for Social Science Students; English for Arts and Humanities Students) or (2) the product of local, ad hoc departmental initiatives that have been forged from often longstanding professional and personal relationships between one or more EAP teachers and their ACL counterparts in the departments concerned. This latter situation makes for uneven and thus inequitable academic literacy support, lacking as it does the kind of systematic and comprehensive provision that can only come about through endorsement by university senior management.

There is, however, a particular realization of the devolved model of EAP provision that offers a more viable, alternative soft form of embedding which, while by no means perfect, is both cost effective in the sense of being scalable, and equitable in that ESAP resource is distributed evenly across the institution.

The Hub-and-Spoke Model of ESAP Provision

Despite the increasing number of articles reporting on embedding initiatives of one kind or another, as I have indicated, these often arise quite sporadically and independently of the kind of centralized provision that remains the mainstay of EAP support in universities and is typically delivered by English language centres, applied linguistics departments and other cognate departments, often complemented by related services offered by libraries, writing centres and careers and skills units. Within these structures, it tends to be EGAP that is taught on the basis of the utilitarian principle that while it may not go far in meeting the particular language needs of a given student or a specific cohort, it will benefit the majority of students *to some degree*. As I have indicated, where there is an attempt to acknowledge the different language needs of students working in different disciplines, this is usually reflected in ESAP classes set up to cater for students working within the same faculties – albeit in a variety of disciplines – with the result that, somewhat paradoxically, the content of these classes necessarily remains quite general in nature. In some cases, and as a complement to the (normally) free EGAP classes on offer to all students, individual departments with large intakes of international students may themselves fund ESAP classes for their own students.

The hub-and-spoke model I describe here was trialled at a higher education institution in Australia. The idea was that while oversight of the initiative would be maintained centrally within its Learning and Teaching Unit (the hub), EAP teachers would be distributed across the four university faculties, where they would be physically based and operate as satellite units (the spokes). Each faculty team would be managed by a Faculty English Language Coordinator who was required to be research active and expected to encourage their team to engage in research relevant to their duties. Although teachers' contracts did not stipulate this as an obligation, it was felt that it would help professionalize the team, encourage reflection on their activities and the benefits and shortcomings of the model and help generate ideas for improving its implementation.

The hub-and-spoke model was seen as having distinct advantages. Being physically located and thus a permanent presence within the faculties meant the teams themselves would feel more integrated and also be seen by faculty staff as 'belonging'. This meant that they could more easily forge productive relationships with academic staff in the various disciplines and would be privy to issues and debates that may have implications for the effective performance of their role and of which they might otherwise remain unaware. Moreover, they would have opportunities to input into those discussions and to influence their direction and outcomes. These kinds of interactions are key in at least two important respects. Firstly, they help ensure that EAP provision is more responsive to the local context by providing a means through which EAP teachers can better understand the nature of knowledge and its expression in relation to the disciplines of their particular faculty and the ways in which students are required to display their mastery of the relevant literacies through the particular types of assessment employed. Thus, over time, EAP teachers develop particular expertise and are able to shape their courses and source materials in such a way that they are optimally relevant and thus engaging for students. Secondly, they serve to raise awareness within the faculty and beyond of the nature of EAP and the specialist knowledge of those who teach it, a growing number of whom are research active (Dunworth et al., 2014). This is often neither sufficiently understood nor acknowledged, and it can mean that, among other things, students' language needs go unaddressed. Furthermore, this lack of understanding and recognition can perpetuate a perception of academic literacy as peripheral to core university business, with the result that EAP teachers are widely associated with service departments – something reflected in their generally disadvantageous conditions of service (part-time, hourly paid contracts, limited promotion prospects etc. [Jordan, 2002; MacDonald, 2016]) and the often modest institutional funding EAP activity attracts. Decentralizing academic literacy provision and locating it in the faculties where EAP teachers can collaborate with staff and be more responsive to the needs of *all* students in their constituent disciplines alleviates this problem while also helping to counteract the common perception of academic literacy tuition as a service activity directed solely at students seen as being in deficit and thus at risk, and designed to 'cure their ills' and ' "fix" problems … which are treated as a kind of pathology' (Lea and Street 1998: 158). These 'at-risk' students are, almost by default, non-native speakers of English who are consequently stigmatized.

Given the fact that financial and logistical constraints militated against tailored academic literacy provision being made available to each and every department in the faculty, a key element of the Faculty English Language Coordinators' role was to liaise closely with departments in order to identify their needs and then to deploy the EAP teachers in their respective teams as effectively as possible. This meant both that there was some variation in provision between different faculties and that the nature of provision in any given faculty would change periodically. In other words, while support could not comprehensively meet the particular academic literacy needs of students in every discipline, the Coordinators worked to secure the best compromise through adopting a strategy based on the principles of agility and flexibility. This meant that provision might, for example, comprise a combination of credit and/or non-credit bearing modules organized for particular departments, a cyclical series of workshops covering literacy practices shared across different disciplines, and individual writing surgeries.

The devolved model described was supported with the creation of a website that was similarly faculty based in its structure and the homepage of which presented students with four links, one for each faculty. Each link was a portal to resources specifically tailored to reflect the academic literacy needs of students studying in disciplines located within that faculty. It was understood from the outset that development of the website was a long-term project and that while the materials posted would initially reflect certain of the faculty's disciplines more than others and/or have relevance for multiple disciplines, in time and through a process of ongoing refinement they would become more focused on individual disciplines and more responsive to students' needs as EAP teachers became more attuned to the different disciplines. What was striking was the creativity and verve with which the four faculty teams applied themselves to the task of developing their online resources, and this was driven in part by a spirit of competitiveness that emerged. As a result, the rate of progress was impressive.

Despite working independently of each other, the faculty teams came together periodically for the purpose of professional development and sharing ideas and learning. Among other things, this led to a degree of cross-fertilization in respect of the content and presentation of the teams' online offerings and provided an opportunity to reflect on and evaluate progress in implementing the hub-and-spoke model.

The Distribution of the Teacher Resource and the Means of Its Funding

Within the hub-and-spoke model, the types and scale of academic literacy provision able to be negotiated by Faculty English Language Coordinators will be dependent on the teacher resource they have available to them. This raises the question as to the basis on which that resource should be distributed across the faculties and ultimately how the model should be funded. A number of issues arise here: firstly, whether provision should be funded centrally or by individual faculties and their constituent departments; secondly, if funded centrally, whether there should be differential funding and if so on what basis, and thirdly, how funding should be raised and/or from which account(s) it should be drawn.

Central Funding

Given that every discipline requires all of its students to become conversant in its particular literacy practices, and that few assumptions can be made about the extent to which students come equipped with knowledge of those practices, there is a strong argument for EAP to be centrally funded. However, this does not necessarily mean that resource should be distributed equally among faculties; rather, it would seem reasonable to take a proportional approach whereby larger faculties are better resourced in terms of the number of EAP teachers assigned to them. This is in sharp contrast to models that base distribution of resources not on student numbers but on faculty type (and its constituent departments) and the longstanding and still quite prevalent belief that students in the more science-oriented disciplines have less need of literacy development – a notion that does not sit comfortably with an academic literacies perspective. Basing resource on *overall* student numbers is significant in that it acknowledges the need for *all* students to become conversant in the literacy practices of their disciplines and is therefore non-discriminatory in a way that approaches which apportion resource according to discipline and the number of international students they recruit are not.

Assuming provision is centrally funded, decisions will need to be made regarding the scale of the teacher resource it requires and how this is quantified – a difficult question as there is no end point as such to academic literacy development or any easy way of measuring how and at what point 'sufficient' control of the relevant practices might reasonably be claimed. Consequently, while more teachers means more input and greater flexibility in meeting the needs of students with varied timetables, any determination of what is adequate resourcing is inevitably going to be quite notional and each institution will have its own view on what is required and financially viable. Historically, institutions have a broad, often quite poorly defined view of the extent to which academic literacy is a priority and simply specify the funding to made available, without undertaking any meaningful exploration of the issue in consultation with the English language units responsible for its delivery and with whom real expertise resides. One senses, however, that this is beginning to change and that universities are not only increasingly seeing the provision of academic literacy support as a moral obligation they have towards their students but also as a marketing tool that can bring reputational benefits by highlighting their concern with maximizing students' academic potential though providing systematic and equitable academic literacy support on an institution-wide basis.

Whatever EAP funding is ultimately deemed appropriate and feasible, the apportioning of it on a per capita basis such that larger faculties receive proportionately more funding would seem to be a sensible and equitable approach the cost of which could be recouped indirectly via student fees or a central service charge levied on faculties. Such an arrangement need not preclude individual faculties or departments investing independently in additional EAP resource where they feel it is required.

Conclusion

Any institutional model of academic literacy provision is almost inevitably going to be a compromise not only because resources will always be limited due to multiple competing institutional priorities and differing understandings and perceptions of the activity itself and the need for it, but also because of logistical factors around such things as timetabling and space in the curriculum. While the hub-and-spoke model is certainly not immune to the effects of many of these factors, it does offer a solution that is both equitable – by virtue of its underpinning belief that academic literacy and its development is relevant and should be equally accessible to all students, whatever their discipline – and scalable, such that the extent of that accessibility will depend on, and can be tailored according to, the financial circumstances of the institution concerned. The model also offers a degree of flexibility in that the faculty-based EAP teams can decide, in consultation with ACLs and based on their developing knowledge of the local context, how the resources at their disposal can best be utilized.

References

Alderman, G. (2010), 'Why University Standards Have Fallen', *The Guardian*, 10 March. Available online: http://www.theguardian.com/commentisfree/2010/mar/10/universities-standards-blair-target (accessed 5 June 2021).

Allan, H., and S. Westwood (2016), 'English Language Skills Requirements for Internationally Educated Nurses Working in the Care Industry: Barriers to UK Registration or Institutionalised Discrimination?', *International Journal of Nursing Studies*, 54: 1–4.

Arkoudis, S., C. Baik, E. Bexley and L. Dougney (2014), 'English Language Proficiency and Employability Framework for Australian Higher Education Institutions', Commissioned Report Prepared for the Australian Government Department of Education. Available online: https://melbourne-cshe.unimelb.edu.au/__data/assets/pdf_file/0008/1489157/ELP_ Employability_Framework.pdf (accessed 5 June 2021).

Arkoudis, S., and P. Kelly (2016), 'Shifting the Narrative: International Students and Communication Skills in Higher Education', Melbourne: International Education Association of Australia. Available online: https://www.ieaa.org.au/documents/item/664 (accessed 5 June 2021).

Baik, C., and J. Greig (2009), 'Improving the Academic Outcomes of Undergraduate ESL Students: The Case for Discipline-Based Academic Skills Programs', *Higher Education Research & Development*, 28 (4): 401–16.

Baty, P. (2004), 'Caught in Vicious Cycle of Declining Standards', *Times Higher Education*, 19 November. Available online: http://www.timeshighereducation.co.uk/news/caught-in-vicious-cycle-of-declining-standards/192504.article (accessed 5 June 2021).

Bohemia, E., H. Farrell, C. Power and C. Salter (2007), 'Embedding Literacy Skills in Design Curriculum', in *ConnectED 2007: International Conference on Design*

Education, 9–12 July, Sydney. Available online: http://nrl.northumbria.ac.uk/25/ (accessed 28 May 2021).

Bourdieu, P. (1986), 'The Forms of Capital', in J. E. Richardson (ed.), *Handbook of Theory of Research for the Sociology of Education*, 241–58, Westport, CT: Green Word Press.

Bruce, I. (2011), *Theory and Concepts of English for Academic Purposes*, London: Palgrave Macmillan.

Coley, M. (1999), 'The English Language Entry Requirements of Australian Universities for Students of Non-English Speaking Background', *Higher Education Research & Development*, 18 (1): 7–17.

Curnow, T. J., and A. J. Liddicoat (2008), 'Assessment as Learning: Engaging Students in Academic Literacy in their First Semester', in A. Duff, D. Quinn, M. Green, K. Andre, T. Ferris and S. Copland (eds), *Proceedings of the ATN Assessment Conference 2008: Engaging Students in Assessment*. Available online: http://www.ojs.unisa.edu.au/index.php/atna/issue/view/ISBN%20978-0-646-504421/showToc (accessed 21 March 2021).

Daller, M. H., and D. Phelan (2013), 'Predicting International Student Study Success', *Applied Linguistics Review*, 4 (1): 173–93.

Dooey, P., and R. Oliver (2002), 'An Investigation into the Predictive Validity of the IELTS Test as an Indicator of Future Academic Success', *Prospect*, 17 (1): 36–54.

Dunworth, K., H. Drury, C. Kralik and T. Moore (2014), 'Rhetoric and Realities: On the Development of University-Wide Strategies to Promote Student English Language Growth', *Journal of Higher Education Policy and Management*, 36 (5): 520–32.

Edwards, E., R. Goldsmith, C. Havery and N. James (2021), 'An Institution-Wide Strategy for Ongoing, Embedded Academic Language Development: Design, Implementation and Analysis', *Journal of Academic Language and Learning*, 15 (1): 53–71.

Gunn, C., S. Hearne and J. Sibthorpe (2011), 'Right from the Start: A Rationale for Embedding Academic Literacy Skills in University Courses', *Journal of University Teaching and Learning Practice*, 8 (1): 1–10.

Halliday, M. A. K. (1978), *Language as a Social Semiotic*, London: Edward Arnold.

Henderson, R., and E. Hirst (2006), 'How Sufficient is Academic Literacy? Re-examining a Short Course for "Disadvantaged" Tertiary Students', *English Teaching: Practice and Critique*, 6 (2): 25–38.

Ingram, D. E., and A. Bayliss (2007), 'IELTS as a Predictor of Academic Language Performance. Part 1: The View from Participants', *IELTS, Impact Studies*, 7, Report 3: 1–68.

Jacobs, C. (2005), 'On Being an Insider on the Outside: New Spaces for Integrating Academic Literacies', *Teaching in Higher Education*, 10 (4): 475–87.

Jenkins, J., and U. Wingate (2015), 'Staff and Student Perceptions of English Language Policies and Practices in "International" Universities: A UK Case Study', *Higher Education Review*, 47 (2): 47–73.

Jordan, R. R. (1997), *English for Academic Purposes*, Cambridge: Cambridge University Press.

Jordan, R. R. (2002), 'The Growth of EAP in Britain', *Journal of English for Academic Purposes*, 1 (1): 69–78.

Kerstjens, M., and C. Nery (2000), 'Predictive Validity in the IELTS Test: A Study of the Relationship Between IELTS Scores and Students' Subsequent Academic Performance', *English Language Testing System Research Reports*, 3: 85–108.

Lambert, H. (2019), 'The Great University Con: How the British University Degree Lost its Value', *New Statesman*, 21 August. https://www.newstatesman.com/politics/education/2019/08/great-university-con-how-british-degree-lost-its-value (accessed 24 November 2021).

Lave, J., and E. Wenger (1991), *Situated Learning. Legitimate Peripheral Participation*, Cambridge: Cambridge University Press.

Lea, M. R., and B. V. Street (1998), 'Student Writing in Higher Education: An Academic Literacies Approach', *Studies in Higher Education*, 23 (2): 157–72. https://doi.org/10.1080/03075079812331380364.

Lea, M. R., and B. V. Street (1999), 'Writing as Academic Literacies: Understanding Textual Practices in Higher Education', in C. N. Candlin and K. Hyland (eds), *Writing: Texts, Processes and Practices*, 62–81, London: Longman.

MacDonald, J. (2016), 'The Margins as Third Space: EAP Teacher Professionalism in Canadian Universities', *TESL Canada Journal/Revue TESL du Canada*, 34 (11): 106–16.

Macnaught, L., Bassett, M., van der Ham, V., Milne, J. and Jenkin, C. (2022), 'Sustainable embedded academic literacy development: The gradual handover of literacy teaching', *Teaching in Higher Education*, DOI: 10.1080/13562517.2022.2048369.

McKay, T. J. (2013), 'Embedding Academic Support within an Academic Discipline: A Teaching Model', *South African Journal of Higher Education*, 27 (3): 682–95.

Murray, N., and S. Nallaya (2016), 'Embedding Academic Literacies in University Programme Curricula: A Case Study', *Studies in Higher Education*, 41 (7): 1296–312.

Murray, N., and A. Muller (2019), 'Some Key Terms in ELT and Why We Need to Disambiguate Them', *English Language Teaching Journal*, 73 (3): 257–64.

Nesi, H., and S. Gardner (2012), *Genres across the Disciplines: Student Writing in Higher Education*, Cambridge: Cambridge University Press.

O'Loughlin, K. (2015), '"But Isn't IELTS the Most Trustworthy?": English Language Assessment for Entry into Higher Education', in A. Ata and A. Kostogriz (eds), *International Education and Cultural-Linguistic Experiences of International Students in Australia*, 181–94, Queensland: Australian Academic Press.

Pearson, W. S. (2021),'Policies on Minimum English Language Requirements in UK Higher Education, 1989–2021', *Journal of Further and Higher Education*, 45 (9): 1240–52.

Quality Assurance Agency for Higher Education (QAA) (2009), 'Thematic Enquiries into Concerns about Academic Quality and Standards in Higher Education in England', *Gloucester: Quality Assurance Agency for Higher Education*. www.qaa.ac.uk/Publications/.../Documents/FinalReportApril09.pdf (accessed 5 June 2021).

Ransom, L. (2009), 'Implementing the Post-Entry English Language Assessment Policy at the University of Melbourne: Rationale, Processes and Outcomes', *Journal of Academic Language & Learning*, 3 (2): A13–A25.

Ryan, J., and S. Hellmundt (2005), 'Maximising Students' "Cultural Capital"', in J. Carroll and J. Ryan (eds), *Teaching International Students: Improving Learning for All*, 13–16, Oxford: Routledge.

Schoepp, K. (2018), 'Predictive Validity of the IELTS in an English as a Medium of Instruction Environment', *Higher Education Quarterly*, 72 (4): 271–85.

Sheridan, V. (2011), 'A Holistic Approach to International Students, Institutional Habitus and Academic Literacies in an Irish Third Level Institution', *Higher Education*, 62 (2): 129–40.

Thies, L. C. (2012), 'Increasing Student Participation and Success: Collaborating to Embed Academic Literacies into the Curriculum', *Journal of Academic Language and Learning*, 6 (1): A15–A31.

Thomas, L. (2002), 'Student Retention in Higher Education: The Role of Institutional Habitus', *Journal of Education Policy*, 17 (4): 423–42.

Trenkic, D. (2018), 'Language Requirements for International Students are Too Low', *Times Higher Education*, 10 May. Available online: https://www.timeshighereducation.com/opinion/language-requirements-international-students-are-too-low (accessed 10 June 2021).

Wenger, E. (2010), 'Communities of Practice and Social Learning Systems: The Career of a Concept', in C. Blackmore (ed.), *Social Learning Systems and Communities of Practice*, 179–98, London: Springer.

Wingate, U. (2018), 'Academic Literacy across the Curriculum: Towards a Collaborative Instructional Approach', *Language Teaching*, 51 (3): 349–64

Wingate, U., N. Andon and A. Cogo (2011), 'Embedding Academic Writing Instruction into Subject Teaching: A Case Study', *Active Learning in Higher Education*, 12 (1): 69–81.

Wingate, U., and C. Tribble (2012), 'The Best of Both Worlds? Towards an English for Academic Purposes/Academic Literacies Writing Pedagogy', *Studies in Higher Education*, 37 (4): 481–95.

5

Proofreading in a UK University Writing Centre: Perspectives and Practices

Chang Liu and Nigel Harwood

Introduction

With the growing number of international students coming to study in the UK, the writing centre has become one of a number of English for Academic Purposes (EAP) resources L2 students can access to help them enhance their academic literacy in higher education. Pre- and in-sessional EAP courses attempt to socialize international students into the wider university culture and to familiarize students with the spoken and written genres that they will be expected to understand and produce; but writing centres provide one-to-one bespoke advice, genre by genre and text by text.

The roles and responsibilities of the writing centre are much discussed in the literature (e.g. Barnawi, 2017; Barnett and Blumner, 2008; Bruce and Rafoth, 2009; Harris, 1986; Murphy and Sherwood, 2008; North, 1984; Ryan and Zimmerelli, 2010). However, the issue of 'proofreading' L2 students' texts in the writing centre is something that remains less discussed. Where it is mentioned at all in classic work on writing centre pedagogy, proofreading is often seen as beyond the pale, and those students expecting a writing centre to offer proofreading are seen to be erroneously equating the writing centre to a 'grammar center' or a 'fix-it shop' (North, 1984: 437). However, more recent discussion of writing centre roles has suggested the need to rethink no-proofreading policies, arguing that classic writing centre L1 tutoring strictures may not be appropriate when working with the diverse range of writers in the contemporary university (see Myers, 2003; Nan, 2012; Powers, 1993). It is therefore worth exploring how various stakeholders associated with writing centres – L2 students, writing tutors and writing centre directors – view the appropriacy of proofreading, as the results of such an investigation will have implications for writing centre policy and for tutor pedagogy. The investigation will enable us to determine the extent to which stakeholders agree among themselves as to the appropriateness of the proofreading role, and where conceptualizations of ethical roles diverge, will suggest ways in which differing views can be acknowledged and addressed via inclusive policy and effective pedagogy.

This chapter duly reports on a research project situated in the writing centre of a research-intensive UK university, examining the beliefs about proofreading by Chinese students, writing tutors and the writing centre director. The university offers students individual sixty-minute one-to-one writing consultations in which they can discuss their draft texts with a writing centre tutor so that students can improve their text prior to submitting it for assessment. The writing centre's policy specifies that the improvements suggested by tutors may cover several areas including language and grammar but that the tutor must not enact the role of a proofreader. However, international students who come to the writing centre and look for help with their writing may have beliefs about the appropriacy of proofreading which are at odds with writing centre policy; indeed, several studies make claims that L2 students may wish for a far more directive, accuracy-focused writing centre pedagogy than classic non-directive approaches (e.g. Eckstein, 2019; Kim, 2014; Linville, 2009; Moussu, 2013; Nan, 2012). In what follows, then, we examine what each group of stakeholders – students, tutors and director – believes about the appropriacy of proofreading in the writing centre, as well as exploring the extent to which writing tutors actually proofread in consultation sessions. We begin though by addressing the tricky issue of defining proofreading.

What Is Proofreading?

Proofreading can be defined differently in different contexts, and more or less substantial forms of intervention may fall under these definitions. Broader conceptualizations of the proofreading of student writing may involve a much wider 'help with writing and thinking' remit which includes asking questions, making suggestions and rewriting text at the level of ideas, content and argumentation (see Harwood, 2018, 2019; Harwood, Austin and Macaulay, 2009, 2010, 2012). However, traditional conceptualizations of proofreading are rather narrow and envisage more limited forms of intervention. According to the Chartered Institute of Editing and Proofreading (2020: 4), for instance, proofreading is 'a process of identifying typographical, linguistic, coding or positional errors or omissions on a printed or electronic proof, and making corrections'. The working definition of proofreading we adopt in this chapter is in line with the latter traditional, narrow definition, as it is this conceptualization of proofreading that appears in the writing centre literature.

Writing Centre Tutoring and Proofreading

According to classic writing centre pedagogy, proofreading is not appropriate in the writing centre (Mack, 2014). In his seminal article 'The Idea of the Writing Center', North (1984) emphasizes that the role of the writing centre is to produce 'better writers, not better writing' (438). For North, proofreading the student's text would be to turn the writing consultation into a mere 'clean-up' or 'fixing' session, with the writer then playing a passive role. Instead, writing centres must prioritize the enhancement of the writer's composing process and educate the writer, rather than simply eliminating errors and thus enhancing the product. In agreement with North, Brooks (1991: 128) argues that 'the goal of each tutoring session is learning, not a perfect paper'. Brooks also argues that the tutor should focus on higher order concerns (HOCs) before lower order concerns (LOCs). HOCs include aspects of writing such as organization, structure, logic, argument and evidence, and information about specific disciplinary conventions and genres. In contrast, LOCs include grammar, syntax and punctuation. In sum, then, orthodox writing centre pedagogy advocates tutors enact process-focused rather than product-focused learning, the pedagogical aim of the tutorial being educative gains by the writer rather than an error-free text.

However, while tutoring L2 students in the writing centre, the issue of proofreading may arise. Many international students come to the writing centre asking for sentence-level assistance and even for proofreading (Eckstein, 2016; Kim, 2014; Severino, Swenson and Zhu, 2009). Indeed, L2 students' texts can present something of a dilemma to writing tutors – tutors may perceive the need for sentence-level grammar help, yet be conscious that their writing centre operates a no-proofreading policy. This conflict has led to frustration on the part of both students and tutors (Bonazza, 2016; Kim, 2014; Voigt and Girgensohn, 2015). Since many L2 students' previous English education consisted of a directive pedagogy aimed at improving grammatical accuracy – often the chief or even sole criterion upon which writing would be assessed – it is hardly surprising that L2 students may expect detailed help with grammar, including proofreading, in consultations offered by their writing centre.

Furthermore, it is argued by Chromik (2002) that proofreading, in the form of helping students identify and correct their own errors, should be part of the writing centre tutorial since too many grammar errors would likely impact on the success of the writing, interfering with the communication of content that the writer wishes to convey. Indeed, especially when it comes to less proficient L2 students, proofreading is sometimes unavoidable, these learners in particular needing more help with grammar and language (Harris, 1995). In cases where language concerns impact upon the clarity of the writer's message, then, the writing tutor may opt for an approach which combines a focus on both LOCs and HOCs, and some line-by-line work may be needed on students' texts (Blau, Hall and Sparks, 2002).

Some empirical studies confirm the existence of writing centre pedagogies at odds with the classic tenets of North American non-directive pedagogy as embodied in North (1984). For example, LaClare and Franz (2013) explored the purpose, function and target tutees of a writing centre of a Japanese university. They used four semesters of data from the writing centre booking system and tutorial logs to explore who used the writing centre and what users consulted tutors for. The findings indicated that users of this writing centre are students and faculty; the main purpose for them consulting the writing centre is for editing and that the writing centre was product-oriented. Indeed, the centre's clients' wish for help with editing (rather than with HOCs) is so strong that LaClare and Franz claim that 'it is hard to imagine that our writing center would survive an outright prohibition on editing' (11). The researchers are of course aware that a focus by tutors on editing/proofreading is at odds with writing centre orthodoxy, but argue that they wish to meet the needs and wishes of their clients, asking 'in circumstances where the vast majority of users are coming in search of a particular service, is it desirable or even feasible to deny it?' (11), since their clients look for tutors to help them produce an error-free text. As a result, LaClare and Franz envisage that 'editing work will remain the cornerstone of what we do' (14). However, relying as it does on quantitative data, this research does not feature an in-depth investigation of how students and writing tutors understand proofreading, how proofreading is enacted in the writing centre, or the reasons why proofreading operates in the way it does in this context.

Kim (2014) is another study which highlights students' preoccupations with receiving proofreading in their writing centre, as well as a tension between expectation and policy. Located in an American university writing centre with an orthodox no-proofreading policy, Kim's participants consisted of eleven native students acting as writing tutors and thirty-six mostly East Asian L2 student tutees. Kim collected videotaped tutorial data and analysed the data using Conversation Analysis, as well as holding post-consultation interviews with both students and tutors about the tutorial experience, and attending weekly tutor staff meetings, during which tutors exchanged experiences of tutoring and asked each other about how to deal with problematic issues arising. Kim concluded that L2 student writers tend to regard writing consultations as a final, quick fix in the writing process to clear up all surface errors and produce an error-free essay when in fact more substantial work was often in order. However,

> Those students usually arrived at the Writing Center at the last moment before having to submit their paper to the class for which it was written, and with a sense of urgency about the correctness of their grammar. Thus, if the tutor pointed out problems other than just grammar – higher-level problems such as flow and the organization of their arguments which require more significant revision in many cases – the students resisted addressing these issues and did not cooperate with the tutor in doing this unexpected work. (Kim, 2014: 74)

Unsurprisingly then, another of Kim's findings is that many L2 students fail to appreciate what the remit of a writing centre is; rather than understanding its mission to be to improve the writer rather than the writing, students may believe the remit to be solely or mainly to clean up grammar. Once students grasp that the centre's remit is different from what they had understood, Kim found that disappointment may follow, and that students may simply never return to the writing centre, since tutors are unwilling to provide the kind of tutorials and help they desire:

> Some of them became angry upon learning that they could not receiv[e] proofreading, which was their only reason for visiting the Writing Center, and some of them even left the Writing Center when it became apparent that they would not receive the 'fix it' work they wanted done. For them, the Writing Center was not perceived as place of learning; it was only about repairing what was wrong at the sentence level. (Kim, 2014: 94)

Interestingly, despite the fact they worked for a writing centre with an orthodox remit (i.e. to improve the writer rather than the writing), Kim reports that not all tutors were comfortable with this or certain in their own minds as to where they stood on the (in)appropriacy of proofreading for students:

> During the staff meetings observed in this study, the tutors had intense debates about proofreading. Various opinions came out as to how they regarded

proofreading and whether it is useful for helping clients learn about English grammar. (Kim, 2014: 145)

While Kim's study sheds light on student expectations and mismatches between these expectations and policy, as well as intriguingly flagging up tutor debate about the ethics of proofreading, it lacks the perspective of the writing centre administrators, which would have shed light on the extent to which the administrators of the centre were aware of the tensions between student expectations and the centre's policy, and the extent to which the administrators may have been able and willing to modify their no-proofreading policy to align their practices more closely to the kind of consultations students wished to receive.

Another study highlighting differences between L2 writers' expectations and writing centre policy is Eckstein (2013). Eckstein evaluated a writing conference programme for L2 writers with different language proficiency levels at a writing centre in Canada featuring weekly one-to-one writing consultations. Eckstein found that lower proficiency students preferred more directive feedback and that tutors generally provided this feedback, focusing on LOCs, despite the fact that doing so ran counter to the centre's policy. Thus, there was a conflict between students' expectations and the writing centre policy of no-proofreading. In a later study comparing and contrasting the expectations of L1, Generation 1.5[1] and L2 writers, Eckstein (2016) found that although all writer groups surveyed expected writing centre tutors to point out grammar errors, L2 writers 'most highly agreed with the statement that tutors should point out their grammar errors or edit their paper' (368), although it should be noted that L2 writers also expected help with HOCs like organization and content. Hence students' expectations of writing tutorials differed according to proficiency level and language status.

The misalignments highlighted in the studies above between writing centres' no-proofreading policies and the expectations of L2 students underline the importance of exploring the reasons for these misalignments as well as whether and to what extent a no-proofreading policy is in fact advisable in an L2 writing centre (Kim, 2014). Previous studies have highlighted tutors' difficulties in sticking to no-proofreading policies when tutoring L2 students in various contexts, including North America (Eckstein, 2013; Kim, 2014), East Asia (LaClare and Franz, 2013) and Europe (Bonazza, 2016). We extend this line of research to focus on a UK university writing centre here. Unlike in Kim's (2014) research, professional, experienced EAP teachers rather than students act as tutors in the writing centre we study, as is typical in the UK. However, in common with North American writing centres, the centre in focus here stipulates that tutors enact classic North

American writing centre non-directive pedagogy and proscribe proofreading. We explore whether there are tensions in understandings within and across the three stakeholder groups in regard to proofreading, as well as examining writing tutors' actual tutoring practice. Our research questions are as follows:

> RQ1. What do international students, specifically Chinese students, believe about the appropriacy of proofreading in the writing centre? What do they want their writing tutor to do, and why?
> RQ2. What do tutors believe about the appropriacy of proofreading in the writing centre?
> RQ3. What does the writing centre's director believe about the appropriacy of proofreading in the writing centre?
> RQ4. To what extent do writing tutors actually proofread in consultation sessions?

We now describe the research context and the research design. These questions will be investigated using a predominantly qualitative approach, by means of interviews with all three parties (students, tutors and the writing centre director), as well as via document analysis and audio recordings of consultations.

Methodology

Research Context

The research was done in the writing centre of a UK research-intensive university. The university offers students individual sixty-minute one-to-one writing consultations in which they can discuss their draft texts with a writing centre tutor so that students can improve their text prior to submitting it for assessment. As explained on the centre's website, the consultation can offer help in logical organization, linking, structure, referencing, register, grammar, punctuation and spelling but not proofreading. Indeed, the centre also states explicitly that tutors are not permitted to act as proofreaders, and that they point out 'general areas for improvement' rather than checking a text word-by-word.

Research Design

In this research, mainly qualitative research methods were used to analyse semi-structured interviews, audio-recorded consultation data and the writing students brought to the consultations. The use of qualitative research methods is appropriate to investigate individuals' ideas and experiences in detail (Mason, 2002). Thirty-three Chinese students (a mixture of undergraduates and postgraduates), eleven writing tutors and the director of the writing centre participated in this research. We focused on Chinese students rather than on other L1 or L2 writers for two reasons: (1) Chinese students make up the largest cohort of international student numbers in our UK context, and (2) the first author is Chinese and so had a particular interest in researching and learning more about Chinese students' attitudes to writing centres in general and to proofreading in particular. The student participants were from various majors and had IELTS scores ranging from 6.0 to 7.5. The tutor participants were all experienced, qualified EAP teachers.

After an initial pre-interview questionnaire to collect information on participants' profiles, the interviews included questions as to the appropriateness of a wide range of various writing tutor roles (reported in detail in Liu and Harwood, 2022), including that of the proofreader. The interview schedule also included a series of questions related to the student–tutor relationship, students' needs and expectations and teaching strategies. To further examine the extent to which consultation data corresponded with interviewees' accounts of proofreading and to increase the validity of this research, audio-recorded consultation data and students' writing were collected. The data were analysed using a thematic analysis approach, which allows researchers to describe and interpret data in great detail and for nuance (Vaismoradi and Snelgrove, 2019). The interviews and audio-recorded consultation data were transcribed, coded and analysed, drawing on techniques described in Saldaña (2009). The instruments can be found in Liu (2020) (see also Liu and Harwood, 2022, for reproductions of questionnaires, interviews and codebooks used in the interview analysis).

The writing tutor participants were recruited through emails sent by the writing centre director and student participants were recruited by the first author through personal connections and social media.

Results

Students' Experiences Of and Beliefs About Proofreading in the Writing Centre

At present, the writing centre advocates a no-proofreading policy (while not specifying on its website what is meant by proofreading). However, in the interviews, (1) twenty-eight of the thirty-three students claimed that they felt the proofreader role (among other roles) was enacted by writing tutors during consultations, and (2) thirty of the thirty-three students believed that writing consultations should include the proofreading role. We now look at each of these two findings in more detail.

To discuss students' experiences of proofreading during writing consultations, we begin with the example of Cici.[2] Cici is an MA Education student who visited the writing centre on three occasions, working with three different writing tutors. She explained how she discussed different texts at each consultation: (1) an annotated bibliography, (2) a reflective essay and (3) an essay. At interview, she discussed her experience of the three writing consultations and brought to the interview her essay ((3) in the list above, a portfolio work on the topic of digital play and early childhood development in contemporary society) to exemplify and evidence her accounts. Cici claimed that the writing tutor played the role of proofreader and helped her proofread her work, as we see from the excerpt below.

Cici: Yes, proofreading. The writing tutor helped to correct grammar in detail, especially the first [text] and the third [text]. My first teacher would ask me when she couldn't understand and I would clarify for her. ...

Interviewer: Did your three writing tutors help you with structure and logic?

Cici: No, all focused on language I think.

To support Cici's claim, when we look at the interventions made by the writing tutor on her draft, reproduced in Figure 5.1, we see that the tutor did indeed act as proofreader.

Several proofreading revisions can be seen in Figure 5.1 by the writing tutor:

- 3rd line: (tense) 'are showing' changed to 'have showed'
- 4th line: (tense) 'use' changed to 'used'
- 7th line: (word formation) 'the cognitive' changed to 'cognition'
- 8th line: (word formation) 'academic' changed to 'academic learning'
- 10th line: (preposition) 'of' changed to 'in'; 'of' changed to 'to'
- 13th line: (tense) 'are taking' changed to 'have taken'; 'tend' changed to 'have tended'
- 14th line: (sentence formation; plural) 'how do the finding' changed to 'how the findings'

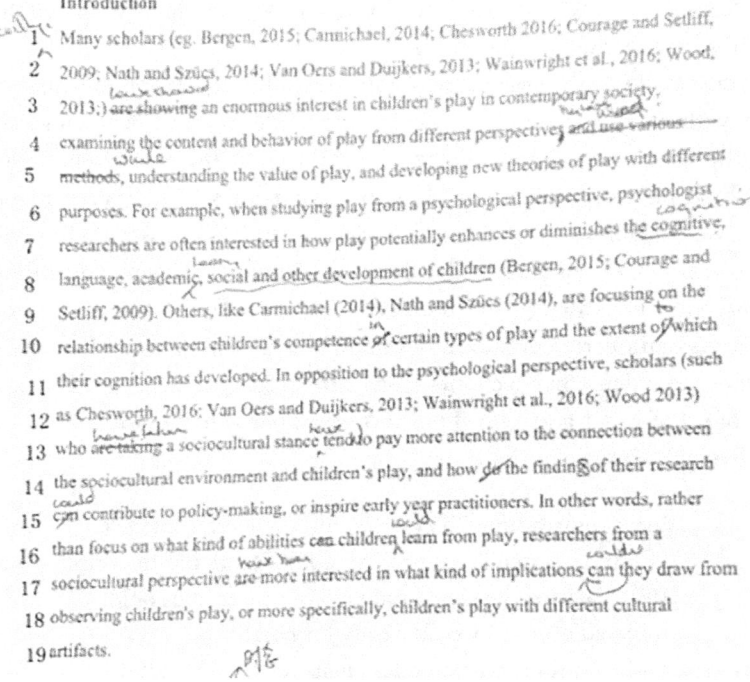

Figure 5.1 Excerpt from Cici's writing

- 15th line: (modal verb) 'can' changed to 'could'
- 16th line: (word order; modal verb) 'can children' changed to 'children could'
- 17th line: (tense; word order; modal verb) 'are' changed to 'have been'; 'can they' changed to 'they could'

Thus we find evidence from Figure 5.1 that the writing tutor acted as proofreader for Cici, marking, underlining and correcting grammatical errors line-by-line. In addition, the writing tutor made the corrections explicitly (rather than using indirect correction techniques such as underlining or deploying metalinguistic correction symbols like 'Gr' to pinpoint a grammatical error and thereby placing the onus on the student to self-correct). Similarly, most of the student participants reported that their writing tutors did the proofreading for them.

However, it should be acknowledged that not all tutors focused on the proofreading role to the extent that Cici's tutor did; from our analysis of other students' texts brought to interviews, we found some of the tutors only pointed out a few language issues rather than engaging in detailed proofreading. There was also evidence from student accounts and textual analysis that, in contrast to Cici's tutor, some tutors not only engaged in far less detailed proofreading, but delivered their interventions orally rather than in writing.

We turn now to our second finding, focusing on Chinese students' beliefs about the appropriacy of proofreading in the writing centre. We identified an obvious disparity between students' preference for proofreading and the no-proofreading policy of the centre, a policy which is in line with orthodox writing centre pedagogy (e.g., North, 1984). As explained earlier, thirty of the thirty-three student participants argued that writing consultations should help with proofreading, and the main reason students gave to justify their position was their lack of confidence in their command of the English language and grammar. For example, Anna felt that writing tutors should help with all language issues and explained that in her view proofreading was the reason for the popularity of the writing centre with international students:

> The tutor should point out all problems, including big ones and small ones. Especially for international students who have limited language competence, we need writing tutors to help us to proofread. And I think this is the main reason for most international students to go to [the centre].

Writing Tutors' Beliefs about Proofreading

In terms of the writing tutors' perspective, no tutors advocated at interview that they should help students with proofreading and distanced their role from that of proofreader, in line with writing centre policy. The main reasons tutors gave in support of these beliefs included: (1) ethical reasons, (2) the wish to encourage learner autonomy, (3) time constraints and (4) the non-proofreading remit of the writing centre. We examine the tutors' reasoning further below.

Tutors' ethical objections to proofreading were associated with the fear that enacting this role led to overdependence and passive learning behaviour on the part of the students and ethically inappropriate interventions on the part of tutors:

> We don't like proofreading. I suppose in the past we did a little bit more, but we have some students who were coming in every week and we've got a little bit

of a problem, and we're basically writing their essays, and so now, the system, I've been working in the writing centre for 6 years now and it's changed a little bit, so it's become a little bit more stricter in how often the students can book appointments, because we don't want to be writing it for them, they've got to be writing it. You know, we're just advising them and pointing things out to them, you know. (Amy)

We see how Amy links proofreading with ethical and pedagogical problems, explaining how the centre seeks to promote the development of learner autonomy.

Time constraints are also an issue: the writing centre used to allow any number of visits per student but has now limited the number of times students can book an appointment each year to avoid overdependence on tutors. Limiting student visits is associated with the avoidance of proofreading in the minds of some tutors because, where students can bring their texts multiple times to a consultation, once the tutor is satisfied the most serious macro issues have been addressed, sooner or later the temptation may be to start correcting/proofreading at the micro-level. Instead, the centre wishes students to take responsibility for their own work: rather than the tutor proofreading all the grammar mistakes, students should try their best to self-edit. As Rosa explained: 'They have to work. And you can say, you could say, "You've got a problem with a tense. What tense do you think it should be? I'm sure you can do that, I can't actually change it."'

In sum, then, for ethical and pedagogical reasons, writing tutors claimed they eschewed proofreading – despite evidence to the contrary from student interviews and tutor interventions on students' texts – and explained they could only focus on HOCs. Tutors suggested that if a student insisted they needed the help of a proofreader, s/he should ask a professional proofreader for help since proofreading is not part of the writing centre's remit.

The Writing Centre Director's Understanding of Proofreading

From the managerial perspective, the centre director said that although the guidance for writing tutors stated that their role does not include that of proofreader, writing tutors have indeed played this role at times formerly:

> We do know that some of our teachers have done this in the past and I have had to contact them and say 'Please don't' because this is not what the … service is … So actually if a tutor starts doing that, they're in trouble.

The director's remarks are consistent with the finding that some writing that the students brought to the interview had been proofread by writing tutors – although our findings indicate that proofreading should certainly not be associated exclusively with former writing centre practices. The director explained how the centre attempted to manage students' expectations regarding proofreading via their website: 'We've made it very clear in the website that this is not an editing and proofreading service.' Furthermore, the centre replied to students' post-consultation feedback requesting more of a focus on proofreading by explaining the tutor's role was not to act as a proofreader, while suggesting students could find a professional proofreader if they were insistent that proofreading was what they wanted:

> Some of the students in the past have written to complain to say that the teacher was not very helpful because the teacher didn't correct anything and then we have to reply to the complaint and then say, 'Well, sorry, but that's not what the [centre] is about, as we've said on the website'. We try to make it very clear but it is sometimes difficult, especially when the students are stressed and they want somebody to correct their work. We say, 'Well, if you want somebody to correct your work, then you need to find a professional proofreader'.

Adding to the tutors' explanations of why proofreading is (reportedly) eschewed, the director mentioned two reasons: first, writing tutors are not professionally trained as proofreaders; second, different departments in the university have different views of tolerances and boundaries as far as proofreading is concerned, and so ethical issues would arise if proofreading was part of the tutors' remit.

To What Extent Do Writing Tutors Actually Proofread in Consultation Sessions?

Based on our analysis of eight audio-recorded consultations, it was found that no writing tutor proofread during consultations, which contrasts with evidence of proofreading from students' interview data and the examination of students' drafts brought to the interviews. Instead, tutors helped more with HOCs while also advising on language issues as necessary.

To exemplify tutors' behaviour, we focus on Yuki, an MA Education student, who discussed a reflective essay during her consultation. The audio-recorded data reveals how the writing tutor pointed out the student's problems with grammar and language but did not proofread for Yuki or revise the text line-by-line. Instead, he tried to encourage Yuki to figure out the problems herself. The strategies he used included three techniques from classic writing centre pedagogy (e.g. see Blau et al., 2001; Mack, 2014; Murphy and Sherwood, 2008), as follows:

1. *Socratic questions to promote writer reflection and to enhance Yuki's ability to self-edit.* For instance, at the beginning of the consultation, the tutor asked Yuki several questions to see if she could identify certain errors and revise them by herself: 'What do you think is wrong with that, the sentence?'; 'Yeah ok, so what do you think it should be?'
2. *Reading aloud.* During the consultation the tutor realized that Yuki was not able to come up with the right grammar as a result of direct elicitation and so tried to help by encouraging her to use the reading aloud strategy: 'Or can you read it and think.'
3. *Implicit error correction.* The tutor used a single grammar mistake as an example, circling it and asking Yuki to then explain the right way to use it throughout her text.

Discussion and Implications

In summary, we found rather a nuanced and complex picture regarding proofreading in our focal university writing centre. Some parts of the picture were as expected, in that the centre policy reflected the tenets of orthodox pedagogy, instructing tutors to focus on HOCs rather than LOCs, to ensure students played an active role in the conferencing talk using techniques like elicitation and Socratic questioning, and to resist student requests for proofreading. However, the kind of consultation most students wanted was in marked contrast to what was on offer. Evidence of a certain amount of student dissatisfaction came not only directly from our student interviews, with thirty out of thirty-three students believing that consultations should include proofreading, but also indirectly from the centre director's mentioning of negative post-consultation feedback from students disappointed that they had not been offered proofreading. Again, though, none of this was particularly surprising in view of the fact that several studies we mentioned at the start of our chapter suggest that L2 students may wish writing tutors to enact more accuracy-focused approaches (e.g. Eckstein, 2019; Kim, 2014; Linville, 2009; Moussu, 2013; Nan, 2012). But what was more unexpected was that, in contrast to how they claimed at interview they acted during consultations, at least some tutors were found to play the role of the proofreader when we analysed their interventions on the students' texts. Our findings therefore uncover some mismatches, not only in terms of expectations, but also in terms of writing centre practices. How then can these mismatches and tensions be confronted and addressed? We consider this question from the perspective of students and of tutors below.

Students' Perspectives

One possible response to the mismatch between policy and students' wishes would be to hold that the centre's orthodox writing centre pedagogy must be retained, students being compelled to appreciate the benefits of an active rather than passive pedagogy which seeks to help them become better writers rather than to quickly fix their writing (see North, 1984). This would entail greater efforts to enable students to appreciate the present policy. An alternative response would be that students' dissatisfaction with the centre's no-proofreading policy should lead to a change in the focus of consultations. Various types of interventions could then be permitted, ranging from a fully permissive policy which enabled tutors to proofread as much of a student's text as was held to be necessary (by student or tutor) to a more educative-focused policy. Where the latter policy held sway, tutors could engage in selective rather than comprehensive proofreading, devoting more of their energies to raising students' awareness of their language errors and equipping students (either by direct teaching or pointing students to resources) to proofread the rest of their errors themselves.

Tutors' Perspectives

Looking at the proofreading issue from the perspective of the tutors, we propose two methods to confront mismatches in terms of expectations and practices: peer observations and videotaping tutoring sessions.

1. Peer Observation

Peer observation of tutoring is a useful way of systematically recording tutor behaviour and enabling post-observation discussion to understand tutors' reasons for adhering to or departing from the writing centre's proofreading policies.

If tutors adhered to the centre's no-proofreading policy, post-observation discussion could focus on the tools and techniques tutors use to avoid proofreading (e.g. Socratic questioning, having students read problematic passages aloud), how successful these tools and techniques are, how well they are received by student tutees and whether any additional techniques could with hindsight have been implemented which tutors may not already have in their armoury. Post-observation discussion could also provide a space for tutors to assess the extent to which the no-proofreading policy is fit for purpose, or whether alternative approaches to debarring proofreading seem worth considering.

If tutors violated the centre's no-proofreading policy, one response would be to try to understand why. Firstly, did they do so *consciously or unconsciously*? If the latter, an obvious fix would be to enhance the existing compulsory tutor training which is offered in-house before tutors are permitted to hold consultations. The training could be broadened out so that it moved beyond initial workshops for novice tutors to include regular continuing professional development (CPD) sessions for experienced staff. In addition to discussing the concepts of orthodox writing centre pedagogy and how far tutors should go when dealing with language and grammar issues, proofreading could be tackled head-on by once again using the method of peer observation. Post-observation, observee and observer could discuss issues which emerged from the consultation relating to proofreading: for instance, what did the tutor do when they noticed proofreading was needed in a text? What did they do when students requested proofreading? Did tutors act in accordance with the centre's policy? How could they have responded in a more pedagogically effective manner than they did? If, on the other hand, tutors violated the centre's no-proofreading policy consciously, peer-observed consultations could be used to enable discussion of the extent to which the centre's no-proofreading policy enabled the tutor observee to meet the needs and expectations of the tutee. If observer and observee agreed that more grammar-focused interventions would have benefitted the tutee, they could discuss how this more directive pedagogy would best be reflected in a reworded writing centre policy. What might be the downsides of a policy permitting more accuracy-focused tutoring styles, including the role of tutor as proofreader? How could those downsides be best addressed and overcome at the level of policy formulation, but also at the level of best practice, that is in the consultation? The policy proposals generated by these discussions could then be fed up to the writing centre director and debated by senior centre tutors.

2. *Videotaping Tutoring Sessions*

A second technique to enable exploration of tutoring policy and practice is to videotape tutoring sessions and then to use videoclips from these sessions for discussion. Should the writing centre decide to open up a debate about continuing with or departing from a no-proofreading policy, video clips of various tutor strategies which are associated with a more proofreading-tolerant role could be used as the basis for debate. These clips could feature tutors enacting the proofreader role with students possessing varied levels of proficiency, and whose texts feature a greater or lesser number of errors. In addition, videotapes of tutors acting very differently by adhering to the centre's current no-proofreading policy could also be made. The videos could then be viewed and discussed by tutors, together with the centre director, in terms of the ethical appropriacy of the tutors' interventions or non-interventions, following which an attempt could be made to come to a consensus on any future changes to centre policy with reference to proofreading.

Conclusion

In this chapter, we have uncovered evidence that a writing centre's no-proofreading policy has failed to attract the consensus of Chinese students – and other student cohorts, whether L1 or L2, may feel similarly. Furthermore, although the tutors we spoke to defended it, there was evidence that at least some tutors were violating the no-proofreading policy. We have explained how the centre's policymakers could choose to accommodate those who wish tutors to adopt a more interventionist role, being permitted to tackle LOCs head-on, whether by permitting tutors to directly correct grammatical errors or by taking a more educative stance and only correcting selectively, then requiring students to proofread most of their texts themselves. Alternatively, the centre could retain its no-proofreading policy and defend its stance more robustly and ensure this policy is more effectively disseminated to both staff and students. We have also proposed methods of stimulating discussion and debate among writing centre tutors and policymakers regarding the centre's stance on proofreading.

However, in addition to writing centre personnel, future policy must also take into account the views of other stakeholders, not least disciplinary faculty, who will ultimately be assessing the written work students are bringing to the writing centre pre-submission. Another important group whose views must be solicited is those university teaching and learning specialists who design assessment criteria, as these academics need to consider the extent to which language and linguistic correctness are referenced in the assessment criteria, and how much weight formal correctness should carry in relation to grading. If writing centre tutors are to be permitted to proofread, they will be able to enhance the accuracy of the language of students' texts; and if assessment criteria reference language accuracy, questions arise about the impact writing centre tutors will have upon students' eventual grades. Harwood (2021, under review) found that most lecturers he spoke to about proofreading claimed that they were not overly concerned with linguistic accuracy when assessing written work, being instead preoccupied with determining students' understanding of disciplinary content; but there were a few lecturers who explained that for some writing it was important to assess accuracy as well as content. For instance, one lecturer set their students public-facing writing assignments, where students were required to write letters to clients. In this case, language accuracy was deemed to be important because of the poor and unprofessional impression errors would create if found in the text. Where a writing centre tutor helped eliminate surface errors from the latter type of writing assignment, this could have far more of an impact on the grade than if they did so on an assignment in which language accuracy was less of a concern for the marker. Hence there are many ethical issues related to formulating proofreading policy, involving issues of consistency and fairness, and arriving at a one-size-fits-all proofreading policy which applies across the university, to all students, to all disciplines and to all kinds of assessed writing may not be realistic, and any top-down attempt to do so on the part of policymakers may fall short of attracting consensus on the part of lecturers. And so if good policy is to be arrived at, it will be important to expand research on stakeholders' views of proofreading to encompass a broader set of university stakeholder groups.

Notes

1 Described by Eckstein (2016) as 'multilingual writers who are not native English speakers per se and not true international students' (363), Generation 1.5 students are long-term residents in English-speaking countries. They may have been born in the English-speaking country or arrived there at a young age. They may sound like native speakers in informal conversational contexts, but their academic language, particularly their academic writing, may be less proficient. See Singhal (2004) for more on Generation 1.5.
2 All names are pseudonyms.

References

Barnett, R. W., and J. S. Blumner (2008), *The Longman Guide to Writing Center Theory And Practice*, New York: Pearson/Longman.

Blau, S. R., J. Hall, J. Davis, and L. Gravitz (2001), 'Tutoring ESL Students: A Different Kind of Session', *Writing Lab Newsletter*, 25 (10): 1–4.

Blau, S., J. Hall and S. Sparks (2002), 'Guilt-free Tutoring: Rethinking How We Tutor Non-Native-English-Speaking Students', *Writing Center Journal*, 23 (1): 23–44.

Bonazza, R. (2016), 'Locating L2 English Writing Centers in German Universities', *Journal of Academic Writing*, 6 (1): 1–16.

Brooks, J. (1991), 'Minimalist Tutoring: Making the Student Do All the Work', *Writing Lab Newsletter*, 15 (6): 1–4.

Bruce, S., and B. Rafoth (2009), *ESL Writers: A Guide for Writing Center Tutors*, 2nd edn, Portsmouth, NH: Boynton/Cook.

Chartered Institute of Editing and Proofreading (2020), 'Ensuring Editorial Excellence: The CIEP Code Of Practice'. Available online: https://www.ciep.uk/standards/code-of-practice/ (accessed 22 October 2020).

Chromik, M. (2002), 'Proofreading, Its Value, And Its Place In The Writing Center', ERIC. Available online: https://files.eric.ed.gov/fulltext/ED476401.pdf (accessed 1 May 2021).

Eckstein, G. (2013), 'Implementing and Evaluating a Writing Conference Program for International L2 Writers across Language Proficiency Levels', *Journal of Second Language Writing*, 22 (3): 231–9.

Eckstein, G. (2016), 'Grammar Correction in the Writing Centre: Expectations and Experiences of Monolingual and Multilingual Writers', *Canadian Modern Language Review*, 72 (3): 360–82.

Eckstein, G. (2019), 'Directiveness in the Center: L1, L2, and Generation 1.5 Expectations and Experiences', *Writing Center Journal*, 37 (2): 61–91.

Harris, M. (1986), *Teaching One-To-One: The Writing Conference*. Urbana, IL: National Council of Teachers of English.

Harris, M. (1995), 'Talking in the Middle: Why Writers Need Writing Tutors', *College English*, 57 (1): 27–42.

Harwood, N. (2018), 'What Do Proofreaders of Student Writing Do to a Master's Essay? Differing Interventions, Worrying Findings', *Written Communication*, 35 (4): 474–530.

Harwood, N. (2019), '"I Have to Hold Myself Back from Getting into All That": Investigating Ethical Issues in the Proofreading of Student Writing', *Journal of Academic Ethics*, 17 (1): 17–49.

Harwood, N. (2021), 'The Views of Lecturers, English Language Tutors, and Students on the Ethics of Proofreading: Preliminary Results'. Paper presented at the BALEAP Conference, University of Glasgow.

Harwood, N. (under review), 'Lecturer, Language Tutor, and Student Perspectives on the Ethics of the Proofreading of Student Writing'.

Harwood, N., L. Austin and R. Macaulay (2009), 'Proofreading in a UK University: Proofreaders' Beliefs, Practices, and Experiences', *Journal of Second Language Writing*, 18 (3): 166–90.

Harwood, N., L. Austin and R. Macaulay (2010), 'Ethics and Integrity in Proofreading: Findings from an Interview-Based Study', *English for Specific Purposes*, 29 (1): 54–67.

Harwood, N., L. Austin and R. Macaulay (2012), 'Cleaner, Helper, Teacher? The Role of Proofreaders of Student Writing', *Studies in Higher Education*, 37 (5): 569–84.

Kim, J. (2014), 'Better Writers or Better Writing? A Qualitative Study Of Second Language Writers' Experiences in a University Writing Center', PhD thesis, Ohio State University.

LaClare, E., and Franz, T. (2013), 'Writing Centers: Who Are They For? What Are They For?', *Studies in Self-Access Learning Journal*, 4 (1): 5–16. Available online: http://sisaljournal.org/archives/mar13/laclare_franz (accessed 1 May 2021).

Linville, C. (2009), 'Editing Line By Line', in S. Bruce and B. Rafoth (eds), *ESL Writers: A Guide for Writing Center Tutors*, 2nd edn, 116–31, Portsmouth, NH: Boynton/Cook.

Liu, C. (2020), 'One-To-One Writing Consultation in a UK University Context: A Study of Chinese Students and Their Tutors', PhD thesis, University of Sheffield.

Liu, C., and N. Harwood (2022), 'Understandings of the Role of the One-To-One Writing Tutor in a UK University Writing Centre: Multiple Perspectives', *Written Communication*, 39 (2).

Mack, L. (2014), 'Importing the Writing Center to a Japanese College: A Critical Investigation', EdD thesis, University of Exeter.

Mason, J. (2002), *Designing Qualitative Research*, London: Sage.

Moussu, L. (2013), 'Let's Talk! ESL Students' Needs and Writing Centre Philosophy', *TESL Canada Journal*, 30 (2): 55–68.

Murphy, C., and S. Sherwood (2008), *The St. Martin's Sourcebook For Writing Tutors*, 3rd edn, Boston, MA: Bedford/St. Martin's.

Myers, S. A. (2003), 'Reassessing the "Proofreading Trap": ESL Tutoring and Writing Instruction', *Writing Center Journal*, 24 (1): 51–70.

Nan, F. (2012), 'Bridging the Gap: Essential Issues to Address in Recurring Writing Center Appointments with Chinese ELL Students', *Writing Center Journal*, 32 (1): 50–63.

North, S. M. (1984), 'The Idea of a Writing Center', *College English*, 46 (5): 433–46.

Powers, J. K. (1993), 'Rethinking Writing Center Conferencing Strategies for the ESL Writer', *Writing Center Journal*, 13 (2): 39–47.

Ryan, L., and L. Zimmerelli (2010), *The Bedford Guide for Writing Tutors*, 5th edn, Boston, MA: Bedford/St. Martins.

Saldaña, J. (2009), *The Coding Manual for Qualitative Researchers*, London: Sage.

Severino, C., J. Swenson and J. Zhu (2009), 'A Comparison of Online Feedback Requests by Non-Native English Speaking and Native English-Speaking Writers', *Writing Center Journal*, 29 (1): 106–29.

Singhal, M. (2004), 'Academic Writing and Generation 1.5: Pedagogical Goals and Instructional Issues in the College Composition Classroom', *Reading Matrix*, 4 (3), 1–13.

Vaismoradi, M., and S. Snelgrove (2019), 'Theme in Qualitative Content Analysis and Thematic Analysis', *Forum: Qualitative Social Research/Socialforschung*, 20 (3), Article 23.

Voigt, A., and K. Girgensohn (2015), 'Peer Tutoring in Academic Writing with Non-Native Writers in a German Writing Center – Results of an Empirical Study', *Journal of Academic Writing*, 5 (1): 65–73.

6

The Positioning and Purpose of EAP across the University Curriculum: Highlighting Language in Curriculum Policies

Bee Bond

Introduction

As its starting point, this chapter takes the position that the higher education curriculum 'will always be to some degree contested and be a political as well as an educational matter' (Young, 1999: 464). The curriculum when presented 'as fact' becomes a politically charged institution in its own right, representing as it does the dominant view of knowledge as codified in policy. It becomes a 'symbolic system' with 'the power to impose (and even inculcate) instruments of knowledge and expression (taxonomies) of social reality, which are arbitrary but not recognized as such' (Bourdieu, 1979: 80). However, the curriculum is also a dynamic, fluid, socially situated and socially real enterprise that reflects the politics of those who create and engage in it (the curriculum as practice). The university curriculum is, therefore, political both in fact and in practice. This has become increasingly self-evident in a polarized world where accusations are made of left-wing academics indoctrinating students with their politics, debates around who should and should not be given a platform to speak at a university, and movements such as 'Rhodes must fall' highlighting issues of institutional and structural racism – including within the curriculum. 'Social Justice' (taken as a broad spectrum of sociopolitical issues needing to be addressed) in higher education (HE) is certainly having an impact on policy and driving strategic changes to institutional approaches to curriculum development.

Meanwhile, English for Academic Purposes (EAP) frequently finds itself at the forefront of the neoliberal policies, global political shifts and market forces that impact on higher education. This includes governmental changes to visa regulations, both within the host country but also globally – with, for example, other countries benefiting from a 'greater market share' when an increasingly hostile environment in the United States under the Trump presidency persuaded international students to apply to study elsewhere (see Chapters 2 and 3 in this volume for further exploration of these issues). Political decisions feed into student choices of where to study abroad. Coming prior to the core period of academic study, EAP pre-sessionals are frequently the test dummy for trends in international student movement and are vulnerable to both sudden increases and decreases in student applications occurring as a result of wider political decisions.

Despite this, EAP has, in the most part, remained steadfastly apolitical. Viewing its role as being one of socialization, enabling students to understand and access methods of knowledge communication within their own academic tribe, EAP *practice* (in contrast to research, see Hamp-Lyons [2015, 2018] for further comment) remains outside the academic tribal system (Becher and Trowler, 2001), hovering on the margins and relatively agentless (Bond, 2020; Ding and Bruce, 2017; Hadley, 2015). Its focus on student need has kept to the confines of consideration of language as a carrier of academic knowledge rather than drawing on wider sociopolitical needs. Its curriculum is empty of its own content, waiting to be filled up with the language and content of an academic other. This pseudo-neutral pragmatism, presenting an ideology of factual objectivity, means that attempts to ethically politicize EAP have been scarce. The notable exception Critical EAP (Benesch, 2001) seems to have been a fleeting moment in time rather than a shift in practices. While Benesch's work continues to be referenced, there is little to suggest it has been widely taken up as an approach to teaching EAP or that it achieved the desired impact of politicizing the international student body.

In 2019, BALEAP supported the development of a range of Special Interest Groups. One of the first of these has Social Justice as its raison d'etre. However, at the time of writing, this remains in its infancy and has yet to establish a clear focus, particularly in relation to how social justice for students rather than for practitioners can be meaningfully developed through EAP practices. To date, neither the Social Justice SIG (Special Interest Group) nor Critical EAP have been able to meaningfully articulate how EAP, learning about language and discourse, can connect to the disciplinary communication and socialization needs of students and enable them to develop a more transformative or transformational position.

Given that the focus of most EAP teaching is on language and discourse, and that subjectivity and power relations are an integral element of any discourse this non-critical, apolitical stance seems bizarre. Discourse is a social as well as a linguistic act. Many working in EAP have, for this very reason, been drawn to and begun to incorporate Academic Literacies (Lea and Street, 1998; Lea, 2004) into their principles and publicized practices. Academic Literacies, viewing discourse awareness at three levels: skills, socialization and transformation, does allow for a more critical and possibly politically aware approach. However, in order to take an Academic Literacies approach to EAP teaching, it is necessary to work in and through specific disciplinary discourses. And here is one of the current difficulties for EAP. A combination of the marginalized status of EAP practitioners (Ding and Bruce, 2017; Hadley, 2015), the lack of visibility of language in the curriculum (Bond, 2020; Turner, 2011) and the consequent lack of impetus to provide any financial, staff or time resources to embed EAP within the curriculum all work to ensure that EAP remains sidelined and disconnected from the wider curriculum. Thus, its status as being reduced to that of a sticking plaster or fix only when language is noticed as being deficient is maintained.

This chapter therefore argues that it is imperative that EAP practitioners work to break this status quo and to develop an academic authority through scholarship, agency and a status within the academy that allows them to advocate for a more central position for language across the curriculum.

The chapter begins with an overview of where language can be shown to be most visible within the policy formation of a higher education curriculum as well as within the wider, 'hidden' curriculum – which could and maybe should itself also inform policy. I then consider the impact on staff and students when language is ignored or dismissed as an irrelevant element of learning and communication. Using my own institution as a case study, I then suggest ways in which the curriculum can be harnessed by EAP leaders and practitioners and used to gain access to institutional power structures and policy makers, particularly within the context of a university's internationalization agenda. I argue that EAP centres and practitioners can work through and within the curriculum to move themselves towards the centre stage, arguing for a re-positioning of EAP as a knowledge-based, scholarly endeavour which is firmly embedded within the structures and educational purposes of higher education.

Connecting the Dots: A Language Aware Curriculum

It should come as no surprise that language is everywhere and impacts every aspect of a university. Because language is everywhere, in everything, it is difficult to separate out into manageable areas for policy work and curriculum development. Essentially, the whole curriculum needs to consider language and those working on both the written, academic curriculum and those involved in surfacing the hidden, more social aspects of a university curriculum all need to consider the impact that language use, language choice and university discourses can have on a diverse student population.

I have previously suggested a heuristic for a language connected curriculum (Bond, 2020: xi) where the university (the dominant culture) is viewed as a site of linguistic struggle for students, in Bourdieuvian terms:

> The dominant culture produces its specific ideological effect by concealing its function of division (or distinction) under its function of communication: the culture which unites (a medium of communication) separates (an instrument of distinction), and legitimates distinctions by defining all cultures (designated as sub-cultures) in terms of their distance from the dominant culture (i.e. in terms of privation), identifying the latter with culture (i.e. excellence). (Bourdieu, 1979: 80)

Within this heuristic, language can maintain the symbolic power of the current elite (Bourdieu, 1979) or help to empower others; it can oppress and marginalize or disrupt the status quo (hooks, 1994). However, in order to empower and disrupt or even, less ambitiously, to allow all students access to the knowledge and dominant culture of their discipline, it is important that language becomes an integral element of the taught curriculum and of teachers' pedagogical content knowledge.

The consequences of not connecting language to academic disciplinary content in a visible and intentional manner are also clear across all elements of this heuristic. A disconnection feeds into narratives frequently reported in the media (e.g Four Corners [2019] in Australia; *The Guardian* [2019] in the UK), emerging both anecdotally and from research around the *perceived* negative impact of an increasingly diverse and internationalized student population on the quality of higher education.

A curriculum that ignores the importance of language as a form of cultural and social capital reduces student confidence in their own academic abilities and in the abilities of their peers; staff confidence in their ability to teach and staff confidence in their students' academic abilities. This ultimately reduces trust in the partnership that should exist and leads to social separation (Bond, 2020; Montgomery, 2010; Ortactepe, 2013) as well as to separation and disconnection within the classroom (Bond, 2020; Hartig, 2017; Kettle, 2017).

Maintaining the current doxa that the language and genre of disciplinary discourses and knowledge communication can be developed through a form of osmosis or implicit rather than explicit socialization (Turner, 2011) denies the time involved in developing an understanding of disciplinary communication practices. The cognitive and conceptual weight behind key disciplinary terms that are not easily translated or broken down is ignored or dismissed.

Largely because it is (un)seen as a carrier rather than an integral element of disciplinary knowledge building, language often then does become seen as 'the catch-all term for problems with unmet standards, and the need for remediation' (Turner, 2004: 99). This in turn becomes connected to dissatisfaction with the perceived imposition of university wide admissions policies and procedures and erosion of agency for academics and individual departments to make localized decisions. Students (most frequently international students who speak languages other than English) who are unable to use and manipulate (academic) English with the ease of those who have the 'culturally embedded and socially embodied "habitus" of being academic' (Turner, 2011: 37) are viewed as being in deficit and the 'system' is seen as being broken with no clear way of fixing it. It is often at this point that the EAP unit is called upon as the cure-all and fixer of language problems.

EAP as Pharmakon

By invoking and highlighting perceived 'language issues' in this way, the purity and authenticity of academic thought is tarnished, and academic literacy becomes a metaphorical pharmakon – a poison and a cure: 'The dilemma for contemporary academic institutions is that with the emergence of the relatively new pedagogies of academic literacy and English for Academic Purposes, the self-sufficiency of the academic mission, mediated through its various and ever multiplying disciplines is endangered by the necessity of acknowledging the substantive role of language and languaging in academic performance' (Turner, 2011: 37).

Conceptualizing EAP as a pharmakon can also have a negative impact on EAP, where it becomes 'a scapegoat for when students are failing to communicate, a poison in perpetuating myths around language as being easily fixed and isolated from academic thought processes and only a remedy as a placebo, providing confidence and emotional "sticking plasters" to students without treating the much more complex cause of their difficulties' (Bond, 2020: 162).

However, as both a cure and a poison, pharmakon 'has an indeterminate meaning in which the opposite meaning is contained within it' (Ding, 2016a). By conceiving language and academic discourse as a pharmakon, the problem and the solution, a faint but visible route to making language a central and acknowledged element of the university curriculum begins to emerge.

Through interviews with university leaders, Nicholls (2019) has identified a responsibility gap when it comes to language. Although when questioned, leaders are able to identify language as having a clear impact on how accessible a curriculum is for students, they were not able to identify who should take on the responsibility of highlighting this as a key need within any curriculum policies or redevelopment programmes. This is not true of all contexts; Australia has (or had) government-led policies that directly relate to language (DEEWR, 2009), English as a Medium of Instruction (EMI) institutions also tend to have clearly expressed language policies and in South Africa there is increasing institutional focus on the accessibility of and power within the use of academic English languages (see e.g. Clarence, 2021; Paxton and Frith, 2015). It is when functioning without a government or institutional language policy that responsibility for linguistic accessibility is at best unclear and at worst abdicated, but also perhaps offers more radical possibilities if responsibility is taken up locally.

I suggest, then, that EAP (or equivalent) centres should take this responsibility for developing policy and the consequent practices of a language aware curriculum seems obvious. That they are not currently doing so, at least in the UK, speaks volumes about the present marginalization and lack of academic authority in EAP, suggesting 'there are not practitioners in place with the agency and capital to enact, develop and critique theories, ideas, research and ideological projects' (Ding and Bruce, 2017: 206).

Nicholls's research (2019) suggests that EAP leadership needs to shift more clearly to taking confident ownership of its area of expertise and its ability to contribute fully to the life of the university. Educational leadership has to start with an understanding of what you want education to look like or to be. It seems clear that it is only those interested in language who can lead others to see it as central to all learning. In this sense, EAP leadership is closely aligned to EAP teaching practice – the required knowledge base (Ferguson, 1997), the importance of collaboration, the ability to connect language and academic knowledge should all stem from a scholarly, moral, ethical, socioculturally and politically aware position. All forms of EAP practice are political because, as Dyches and Boyd argue (2017: 476), 'all instructional manoeuvres are politically charged and therefore never neutral'.

Principled Pragmatism

I suggest that EAP leaders can effect change to university education, policy and politics via a route of 'principled pragmatism'. This requires reflexivity, a kind of praxis where feedback is incorporated and learned from. It is not a method, approach or style of teaching or leadership but an orientation or stance. More concretely, principled pragmatism involves walking a thin tightrope between harnessing some of the more negative rhetoric within the university around, inter alia, linguistic deficit, problem fixing, international students as pipelines, as intentional academic cheats and using these perceived problems as a route into conversations. Suggesting 'we can help with that' does not necessarily mean we can fix the problem or even agree the problem identified is the actual problem to be addressed; it does provide an opportunity for discussion.

While ideally these discussions would be institution-wide, in reality the route into change is likely to be at the meso-level of school or faculty as it is at this level that the 'language problem' is noticed and seen as having an impact on education. It is here that it is possible to have the 'significant conversations' (Roxå and Mårtensson, 2009) that can have a direct impact on disciplinary approaches to teaching and learning and where the principles that are central to ensuring change are likely to resonate the most.

As with most aspects of EAP practice, the principles you work from are likely to be context specific. However, as an example, I outline here the principles we use in my own institution for opening up discussion within a disciplinary context.

EAP Provision: Vision

These concepts are further defined and explained below:

1. **Challenge** moves beyond awareness raising, pushing teachers and students towards a critical analysis of all learning materials, encouraging constant questioning of current norms and beliefs, stretching students beyond their comfort zone.
2. **Collaboration** is vital to ensure understanding of the discipline and the language needs of students. Collaboration includes between EAP/subject and students.

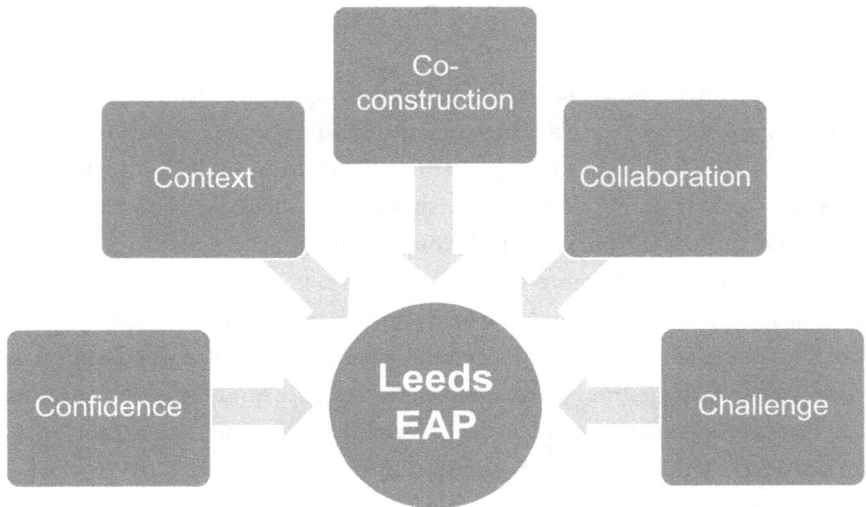

Figure 6.1 The 5Cs principles for an EAP curriculum (Bond, 2021)

3. Learning is **co-constructed** between the EAP specialist and the students who bring their specific disciplinary background knowledge to the EAP classroom, and with subject specialists across campus.
4. **Context** is vital to teaching and learning EAP, incorporating (inter)cultural understanding, acknowledging institutional constraints and power as well as the authenticity and relevance of academic communication. In this way both a pragmatic and critical approach to context can be taken.
5. **Confidence** to communicate knowledge and understanding is built and is seen as key to removing affective filters to study. This includes awareness of and focus on the confidence of teachers working through the content of an unfamiliar discipline as well as the confidence of students working in an unfamiliar language and context.

These concepts are then connected and woven through the principles, aims and intended outcomes presented during discussions and planning for collaborations with disciplinary schools and used in the development of an embedded EAP curriculum.

Academic Language and Literacy Development

1. Is offered to all students
2. Values the diverse nature of our students and works to be inclusive of all

3. Is developed in partnership with disciplinary academic programmes
4. Acknowledges disciplinary differences but builds on cross-disciplinary connections
5. Is student-centred and driven by student need
6. Is participatory, collaborative and co-constructed
7. Is holistic and embodied, acknowledging cognitive, emotional and social factors of learning
8. Is core to knowledge creation and communication.

Aims

1. To enable students to take ownership of their own learning
2. To surface occluded cultural practices and processes and thereby reduce cultural and linguistic barriers to learning
3. To enable students to develop their ability to achieve the 'appropriate arrangement of both content information and language in order to create extended spoken or written discourse' (Bruce, 2008: 4)
4. To enable students 'to develop the means to negotiate and respond to the requirements of assignment genres' (Bruce, 2011: 67).

Outcomes for Students

Students are better able to:

1. organize their own learning
2. interact more successfully with the discourse and practices of the institution
3. activate their linguistic knowledge and employ it effectively in an academic context
4. achieve better outcomes for their programme of study

In taking a principled yet pragmatic approach it is important to recognize that you are knowingly developing an 'elective affinity' (Zepke, 2015) with rhetoric, perceptions and structures that are highly problematic. As Mackay argues: 'Blanket labels like neoliberal academy may speak a truth at a macro-level but fail to capture the nuance and variability of these tendencies. In so doing, they miss the "institutional openings", crisis tendencies, "soft spots" and contradictions on the ground through which agency can be exercised and progressive change promoted.' (2021: 90).

Therefore, pragmatically, you may be providing EAP with a space to grow within the university and moving it away from the edges of the institution. However, it is vital that this is done through a principled and determinedly reflexive lens, in the knowledge that you are working within neoliberal structures and, more locally, with deficit perceptions of the students you are working to support. Principles, in terms of what needs to be achieved and how it can be achieved, need to be the starting point and the points to which all discussions and negotiations return in order to avoid getting lost in the bureaucratization of the institutional dialogic process. to avoid policy-making without political content that engenders and enacts a commitment to change. It is necessary to allow a freedom of choice and orientation to colleagues and Schools within that; an awareness of competing epistemologies that need, in equal measure, to be embraced, adapted to and defended against is essential.

EAP Leadership as Guerrilla Gardening

I have suggested that a pragmatic approach to developing a more embedded focus on language and academic literacies is developed initially through conversations at the meso rather than macro-level of a university. This does not mean that the ultimate aim should not be to develop an institution-wide language aware curriculum, rather that it is important for changes in understanding to be seen as useful, impactful and relevant to those involved in teaching and learning. This seems to be best done incrementally through collaboration at point of perceived need rather than via a top-down approach that can often be viewed by those who need to implement it as impracticable and unnecessary in reality. Effecting change to educational practices in this sense requires 'guerrilla' tactics (Smith et al., 2018).

Smith et al. (2018) outlined these tactics using the metaphor of guerrilla warfare, asking the following questions:

1. What will the goal look like?
2. Who are your allies?
3. Where are the contested territories?
4. What help will you need?
5. What are the barriers?
6. What could you do? How?

However, in terms of EAP practice where the approach should be to intertwine language knowledge throughout the curriculum and disciplinary practices, the metaphor of guerrilla *gardening* seems to be more appropriate. It is important to get to know the 'garden' (i.e. discipline and School) before making decisions about the approach you will take with them (which seeds to plant). Decisions need to be made around what interventions will work quickly and where longer-term work needs to be focused. It is necessary to revisit this question frequently and continue to look for other fertile ground while allowing previous work to bed in. Growth should be expected to be patchy, and it needs to be understood that not all attempts will be successful; it may be necessary to change tactics, to restart, to weed out. The aim should be for collaborations and curricula developments to be organic; however, this needs careful tending to and constant revisiting to maintain and nurture. It is through sharing the results with others that further growth, across the institution, can occur.

This approach to collaborating with other disciplines needs to be developed and built in across the range of EAP roles, essentially infiltrating the academy at all levels: micro, meso and macro. This includes planting an EAP practitioner into a discipline in order to nurture relationships with individual module or programme leads at the micro-level. Here it is important that time is given to developing an understanding of student and faculty perceptions of the needs, the pedagogies, the epistemology and the discourses. Essentially, developing

1. a knowledge of disciplinary cultures and values; a form of knowledge which is essentially sociological or anthropological.
2. a knowledge of the epistemological basis of different disciplines; a form of knowledge which is philosophical in nature.
3. a knowledge of genre and discourse, which is mainly linguistic in character (Ferguson, 1997: 85).

At the meso-level, it involves establishing more formal partnerships with heads of School and those involved in leading student education within the discipline in order to establish resourcing arrangements and ensure that EAP colleagues are embedded into School structures and strategies – ensuring their visibility in the discipline. Again, this requires the development of and involves drawing on Ferguson's (1997) three areas of EAP knowledge outlined above. I would argue that it is vital that any discussions here are not approached from a merely transactional position but are firmly rooted in scholarship; academic leadership here needs to have clear academic origins to ensure the ability to speak with authority and be viewed as an equal partner. So, while the message may be the clear and pragmatic: 'we can help', and necessarily connected to finance as well as education, it also requires the ability to demonstrate a research-informed, nuanced understanding of disciplinary linguistic and discourse practices, of student need and of the need to engage in ongoing scrutiny and scholarship around suggested changes to teaching and learning.

This approach may then eventually feed into the wider university structures at a more macro-level of institution-wide policy-making, but initially should draw from institution-wide conversations. Ferguson's knowledge base here extends beyond the disciplines to encompass an anthropological and sociological knowledge of the cultures, values and discourses of the university within which the EAP unit is situated. Examples of this include moves towards inclusive practices, decolonization of the curriculum, a focus on equality and diversity and to better addressing issues around academic integrity. This is not suggested cynically; EAP practices and practitioners have much to contribute towards this more socially just approach to higher education; EAP leadership is needed to make these connections and push for a more language-focused university.

Historically EAP centres, situated somewhat arbitrarily within a higher education institution and 'operating on the edges of academia' (Ding and Bruce, 2017), seem to have found it difficult to exert any influence over institutional strategy and policy-making. This is, in part, due to EAP's own lack of confidence and avoidance of taking a political position or of outlining its own professional ethics (see Chapter 10 in this volume). EAP practice and practitioners need to move away from ideologically colluding in their own marginalization (Turner, 2004). A slight repositioning of EAP practitioners as serious scholars, able to bring academic weight as well as practice-based experience, could bring a realization that EAP is ideally placed to undermine the more neoliberal practices of current higher education policies by working through the systems. This positioning then moves EAP away from 'Third Space' leadership (MacDonald, 2016) towards the use of guerrilla tactics that are aligned to the 'feminist leadership' described in Mackay (2021), to becoming a small, if slightly less radical than intended by Harney and Moten (2014), part of the 'undercommons', working underground to critique, educate and professionalize.

Language as a Pharmakon Versus Language as a Rhizome

Through this guerrilla gardening approach to leadership in EAP, working as part of an 'undercommons', balancing critique and education, it may be possible to shift perceptions of EAP away from that of a fixer of language problems towards an understanding of language and discourse as something that is threaded throughout the higher education curriculum. Rather than being viewed as a pharmakon – a poison or a cure – EAP, language and discourse become a rhizome.

In nature, a rhizome is a stem that grows underground, usually horizontally below the surface of the soil. This stem puts out nodes that usually then grow straight up and become visible above the ground. In this way they present the appearance of being multiple individual plants where in fact they are all shoots of the same rhizome. Once established, they spread stealthily and are hard to kill.

The difference between viewing language as a pharmakon or language as a rhizome then lies between language being viewed as something that is either taken to cure a problem or make an issue worse and something that is always there, always present, built into the fabric of the curriculum, occasionally causing issues if left unattended to, but also providing lasting, tenacious fertility and growth. There are no beginning and endpoints, just a middle in perpetual transformation or *becoming* (Strom, 2018); 'the fabric of the rhizome is and … and … and' (Deleuze and Guattari, 1987, in Strom, 2018: 25)

This Deleuzian view of language seems to connect well to both the metaphor of guerrilla gardening as a form of EAP leadership and to the need to take a principled yet pragmatic approach to developing a higher education curriculum that is language aware. There is no specific route in or out, but a need to look for and develop connections where they naturally arise: 'roots are taproots with a more multiple, lateral, and circular system of ramification, rather than a dichotomous one' (Strom, 2018: 106).

Strom also suggests that Deleuzian approaches allow for a pragmatism and enable a 'pick and mix' method of problem solving, something that is vital when working with multiple disciplines and attempting to align often competing epistemologies. As she suggests, quoting Deleuze (1990),

> 'Something comes through or it does not. There is nothing to explain, nothing to understand, nothing to interpret. It is like plugging in to an electric circuit' (1990: 8). Take what connects with you and that you can use at that moment, asking if it (a concept) works within the particular problem you are grappling with, what it might do in the context of that problem, and what it might do for YOU. (2018: 106).

In this way, language needs to be seen to connect, to be of use in the moment within the context of the discipline rather than viewed as something that needs to be explained or interpreted separately. Language needs to be made visible and highlighted as part of academic knowledge building and disciplinary communication. Theories, research, scholarship can all be drawn on within the context that discussions take place in order to provide a connection to that context. The seeds planted, the methods used may vary depending on the conditions presented; the principles remain the same.

Planned Serendipity: An Autoethnographic Example

Theoretical metaphors for EAP leadership and policy influencing are, however, no use if not put into practice. Here I provide an outline of where seeds were planted and connections made, seemingly at random, in my own institution. While the guerrilla tactics used were intentional and purposeful, the (emerging) impacts are perhaps more accidental and serendipitous.

I have previously detailed a journey through 'accidental scholarship' (Bond, 2020), and the need to engage in scholarship in order to provide EAP practitioners and leaders with greater agency and academic authority has also been highlighted elsewhere (Ding, 2016b, 2019; Ding and Bruce, 2017). In my own case, this scholarship gave me greater confidence and evidence to support the arguments I wished to make within my institution but also provided me with more tangible and instrumental affordances. Undertaken and supported by a university institute for teaching excellence, my scholarship was institutionally visible and resulted in invitations to present, advise and work with a range of groups and committees.

Possibly serendipitously, this personal visibility coincided with the increased prevailing focus within the higher education sector and my own institution on issues that clearly connected with questions of language and internationalization, including, inter alia: inclusive learning and teaching, moves to decolonize the curriculum, a focus on equality and diversity in all areas and questions around academic integrity. Therefore, at the macro-level, I spoke to deputy vice chancellors and pro-deans for Student Education and for internationalization and at university-wide student education conference plenary sessions. I was invited to work with university groups around developing inclusive practice. In this way, my individual practice and scholarship began to merge with my leadership roles. I was able to use my scholarship and increased visibility to represent and highlight the importance of language and EAP at the macro and meso-levels of the university.

This work was not individual. It involved drawing on the knowledge and expertise of other EAP colleagues who all worked and contributed to discussions with the institution at different levels and in different arenas. My own visibility was not only due to my own scholarship but also the careful leadership of others that ensured the Language Centre was already considered a central element of the university.

At the meso-level, we gained access to Faculty and School Student Education Boards where, rather than focusing on evidence from scholarship, we presented the principles developed for working within disciplines to support and develop language, discourse and academic literacies (see above). It is in these meetings and discussions that decisions to put suggestions into practice or not are made. This inevitably includes decisions around finances and whether it is worth a School resourcing input from EAP practitioners into their module teaching. So, it is also here that the uncomfortable juxtapositions around deficit understandings of students' language levels are likely to be encountered. It is necessary to work with an ambiguity around what we are doing and trying to achieve, taking the position 'that accounts for the limitations, compromises and intended and unintended consequences of insider actions and strategies, at the same time as being clear about the need to engage with *actual existing* institutions, the significance of small shifts in context over time and the necessity of compromises at other times to achieve "the least worst outcomes"' (Mackay, 2021).

These discussions then continue at the micro-level, between EAP practitioners and Directors of Student Education, programme and module leaders within a specific School. Here, EAP teaching and leadership again merge as colleagues use their knowledge and expertise 'where the work gets done, where the work gets subverted' (Harney and Moten, 2014: 26) – simultaneously teaching students and working with other-disciplinary colleagues to educate them and make their tacit expectations around language and disciplinary discourses more explicit. This involves hard, consistent and persistent work, creating networks of allies within a School who will support our work and also doing work that combines providing practical solutions to immediate perceived problems while concurrently addressing wider problems within these perceptions. The existence of this network of collegial connections is not taken as given but is 'the product of endless effort' required 'in order to produce and reproduce lasting, useful relationships that can secure material or symbolic profits' (Bourdieu, 1986: 90). Collaborating through and being instrumental in developing these informal, rhizomatic networks, EAP practitioners work to both understand and to change institutionalized beliefs, cultures and forms of behaviour; these networks 'are made up not simply of pragmatic relations, but also constitute moral and epistemic communities' (Ball, 2017: 37).

Impact

Measuring the impact of EAP teaching practices is notoriously difficult. Extrapolating knowledge or ability to use language and discourse(s) from the other learning that students are doing is, more or less, impossible. However, the impact of positioning EAP practices more centrally to the university endeavour and working to make language visible within the curriculum is wider reaching than simply measuring student successes and outcomes (although it is important to be able to demonstrate impact here as well). Work does need to be done on collecting quantitative data that better speaks to those working within an epistemological framework that values this, but this data should be presented alongside qualitative data as being equally valid.

Here again, the interconnection between scholarship, teaching practice and leadership is clear and necessary. The need for all three of these to also be a collaborative endeavour is also clear – involving EAP practitioners working in partnership with each other, with students and with other-disciplinary teachers.

Disciplinary colleagues in Schools have reported improvements in grades in comparison to previous years when there was no insessional EAP teaching. While it is difficult to prove a direct correlation, the fact that this is unsolicited communication, with Schools making the connection themselves, is hugely encouraging.

Outside student outcomes, impact can also be seen through reported increased confidence for students. It is becoming clear that students tend to find their EAP teachers less intimidating, are more open about the difficulties they face and more willing to ask questions around assessment requirements. This feeds into an increased 'sense of belonging', something that was particularly noteworthy during the shift to online learning during the Covid-19 pandemic.

Other-discipline teachers also report the value of having a critical 'outsider within' to talk to about teaching within a safe space and report developing skills and pedagogical techniques through these conversations as per Roxå and Mårtensson's (2009, 2016) findings while the availability and access to the disciplines is enabling EAP colleagues to develop their knowledge base as outlined by Ferguson (1997) and improve both in-sessional and pre-sessional provision, better meeting student needs. By being clear with the university about the position and purpose of EAP within the curriculum we are further enabled to develop our own confidence and understanding of what our position and purpose should be across the institution and within specific disciplinary boundaries. EAP practitioners who work in this context are experiencing a shift in their own identities and sense of agency, moving from a position of agency denial to embracing the challenges of quietly and pragmatically bringing about principled changes to how language is considered within the curriculum. The work done at this micro-level ripples back up through the meso to the macro-level, with conversations around embedding academic literacies and the importance of language learning now threaded into strategic plans for changes to the institution-wide curriculum.

Towards a Symbiosis

This, then, is an ongoing project that requires persistent leadership at all levels and leadership that includes expertise and knowledge of EAP practices and epistemology. It involves the ability to cross boundaries, to move between third spaces and underground spaces, placing roots and sprouting shoots when opportunities arise. Successes in highlighting the importance of language can often (seem to) be due to serendipity or accidental opportunities as much as carefully planned strategies.

For this approach to work, EAP practice needs to professionalize, developing an academic authority that allows us 'to be in multiple places and all levels, including in middle and senior management, seeking to hold and exercise power "helpfully" to bring about structural and cultural change' (Mackay, 2021: 90). We also need to work in collaboration with others, creating a rhizomatic network through which to thread our EAP practices and acknowledging the importance of this collective activity in visibly establishing the unbreakable symbiosis of language and disciplinary knowledge.

References

Ball, Stephen J. (2017), 'Laboring to Relate: Neoliberalism, Embodied Policy, and Network Dynamics', *Peabody Journal of Education*, 92 (1): 29–41.

Becher, T., and P. R. Trowler (2001), *Academic Tribes and Territories: Intellectual Enquiry and the Culture of Disciplines* (2nd edn), Buckingham: The Society for Research into Higher Education and Open University Press.

Benesch, S. (2001), *Critical English for Academic Purposes: Theory, Politics, and Practice*, London: Blackwell.

Bond, B. (2020), *Making Language Visible in the University: English for Academic Purposes and Internationalisation*, Bristol: Multilingual Matters.

Bond, B. (2021), 'Making Language Visible in Higher Education: Connecting EAP and the Disciplines', *British Association of Applied Linguistics and Cambridge University Press Symposium: Language, Literacies and Learning in the Disciplines: A Higher Education Perspective*. University of Surrey (online), 8–9 July 2021.

Bourdieu, P. (1979), 'Symbolic Power', *Critique of Anthropology*, 1 (4) (13–14): 77–85.

Bourdieu, P. (1986), 'Forms of Capital', in J. Richardson (ed.), *Handbook of Theory and Research for the Sociology of Education*, 241–58, New York: Greenwood Press.

Bruce, I. (2008), *Academic Writing and Genre: A Systematic Analysis*, London: Continuum.

Bruce, I. (2011), *Theory and Concepts of English for Academic Purposes*, Basingstoke: Palgrave Macmillan.

Clarence, S. (2021), *Turning Access into Success: Improving University Education with Legitimation Code Theory*, Abingdon: Routledge.

DEEWR (2009), *Good Practice Principles for English Language Proficiency for International Students in Australian Universities*, Canberra: Department of Education, Employment and Workplace Relations. Accessed online: http://www.aall.org.au/sites/default/files/Final_Report-Good_Practice_Principles2009.pdf (accessed 10 June 2019).

Deleuze, G. (1990), *The Logic of Sense*, New York: Columbia University Press.

Deleuze, G., and F. Guattari (1987), *A Thousand Plateaus*, trans. B. Massumi, Minneapolis: University of Minnesota Press.

Ding, A. (2016a), 'EAP as Pharmakon: Are We All Neoliberals Now?', *Teaching EAP: Polemical. Questioning, Debating and Exploring Issues in EAP*, Wordpress blog. Available online: https://teachingeap.wordpress.com/2016/02/19/eap-as-pharmakon-are-we-all-neoliberals-now/ (accessed 8 September 2021).

Ding, A. (2016b), 'Challenging Scholarship: A Thought Piece', *The Language Scholar*, 0: 6–19.

Ding, A. (2019), 'EAP Practitioner Identity', in K. Hyland and L. L. C. Wong (eds), *Specialised English: New Directions in ESP and EAP Research and Practice*, 69–77, London: Routledge.

Ding, A., and I. Bruce (2017), *The English for Academic Purposes Practitioner: Operating on the Edge of Academia*, London: Palgrave Macmillan.

Dyches, J., and A. Boyd (2017), 'Foregrounding Equity in Teacher Education: Toward a Model of Social Justice Pedagogical and Content Knowledge', *Journal of Teacher Education*, 68 (5): 476–90.

Ferguson, G. (1997), Teacher Education and LSP: The Role of Specialized Knowledge, in R. Howard and G. Brown (eds), *Teacher Education for Languages for Specific Purposes*, Clevedon: Multilingual Matters.

Four Corners (2019), *Cash Cows: Australian Universities Making Billions Out of International Students*, ABC News. Available online: https://www.youtube.com/watch?v=Sm6lWJc8KmE (accessed 8 October 2021).

The Guardian [online] (2019), 'My University Accepts Overseas Students Who Are Doomed to Fail'. Available online: https://www.theguardian.com/educat ion/2019/feb/08/my-university-accepts-overseas-students-who-are-doo med-to-fail?CMP=share_btn_tw (accessed 10 June 2019).

Hadley, G. (2015), *English for Academic Purposes in Neoliberal Universities: A Critical Grounded Theory*, Heidelberg: Springer.

Hamp-Lyons, L. (2015), 'The Future of JEAP and EAP', *Journal of English for Academic Purposes*, 20: A1–A4.

Hamp-Lyons, L. (2018), 'Why Researching EAP Practice?', *Journal of English for Academic Purposes*, 31: A3–A4.

Harney, S., and F. Moten (2014), *The Undercommons: Fugitive Planning and Black Study*, New York: Minor Compositions.

Hartig, A. J. (2017), *Disciplinary Language and Disciplinary Knowledge in English for Specific Purposes: Case Studies in Law*, Bristol: Multilingual Matters.

hooks, b. (1994), *Teaching to Transgress: Education as the Practice of Freedom*, New York: Routledge.

Kettle, M. (2017), *International Student Engagement in Higher Education: Transforming Practices, Pedagogies and Participation*, Bristol: Multilingual Matters.

Lea, M. R. (2004), 'Academic Literacies: A Pedagogy for Course Design', *Studies in Higher Education*, 29 (6): 739–56.

Lea, M. R., and B. Street (1998), 'Student Writing in Higher Education: An Academic Literacies Approach', *Studies in Higher Education*, 23(2): 157–72.

MacDonald, J. (2016), 'The Margins as Third Space: EAP Teacher Professionalism in Canadian Universities', *TESL Canada Journal*, 34 (11): 106–16.

Mackay, F. (2021), 'Dilemmas of an Academic Feminist as Manager in the Neoliberal Academy: Negotiating Institutional Authority, Oppositional Knowledge and Change', *Political Studies Review*, 19 (1): 75–95.

Montgomery, C. (2010), *Understanding the International Student Experience*, Basingstoke: Palgrave Macmillan.

Nicholls, K. (2019), 'You Have to Work from Where They Are: Academic Leaders' Talk about Language Development', *Journal of Higher Education Policy and Management*, 42 (1): 67–84.

Ortactepe, D. (2013), ' "This Is Called Free-Falling Theory Not Culture Shock!": A Narrative Inquiry on Second Language Socialization', *Journal of Language, Identity and Education*, 12 (4): 215–29.

Paxton, M. and V. Frith (2015), 'Transformative and Normative? Implications for Academic Literacies Research in Quantitative Disciplines', in T. Lillis, K. Harrington, M. R, Lea and S. Mitchell (eds), *Working with Academic Literacies: Case Studies towards Transformative Practice*, Colorado: WAC Clearinghouse.

Roxå, T., and K. Mårtensson (2009), 'Significant Conversations and Significant Networks – Exploring the Backstage of the Teaching Arena', *Studies in Higher Education*, 34 (5): 547–59.

Roxå, T., and K. Mårtensson (2016), 'Peer Engagement for Teaching and Learning: Competence, Autonomy and Social Solidarity in Academic Microcultures, *Uniped*, 39 (2): 131–43. Available online: www.idunn.no/uniped (10 accessed June 2019).

Smith, H. A., C. Hamshire, R. Forsyth, J. Riddell and P. Taylor (2018), *Guerrilla Leadership and Culture Change in Higher Education: An International Perspective*, ISSOTL conference, 24–7 October, Bergen.

Strom, K. J. (2018), '"That's Not Very Deleuzian": Thoughts on Interrupting the Exclusionary Nature of "High Theory"', *Educational Philosophy and Theory*, 50 (1): 104–13.

Turner, J. (2004), 'Language as Academic Purpose', *Journal of English for Academic Purposes*, 3 (2): 95–109.

Turner, J. (2011), *Language in the Academy: Cultural Reflexivity and Intercultural Dynamics*, Bristol: Multilingual Matters.

Young, M. (1999), 'Knowledge, Learning and the Curriculum of the Future', *British Educational Research Journal*, 25(4): 463–77.

Zepke, N. (2015), 'Student Engagement Research: Thinking beyond the Mainstream', *Higher Education Research and Development*, 34 (6): 1311–23.

Part 3

EAP Programmes: Conceptualization, Organization and Delivery

The Differing Discursive Constructions of EAP within the University: Contrasting Institutional and Language Centre Perspectives

Jennifer J. MacDonald

Introduction

Language and language work are marginalized within higher education (HE) in many Anglophone contexts, including Canada. Language policy is largely invisible in Anglophone Canadian universities, with a large number of de facto and informal policies shaped by reluctant language policy-makers dispersed across the university (MacDonald, 2020). This is against a backdrop of English monolingualism where native speakers of the dominant, local variety of English are considered the default students, students from other linguistic backgrounds are viewed through a deficit lens and the goal of language work is to assimilate and integrate multilingual users of English as an additional language to this monolingual English norm (MacDonald, 2020). As a result, international students who use English as an additional language are often marginalized (Anderson 2015, 2017; Guo and Guo, 2017) or experience a discrepancy between the transformative multicultural experience they were promised they would have studying in Canada, and what they experience on the ground (Stein, 2017; Sterzuk, 2015). Similarly marginalized are the EAP programmes, structures and practitioners who serve multilingual users of EAL from the margins: often non-credit-bearing or adjunct programming, taught by precariously employed practitioners with unclear professional roles and identities (Bond, 2020; Ding and Bruce, 2017; Hadley, 2015).

At the same time, neoliberalism is an increasingly pervasive force in higher education in Anglophone contexts such as Canada. Among the multiple effects of neoliberalism is the fact that the English language is commodified: it is seen as a resource with market or exchange value (Heller, 2010), and therefore, English is 'a terrain where [one's] individual and societal worth are established' (Piller and Cho, 2013: 23). Those who enjoy more of this commodity – a higher level of English language proficiency – are in a position of privilege within Anglophone Canadian HE and have access to more academic and professional opportunities.

Similarly, language work such as pre-sessional or in-sessional EAP support from university English language centres, writing resource centres or English language or writing courses built into the curriculum, seen through the lens of this commodification of English, is seen as 'adding value' to students as their English language ability grows and therefore their worth and access to opportunity increases (Ding and Bruce, 2017; Hadley, 2015). Among other effects in the neoliberal view of HE (such as a curricular emphasis on entrepreneurship and innovation), the university is also seen as training for the labour market, which privileges 'vocational training over the ideals of Western Cultural Humanism' upon which HE was originally built (Hadley, 2015: 6); the objective of HE is no longer to benefit society or individuals' intellectual development, but rather to increase students' value to the economy as skilled workers.

Neoliberalism in Anglophone higher education in Canada leads to contradictions and paradoxical discourses in both formal and de facto language policies and practices. This chapter details part of a larger study in which I applied a discursive approach to the examination of these paradoxical and contradictory discourses around language in Canadian HE under neoliberalism. I carried out a critical discourse study of texts and contexts, drawing on Gee (2005) and Fairclough (2015) and the concept of 'discourse-in-place' (Scollon and Scollon, 2004: 10). In a multiple case study of three Anglophone institutions in Eastern Canada, I examined a variety of policy documents related to language, academic literacy and internationalization at the provincial (macro) and institutional and faculty levels (meso), analysed EAP centre websites and interviewed language, literacy and internationalization stakeholders at the institutions. I mapped 'discourse itineraries' (Scollon, 2008: 234): the taken-for-granted ideas, starting points, constraints and allowances at play around language, language work and EAP in the institutional language policy at these three universities.

I found a discrepancy between how the roles of university English language centres were characterized in institutional policy documents and how those language centres are discursively framed via their websites. Institutional policy framed the English language centres, and by an extension language work at the universities, instrumentally: their primary function being their contribution to marketing and recruitment of international students for the university. In contrast, the English language centres offer a more nuanced portrayal of themselves and their language work via their websites. They are both sites for academic preparation, transformative learning and cultural exchange, while also acknowledging their instrumental role in preparing students for the neoliberal university environment marked by English monolingualism.

Neoliberalism, EAP and Critical Approaches to the Internationalization of Canadian Higher Education

With a focus on applied linguistics, Kubota (2016: 485) defines neoliberalism as an 'ideological and structural apparatus that promotes a free-market economy by privatizing public services, creating a flexible workforce, and increasing individual and institutional accountability for economic success while reducing social services and producing disparities between the rich and the poor'. This economic activity is carried out across borders – globalization – and this neoliberal globalization has led to the internationalization of HE in Canada and elsewhere, with its resultant flows of international students from the Global South to study in more developed nations, such as Canada (Zheng, 2010).

Heller (2010), Piller and Cho (2013), Kubota (2016) and Holborow (2015) (among others) criticize the narrow view of language within neoliberalism, which sees it as an instrument or commodity. This prioritizes just one aspect of the many types of value a language may hold – to individuals, identities, societies and cultures, for example – raising a language's value to the economy over the other forms of value it may carry. Similarly, a hierarchy of language(s) is created by this view of language within neoliberalism, wherein the language(s) with more market value are prioritized in policy and practice, creating tensions in workplaces, schools and even within personal relationships.

Neoliberalism's influence on EAP teaching, practitioner professionalism and identity and pedagogy, as well as on the role of EAP within institutions, is documented by Hadley (2015), Chun (2009, 2013), Rauf (2020), Ding and

Bruce (2017), Riddle (2020) and others. Ding and Bruce (2017: 40) discuss the macro-influences of neoliberalism on EAP: that English language centres must be financially self-sufficient and profit-generating; that they must attract increasing numbers of international students; that centres should operate efficiently (in business terms); and participate in the marketization imposed on universities 'requiring them to compete for students in the belief that this type of competition will somehow raise the quality of university education' (43). These macro-influences constrain the role of EAP institutionally and limit it to an instrumental function, a tool used to achieve something else; in this case, EAP is a tool to obtain revenue and increased international student enrolment numbers for the university.

Another area of influence of neoliberalism is on the language of international higher education. Several recent pieces of research (Chiras and Galante, 2021; Conceição, 2020; Liyanange, 2018; Sterzuk and Shin, 2021) describe the dominance of English and the English monolingual nature of international higher education and internationalization. Ding and Bruce (2017) link this to globalization, the rise of English as the world language and other factors such as colonialism, neoliberal economic policies and direct promotion by state actors such as the British Council.

Many researchers take a critical stance on internationalization in Canada, exploring the areas of diversity, language and power and the paradoxical Discourses that occur against the backdrop of neoliberalism. Language is often 'overlooked, assumed, or not considered at all' (Byrd Clark, Haque and Lamoureux, 2013: 2) in these processes; many policies are de facto, implicit and informal (MacDonald, 2020; Miranda, 2018). Several researchers, including Anderson (2015), Guo and Guo (2017) and Tsushima and Guardado (2015) have recently critically examined internationalization at various institutions in Canada and its interplay with language in terms of educational marketing, internationalization of the curriculum, student support provision and the discrepancy between internationalization policy and student experience. Discursive contradictions are also an issue: the macro and meso-policy backdrop in Canada is one which prioritizes discourses around diversity and multiculturalism and the benefits of internationalization (Larsen, 2015; Stein, 2017; Sterzuk, 2015). However, the settler colonial foundations of the Canadian state (Sterzuk, 2015) and the marginalizing experiences of racialized Canadians and international students (Stein, 2017; Zhang and Beck, 2014) within Canadian universities form a stark contrast with the positive Discourses of diversity that abound in policy documents.

Critical Discursive Studies of Language Policy

Critical discourse studies of language policy provide a very fruitful approach to the critical exploration of phenomena related to neoliberalism, language and EAP and the internationalization of higher education. Foucault defines discourses as social practices – ways of orienting oneself to the world – that include not just words but actions and behaviours (1972). Gee (2005: 7) differentiates between '"Discourse" with a "big D" and "discourse" with a "little d"'. 'Little d' discourse, the non-count form of the word, refers to language-in-use, and to 'semiosis, i.e., all forms of meaning construction in their social context, and of which language is one instance' (O'Regan and Betzel, 2015: 13). In contrast, 'Big D Discourses', the count-noun form of the word, refer to 'perspectival ways of seeing and knowing as they are constituted through semiosis' (13); they are the 'patchwork of thoughts, words, objects, events, actions and interactions' that constitute a 'form of life' or 'way of being in the world' (Gee, 2005: 7). 'Big D' Discourses are therefore enacted via discourse (semiosis) but include much more than semiosis, such as 'ways of acting, interacting, ways of feeling, believing, [or] valuing' (Gee, 2005: 7).

A 'policy as discourse' approach (Ball, 1993, 2015) suggests moving away from a conception of policy merely as 'textual intervention into practice' (Ball 1993: 12) towards a view that sees policy as a 'scripted mixing and matching of cultural codes derived from (and deriving) the schooling context, community, traditions and practices' (Jones, 2013: 10). Therefore, the term 'policy' can be conceptualized as a set of discursive strategies, a 'set of texts, events, artefacts and practices' (Ball, 2015: 308) that play a fundamental role in HE institutional life. Critical discourse studies of language policy which take into account not only policy texts, but policy discourses are less descriptively focused and 'more about examining ... how social inequalities, power relations, and value systems are intertwined in policy making, interpretation, and implementation' (Hult, 2017: 113).

A Multiple Case Study in Anglophone Canadian Higher Education

The findings presented in this chapter are part of a larger critical discourse study of language policy at three public universities in Anglophone universities in Eastern Canada. The study mapped the discourses at play in institutional language policy via critical discourse analysis of a variety of policy documents related to language, academic literacy and internationalization at the provincial (macro) and institutional and faculty (meso) levels as well as of language and internationalization stakeholder interviews.

I drew on Fairclough (2015) and Gee (2005) approaches to discursive analysis of texts and spoken data, and combining them with 'discourse-in-place', from Scollon's mediated discourse analysis (MDA). Scollon and Scollon (2004) conceptualize 'discourse-in-place' with regards to physical places, 'constituted not only by ... built structures, furniture and decorative objects but also by the discourses present in that place' (10). I am extending this idea of 'place' to include the meso-policy space of institutional and faculty-level policy. There are a variety of covert, overt, implicit, explicit, de facto formal and informal policies found in that place: course requirements, teaching units and structures, committees, reports, strategies, testing regimes and so forth. A guiding question for investigation is, therefore, which discourses are internalized as practice: which 'discourses are "invisible" in this action [or policies] because they have become submerged in practice' (Scollon and Scollon, 2004a: 11)? I also mapped 'discourse itineraries' or 'resemiotized displacements' (Scollon, 2008: 234). Similar to intertextuality, whereby discourses are traced across multiple and diverse texts, discourse itineraries simply expand this displacement beyond the text to include a variety of semiotic media, as well as objects, spaces, events, people, actions and so forth. In this study, to find out how different discourses are resemiotized, I mapped how they appeared in different policies – texts, reports, documents, strategies, reports, course requirements and structures.

In this critical discourse study, document and interview data complement each other and allow for triangulation in order to paint a full and detailed picture of the discourses at play at each institution around the issue of the language and their displacements across various semiotic media. A body of texts was gathered from documents and interviews, which included both written and spoken data. The following documents were gathered via the web and were in the public domain or were provided to me by interview participants: provincial or regional HE authorities' policy such as graduate outcomes or quality assurance criteria; institutional internationalization policy or strategy; admissions policies and documents, teaching, learning and assessment policies at the institutional and faculty level; academic calendars and university web pages related to English language and literacy, teaching and learning, and internationalization. Interviews allowed me to access to the discourses of meso-level institutional language stakeholders, whose discourse was analysed discursively and complemented the publicly available data from reports, websites and other documents. Interviews with ten stakeholders in the following roles were carried out: heads of English language teaching centres and writing resource centres, educational developers at centres for teaching and learning, head of the university international office.

Data analysis was not a linear process in this study. Using an abductive approach (Rose, McKinley and Baffoe-Djan, 2020) and supported by NVivo, I applied 'a constant movement back and forth between theory and empirical data' as suggested by Wodak and Meyer (2016: 30). I also moved back and forth between the text and spoken data, as well as considering discourse-in-place in terms of identifying which discourses may have been 'submerged' in non-text-based language policies (Scollon and Scollon, 2004).

Three Case Institutions

The cases identified for this multiple case study were three public English-medium universities in cities in different provinces in Eastern Canada, one a medium-sized institution with a comprehensive variety of programmes including professional programmes, the second a small and teaching-focused university and the third a larger, research-focused institution. The names presented here are pseudonyms and all statistical data on these universities is drawn from the university websites, or relevant provincial or regional higher educational authorities. Statistics are from the time of analysis in 2018.

The first institution, Hillside University, is a comprehensive university with a variety of undergraduate, graduate and professional programmes, including a medical school. The student population of Hillside is approximately 18,000, in a city of 108,860. International students account for 2,961 of the total students, or 16 per cent of the student population. The Hillside English Language Centre (ELC) sits in the Faculty of Arts and Social Sciences, but delivers non-credit-bearing programming focused on a pre-sessional admissions pathway into the university. The second university, Forest, is located in a city with a population of approximately 400,000. A primarily teaching-focused undergraduate institution, it touts itself as 'Canada's most international university', as in October 2018 approximately 28 per cent (1,968) of its 7,030 students were international. Forest's ELC is a standalone unit, which delivers non-credit-bearing programming, which, like Hillside, is also focused on pre-sessional admissions pathway EAP courses. Finally, Lakeview University is a large comprehensive university with a wide variety of undergraduate and graduate degree programmes and professional schools and a student population of 37,970 in a city of approximately 535,154. It is a member of the U15, a group of Canada's top fifteen research-focused institutions. International students make up 7,658 of the total student population, or 20 per cent. Lakeview has two English language teaching units within the same university-affiliated college: one which delivers credit-bearing courses, and the other non-credit-bearing courses including multiple pre-sessional admissions pathways.

Pervasive Discourses of Neoliberalism

As described above, in this globalized economy that university students are being prepared for, language – and specifically the English language – is of high value, as English has become the language of global HE, as well of global business, science and technology and academic research (Holborow, 2015). It is perhaps not surprising, then, that discourses of neoliberalism could be traced throughout the varying policies at the three universities at the centre of this study. The instrumental view of EAP, language and language education was identified in institutional policy as a tool to generate increased international student enrolment numbers. This is the case in the Hillside *Internationalization Plan*, the past two Forest *Academic Plans* and the Lakeview *Internationalization Plan*. However, instrumental discourses were also identified in the ELCs' portrayal of themselves. Some centres emphasized EAP study as a tool to obtain academic success; in other words, the means to an end in an environment where English language proficiency is commodified. This instrumental orientation was at odds with some of the discourses employed in the webpages these English language teaching units use to promote themselves, framing the work of these units in terms of transformative learning. In the following section, I will provide examples of the itineraries of discourses of neoliberalism through the language policy at the three institutions I studied.

Hillside University

The Internationalization Strategy document for Hillside University contains four thematic areas (people, environment, partnerships, strategic initiatives) and six specific recommendations. Of the opportunities and recommendations in this plan, numbers one and six involve teaching, learning and curriculum. Language, academic literacy and linguistic diversity are mentioned in the action point for number 6: 'Review, restructure and improve Hillside's current pre-degree [English as an additional language (EAL)] pathway, in particular, to provide a seamless transition to degree programmes and revenue in support of pan-university international activities.' Similarly, it is noted that 'the [ELC] programmes are generally good revenue generators for universities, and can be harnessed to support a wider range of international activities'. The metaphor of a machine – 'revenue generator' – or work animal – 'can be harnessed' – are examples of an instrumental discourse around EAP: EAP is simply an instrument for increased revenue, recruitment and enrollment.

This is in contrast with the role of the ELC at Hillside, as described on the ELC's own webpage: 'Become a student at Hillside University! We look forward to helping you achieve your language goals and providing you with a rewarding cultural experience.' On the ELC website, the objectives of the centre are educational: providing students with the possibility of learning language or experiencing a new culture. They are also presented with the opportunity for self-transformation in achieving their goals, however, the student themselves might define them. This educational view of language as a resource for achievement and cultural exchange contrasts with the narrow, instrumental view of language in the *Internationalization Plan*.

Forest University

The University's ELC was largely absent from the policy documents I analysed from Forest University. An examination of the policies and practices at Forest shows that the ELC and its activities and expertise do not seem to play much of an in-sessional role for students who have been admitted and are studying on degree programmes. One could imagine a scenario where a centre such as The Language Centre might be framed as an academic resource for the university community; in the case of Forest, it is not. In the 2012–17 and 2008–11 *Academic Plans*, there is only a passing reference to the ELC, and in these references, it is primarily framed as a tool for contribution to recruitment and enrollment:

> Our [ELC] brings hundreds of additional international students on campus each year and serves for many as a stepping-stone into our degree programs. (Academic Plan 2008–11: 8; Academic Plan 2012–17: 16)

This limiting instrumental discourse, which frames language as an instrument to facilitate the recruitment of international students and increase the numbers of these students enrolled at Forest, minimizes the role of language and academic literacy deeply woven into the fabric of the academic endeavour. The choice of the verb 'bring' frames the ELC as a vehicle for students to enter the university.

Describing the ELC as a 'stepping stone' minimizes the Centre as a destination unto itself; it is simply a step on the way to the final destination: university study.

In terms of how the ELC describes itself and its activities on its website, the fact that they are a pathway to admission to Forest is an important part of their mission: 'We offer a variety of programmes and provide all students with the option to embark on a pathway to university' (ELC Website, 'Learn English'). However, they do not limit the description of their programmes to emphasizing them instrumentally as a vehicle or a path to degree studies at the university. They describe themselves instrumentally with regards to the teaching of important skills of the linguistic and academic variety that will help students meet their personal and academic goals, both in Canada and on the global stage. On the ELC webpage, addressing students directly, they urge students to study at the ELC to 'prepare [themselves] for university success' (ELC Website, 'Learn English') or to 'have an opportunity to build confidence before embarking on full-time degree studies' (ELC Website, 'Experience University Life'). They also describe the teaching and learning work done at the ELC in terms of its future academic and economic value on an international scope, evoking the global economic stage that characterizes neoliberalism:

> The [ELC] offers English language training that is recognized and respected by educational institutions and employers around the world. Because our programs are mapped to the Common European Framework of Reference (CEFR) you will be able to communicate your English achievements in terms that are internationally recognized. (ELC Website, 'Learn English')

Forest University takes an instrumental view institutionally of the role of the ELC as a simple tool for recruitment, while also portraying itself as a site for academic work enhancing students' possibilities for academic and professional success.

In the policy at Forest University there are also examples of the monolingual nature of international higher education in the context of neoliberalism. Not only is English discursively framed as an instrument for recruitment, admissions and marketing for Forest, but other languages are as well. Forest has links in Chinese, Arabic, Russian, Spanish and French on its International Welcome page. This is an admissions page with admissions information about requirements and procedures. Of note is the fact that the intended audience of this page is prospective students rather than currently enrolled students who would benefit from information about academics or student services. In only featuring languages other than English on its admissions pages and nowhere else on its institutional website, Forest shows another example of an instrumental view of language. Linguistic diversity and multilingualism are only of value inasmuch as they contribute to marketing, recruitment and admissions.

This instrumental view of languages as an admissions, recruitment and marketing tool is in striking contrast with the 'global citizenship'/'citizen of the world' Discourse prominent for currently enrolled students at the institution that can be traced throughout various policies. In Forest University's policy documents, these two phrases describe a characteristic that is highly valued as an attribute for prospective and current students as well as graduates.

> We want our students to be informed and compassionate *global citizens*, learning from other cultures and historical periods as well as their own localities. (Faculty of Arts Strategic Plan; emphasis added)
>
> Internationalization involves shaping policies and procedures that establish the Faculty of Science as one that supports and attracts international students and prepares its graduates to be *global citizens*. (Faculty of Science Strategic Plan; emphasis added)
>
> The [Faculty of Business], through active learning and the creation and mobilization of scholarship, prepares *citizens of the world* to lead sustainable, entrepreneurial businesses and communities. (Business Strategic Plan; emphasis added)

What is an interesting point of examination here is the role English and other languages play in this definition of 'global citizens'. One might expect languages to play a role in any type of global citizenship initiative; or at least I would, as a language stakeholder in HE. However, with the exception of the Faculty of Arts *Strategic Plan*, in none of the nineteen instances of the phrases related to this concept occurring in various policy documents, is there a concordance with a mention of language (English or other) in the same or adjacent sentences. It seems to be an unspoken assumption that English is the language of this 'global citizenship', and in this way, the linguistic and cultural capital of English is 'invisible' (Liddicoat and Crichton, 2008: 347) or taken for granted. Similarly, discourses of global citizenship might be linked to the promotion of multilingualism or language learning at the university: however, as described above, the university website is all in English aside from the recruitment pages. As well, some but not all degree programmes have a requirement that students learn a 'language other than English' to graduate. It seems, therefore, that 'global citizenship' at Forest University is enacted in English, that intercultural learning and sharing described in the policy document above will happen in English, and the businesses and communities being built by the aspiring global citizens will use English as their dominant language. Therefore, the instrumental discourses on the ELC website framing the role of EAP study as essential for academic success become even more salient in this environment where English plays a dominant role.

Lakeview University

Within some policy documents at Lakeview, their ELC's pathway EAP programmes are framed as tools for recruitment (similar to Hillside and Forest). An instrumental conception of language can be traced through the *Report on Internationalization*, where under the category 'International student recruitment and diversification strategies', one strategy listed is 'Utilize English language pathway programmes or student exchange as pipelines'. The word choice 'pipeline' is striking, as it denotes a conduit or a tool for transmission of a substance from one point to the next. The commodification of international students in this metaphor stands out, as pipelines are often used to transport commodities such as oil and gas. The contents of a pipeline move through it passively. The ELC, and as an extension, the academic activities carried out there – teaching and learning of academic English – are stripped of their value as anything other than a recruitment tool. The academic activities are stripped of their humanity as inherently social endeavours.

The human and the social aspects of the ELC are very much present in the descriptions offered by the ELC at Lakeview. This is in contrast with the commodified pipeline view offered elsewhere. The ELC emphasizes their focus on a 'unique language learning experience', 'excellence' in teaching and learning and cultural immersion:

> Excellence in English language learning
>
> As an [ELC] student, you will receive a unique language learning experience. Your English language classes will engage you in exciting university topics in liberal arts, science, business, and technology. You will meet students from different countries, allowing you to explore and understand new cultures through the use of English. You will also become a part of the student community at the University of Lakeview, one of the world's leading institutions for research, technology, and innovation. (ELC web page)

This description uses verbs and adjectives of engagement: 'engage', 'exciting', 'explore', 'understand' and 'become part of'. This text centres the student in terms of describing what the student will do at the ELC, what they will study and how they will become engaged. The student is active in this description. As well, the transformative learning experience associated with learning language is emphasized. This contrasts strongly with the simple instrumental view of language and the ELC's pathway programmes present in the policy discourse of the *Internationalization Plan*.

However, similar to Forest, there is an assumption that English is the language of intercultural sharing and exchange at Lakeview: 'You will meet students from different countries, allowing you to explore and understand new cultures through the use of English.' There seems to be a monolingual nature to the diverse, multicultural environment at Lakeview University: one where English dominates.

Reconciling Contradictory Discourses

There are several discursive contradictions described at these three institutions, stemming from this simultaneous commodification of English, alongside narrowing of the value of English and language work to its instrumental contribution to marketing, recruitment and academic success in the monolingual university environment. Global citizenship competency development and intercultural encounters are both vaunted while at the same time the linguistic diversity that could characterize these aspects of international education in Canada are flattened into one of monolingualism. This can lead to unmet expectations on behalf of students, and frustration and unmet potential with regards to the roles and activities of English language centres within their institutions.

Canadian universities are often dependent on international students for their tuition fees (Crawley, 2017), but they deny viewing them as cash cows (Brown, 2014). They instead promote Discourses of intercultural exchange and global citizenship arising from the internationalization of Canadian universities (Stein, 2017); they promote the mutual benefits of increased numbers of international students in Canada for both international and domestic students alike. If mutual benefit is what motivates increased international student enrollment, then institutions have a responsibility to provide the political leadership and self-examination to ensure that both international and domestic students can have a positive student experience and obtain the same outcomes. Part of this is the examination of the taken for granted assumptions around EAP, the English language and language work in universities under neoliberalism, be they in Anglophone Canada or elsewhere in the Anglophone world where the effects of neoliberalism on HE and EAP have been observed (Ding and Bruce, 2017).

As Hamp-Lyons (2015) urged, EAP practitioners and leaders should examine the roles they play in maintaining an unproblematized monolingual backdrop to international education, and an instrumental approach to English language and training devoid of the transformative potential of language education. Where possible, EAP practitioners and leaders can work with institutional policymakers and language stakeholders to re-examine and reimagine the linguistic policy environments on our campuses. Intentional critical linguistic and discursive awareness raising around the pervasive discourses of neoliberalism and their effects can take place formally or informally, in the classroom, or through outreach to faculty and staff via continuous professional development training or involvement in institutional committees and policy-making initiatives (MacDonald, 2020). EAP practitioners and leaders are well placed to lead this reimagining of the linguistic policy environment, bringing about improved international student experience and outcomes and contributing to a more comprehensive internationalization.

References

Anderson, T. (2015), 'Seeking Internationalization: The State of Canadian Higher Education', *Canadian Journal of Higher Education*, 45 (4): 166–87.

Anderson, T. (2017), 'The Doctoral Gaze: Foreign PhD Students' Internal and External Academic Discourse Socialization', *Linguistics and Education*, 37 (Supplement C): 1–10. https://doi.org/10.1016/j.linged.2016.12.001.

Ball, S. J. (1993), 'What Is Policy? Texts, Trajectories and Toolboxes', *Discourse: Studies in the Cultural Politics of Education*, 13 (2): 10–17. https://doi.org/10.1080/0159630930130203.

Ball, S. J. (2015), 'What Is Policy? 21 Years Later: Reflections on the Possibilities of Policy Research', *Discourse: Studies in the Cultural Politics of Education*, 36 (3): 306–13. https://doi.org/10.1080/01596306.2015.1015279.

Bond, B. (2020), *Making Language Visible in the University*, Bristol: Multilingual Matters.

Brown, L. (2014), 'International Students or "Cash Cows"?', *The Star*, 11 September. Available online: https://www.thestar.com/yourtoronto/education/2014/09/11/international_students_or_cash_cows.html (accessed 27 February 2022).

Byrd Clark, J., E. Haque, and S. A. Lamoureux (2013), 'The Role of Language in Processes of Internationalization: Considering Linguistic Heterogeneity and Voices from within and Out in Two Diverse Contexts in Ontario', *Canadian and International Education/Éducation Canadienne et Internationale*, 41 (3): Article 5.

Chiras, M., and A. Galante (2021), 'Policy and Pedagogical Reform in Higher Education: Embracing Multilingualism', in K. Raza, C. Coombe and D. Reynolds (eds), *Policy Development in TESOL and Multilingualism: Past, Present and the Way Forward*, 13–24, Singapore: Springer. https://doi.org/10.1007/978-981-16-3603-5_2.

Chun, C. W. (2009), 'Contesting Neoliberal Discourses in EAP: Critical Praxis in an IEP Classroom', *Journal of English for Academic Purposes*, 8 (2): 111–20.

Chun, C. W. (2013), 'The "Neoliberal Citizen": Resemiotising Globalised Identities in EAP Materials', in J. Gray (ed.), *Critical Perspectives on Language Teaching Materials*, 64–87, London: Springer.

Conceição, M. C. (2020), 'Language Policies and Internationalization of Higher Education', *European Journal of Higher Education*, 10 (3): 231–40. https://doi.org/10.1080/21568235.2020.1778500.

Crawley, M. (2017), 'Universities Growing More Reliant on Foreign Student Fees', CBC News, 12 July. Available online: https://www.cbc.ca/news/canada/toronto/international-students-universities-ontario-tuition-1.4199489 (accessed 27 February 2022).

Ding, A., and I. Bruce (2017), *The English for Academic Purposes Practitioner: Operating on the Edge of Academia*, New York: Springer.

Fairclough, N. (2015), *Language and Power*, 3rd edn, Abingdon: Routledge.

Foucault, M. (1972), *The Archaeology of Knowledge*, London: Tavistock Publications.

Gee, J. P. (2005), *An Introduction to Discourse Analysis Theory and Method*, 2nd edn, Abingdon: Routledge.

Guo, Y., and S. Guo (2017), 'Internationalization of Canadian Higher Education: Discrepancies between Policies and International Student Experiences', *Studies in Higher Education*, 42 (5): 851–68.

Hadley, G. (2015), *English for Academic Purposes in Neoliberal Universities: A Critical Grounded Theory*, New York: Springer.

Hamp-Lyons, L. (2015), 'The Future of JEAP and EAP', *Journal of English for Academic Purposes*, 20: A1–A4.

Heller, M. (2010), 'The Commodification of Language', *Annual Review of Anthropology*, 39 (1): 101–14.

Holborow, M. (2015), *Language and Neoliberalism*, Abingdon: Routledge. Available online: https://www.taylorfrancis.com/books/9781317512172 (accessed 27 February 2022).

Hult, F. M. (2017), 'Discursive Approaches to Policy', in S. E. F. Wortham, D. Kim and S. May (eds), *Discourse and Education*, 111–21, New York: Springer.

Jones, T. (2013), *Understanding Education Policy*, New York: Springer.

Kubota, R. (2016), 'The Multi/Plural Turn, Postcolonial Theory, and Neoliberal Multiculturalism: Complicities and Implications for Applied Linguistics', *Applied Linguistics*, 37 (4): 474–94. https://doi.org/10.1093/applin/amu045.

Larsen, M. A. (2015), 'Internationalization in Canadian Higher Education: A Case Study of the Gap between Official Discourses and On-the-Ground Realities', *Canadian Journal of Higher Education*, 45 (4): 101–22.

Liddicoat, A. J., and J. Crichton (2008), 'The Monolingual Framing of International Education in Australia', *Sociolinguistic Studies*, 2 (3): 367–84.

Liyanage, I. (2018), 'Internationalization of Higher Education, Mobility, and Multilingualism', in I. Liyanage (ed.), *Multilingual Education Yearbook 2018: Internationalization, Stakeholders & Multilingual Education Contexts*, 1–20, Cham: Springer. https://doi.org/10.1007/978-3-319-77655-2_1.

MacDonald, J. J. (2020), *Monolingualism, Neoliberalism and Language-as-Problem: Discourse Itineraries in Canadian University Language Policy*, unpublished doctoral thesis, University College London.

Miranda, C. de C. (2018), 'Language Issues in the Internationalizing University: Experiences of Students, Faculty, and Staff', unpublished master's thesis, Simon Fraser University, Vancouver. Available online: http://summit.sfu.ca/item/17969 (accessed 27 February 2022).

O'Regan, J. P., and A. Betzel (2015), 'Critical Discourse Analysis: A Sample Study of Extremism', in *Research Methods in Intercultural Communication*, 281–96. https://doi.org/10.1002/9781119166283.ch19.

Piller, I., and J. Cho (2013), 'Neoliberalism as Language Policy', *Language in Society*, 42 (1): 23–44.

Rauf, M. (2020), 'A Critical Discourse Analysis of Neoliberal Discourses in EAP Textbooks', in *Critical Issues in Teaching English and Language Education*, 179–206. https://doi.org/10.1017/S0047404512000887.

Riddle, S. (2020), 'English for Academic Purposes (EAP) in UK Higher Education: Examining the Impact of EAP's Position within the Academy on Service Delivery, Identity and Quality', *Imagining Better Education Conference Proceedings 2019*, Durham University, 71–85.

Rose, H., J. McKinley and J. B. Baffoe-Djan (2020), *Data Collection Research Methods in Applied Linguistics*, London: Bloomsbury.

Scollon, R., and S. W. Scollon (2004), *Nexus Analysis: Discourse and the Emerging Internet*, Abingdon: Routledge.

Scollon, R. (2008), 'Discourse Itineraries: Nine Processes of Resemiotization', in V. K. Bhatia, J. Flowerdew and R. H. Jones (eds), *Advances in Discourse Studies*, 233–44, Abingdon: Routledge.

Stein, S. (2017), 'National Exceptionalism in the "EduCanada" Brand: Unpacking the Ethics of Internationalization Marketing in Canada', *Discourse: Studies in the Cultural Politics of Education*, 1–17. http://dx.doi.org/10.1080/01596306.2016.1276884.

Sterzuk, A. (2015), 'The Standard Remains the Same: Language Standardisation, Race and Othering in Higher Education', *Journal of Multilingual and Multicultural Development*, 36 (1): 53–66. https://doi.org/10.1080/01434632.2014.892501.

Sterzuk, A., and H. Shin (2021), 'English Monolingualism in Canada: A Critical Analysis of Language Ideologies', in U. Lanvers, A. S. Thompson and M. East (eds), *Language Learning in Anglophone Countries: Challenges, Practices, Ways Forward*, 53–70, New York: Springer. https://doi.org/10.1007/978-3-030-56654-8_4.

Tsushima, R., and M. Guardado (2015), 'English Language "Education" or "Industry"? Bridging Parallel Discourses in Canada', in L. T. Wong and A. Dubey-Jhaveri (eds.), *English Language Education in a Global World: Practices, Issues and Challenges*, 239–50, New York: Nova Science.

Wodak, R., and M. Meyer (eds) (2016), *Methods of Critical Discourse Studies*, 3rd edn, London: Sage.

Zhang, Z., and K. Beck (2014), 'I Came, But I'm Lost: Learning Stories of Three Chinese International Students in Canada', *Canadian and International Education /Éducation Canadienne et Internationale*, 43 (2): Article 6.

Zheng, J. (2010), 'Neoliberal Globalization, Higher Education Policies and International Student Flows: An Exploratory Case Study of Chinese Graduate Student Flows to Canada', *Journal of Alternative Perspectives in the Social Sciences*, 2 (1): 216–44.

8

Perspectives on Directing an EAP Centre

Richard Simpson

Introduction

This chapter will consider management issues in English for Academic Purposes (EAP) from the perspective of a large English language teaching unit situated within a research-intensive (Russell Group) UK university. The portrait of the field which is presented here is based on over twenty-five years' experience managing programmes and services, with more than half of that time as director of the centre. I also draw on the experience of former and cognate institutions, insights gained from conferences, workshops, professional networks, blogs and professional publications.

One of the professional networks is a very informal group of directors of university EAP centres. The group met for the first time a matter of weeks before the UK went into lockdown due to the Covid-19 pandemic. The network members have continued to share experiences by email and some broad reference to themes we have discussed will be made, without revealing identities or compromising any confidentiality.

It should be noted that this chapter also draws on analysis of the sector included in my doctoral thesis, of which work is close to completion (Simpson, forthcoming). Within that work, I juxtapose the positions of two authors who, by coincidence, are contributors to this volume. Their positions are germane to the topic discussed here and will be examined briefly.

Murray (2016) comments on the increase in numbers of international students thus: '[It is] an undeniable fact (no doubt unpalatable to many) that international students, and the considerable fees they bring with them, are today something of a "cash-cow" for universities – and indeed for the local economies ... in which they operate' (14).

Drawing on analysis of government policy on international students, Lomer (2016) identifies different motivations for the recruitment of those students into UK higher education (HE). She describes a variety of ways in which international students are represented discursively in policy, positively and negatively, and highlights how international students are 'othered'. Her thesis concludes with a stipulation of obligation: 'It is the ethical responsibility for those of us who participate in international higher education to critically examine how ... policy represents students, and if necessary, to resist and disrupt it' (14).

These two positions are some considerable distance apart in their representation of the students we EAP practitioners teach. It is not an uncommon experience for EAP professionals to find themselves in between opposing or incompatible positions. Both works express a concern that students are treated responsibly by the institutions that recruit them; EAP providers are intimately involved in that treatment and the responsibility is borne in part by EAP managers.

There are three key areas of EAP work which will be considered in the chapter:

Pre-sessional provision – the potential conflict between institutional demands for quantity and quality of students is a key focus.
Pathway provision – the author's own institution has an unusual relationship with the private pathway provider; a range of 'business' models will be compared and evaluated.
In-sessional provision – the locus of the EAP unit, the funding model and the degree of integration of EAP into academic programmes will be examined.

In particular, the challenges of managing these areas of work in the context of marketization and massification will be considered, as will a look ahead to a post-Covid environment.

Pre-sessional Provision

Pre-sessional provision is mostly offered to students who have not met the English language proficiency standard required for entry to their prospective degree programme. The cost of these courses is such that the number of students taking a course without actually needing to meet such a requirement is relatively small, though many institutions do offer shorter pre-sessionals for students who already have unconditional offers.

The English language proficiency standards required for entry to degree programmes are described by almost all UK higher education institutions (HEI) in terms of the International English Language Testing System (IELTS) (Hyatt, 2013; IELTS, 2013) With significant growth in the number of overseas students coming to UK universities (Hyland, 2018; Sweeney, 2012), the industry supporting IELTS preparation has grown considerably (Hamid, 2016). Consequently, many students and some teachers have come to equate the (academic) IELTS with Academic English and, by association, with EAP. Furthermore, staff with admission tutor roles within academic departments have become somewhat familiar with IELTS scores; some imagine these scores to be a hard measure of ability rather than the rather less reliable approximation that many who work more closely with the test takers believe them to be (Hyatt, 2013).

Pre-sessional candidates generally need to successfully complete their course in order to secure progression to their degree studies. In some UK HEI this is via an external examination such as IELTS; in many there is an internal examination which approximates the IELTS proficiency level required; in others there is an assessment of activities modelled on academic assignments. With much resting on the outcome of the pre-sessional these assessments are often described as *high-stakes* (Hyatt, 2013; Hyland, 2009). In these circumstances the pre-sessional provider might assume the role of *gatekeeper*, with responsibility for deciding which candidates can proceed and which must defer.

The gatekeeper role is a heavy responsibility and the quality of the assessment used must be high. The implications for students who do not successfully complete their pre-sessional can be extreme. For example, students who have undertaken a pre-sessional course with funding from a sponsor such as their home country's government often report that they will be obliged to repay their sponsor if they fail to proceed. Staff who have to deal with making and communicating high stakes decisions are vulnerable to pressure from students, from sponsors and even from their peers – the tutors who have taught the candidate. EAP managers need to protect such staff from possible pressure to be lenient with students who may have failed, for example, by operating a process akin to an academic exam board.

An alternative to the high stakes proficiency test is an assessment for learning approach, which requires students to demonstrate that they have achieved the course learning outcomes by completing assignments and tasks during the programme.

Our local context is such that we offer full-time pre-sessional courses to prospective university entrants for very large numbers of overseas students (in summer 2019, n > 2,500). Although substantial, the permanent teaching staff is not large enough to provide for this number of students, and a major recruitment of temporary teachers is necessary. The same is true at very many other UK HEI; even if they do not all operate such large programmes, most recruit additional teachers for their pre-sessional programmes. As a result, the recruitment exercise is often competitive, with teachers looking around for the best packages and institutions offering incentives such as free temporary accommodation. This is an example of the commercialized and marketized context in which EAP units within UK HEI are operating.

Many of the temporary teachers we recruit for our pre-sessionals come to the UK for the summer and return to their substantive posts afterwards. The changes in immigration rules following Brexit have added a level of complexity for those teachers and have added to the precarity many of them experience (Ding and Bruce, 2017).

The marketized context includes the necessity to strike a balance between meeting the demand for places from students (to assist the institution's recruitment/income targets) and maintaining the quality standards demanded by the home institution and by any external validating bodies. Murray (2016) has expressed concern that language proficiency levels have been falling as international student numbers have grown. He suggests that degree programmes may suffer from 'dumbing down' as a result (29). EAP providers within institutions are caught between those who want (or need) to maximize international student recruitment and those who argue that standards are being compromised.

A complicating factor is the student visa regulatory framework, the Points Based System (PBS), which imposes a high degree of regulation. The language of the policy documents which set out guidance for institutions is explicitly threatening: 'UKVI compliance officers are trained to refer cases for civil penalties or prosecutions if they find evidence of wrongdoing or criminal activity … The compliance officer will consider information about abuse of the sponsorship arrangements and investigate and, if appropriate, inform the police and/or any relevant authority' (Home Office, 2019: 58). (This wording has been unchanged since the policy was first published in 2013.)

The regulation imposed on universities is part of the wider 'hostile environment' (National Audit Office, 2012) which was introduced as part of the attempt to attain the (former prime minister) David Cameron's policy pledge to reduce net migration to 'tens of thousands' (Conservative Party, 2009). The regulation effectively imposed on HEI a role in the policing of the immigration system.

Being the institution's first point of contact for many international students, EAP providers have been obliged to negotiate and comply with the frequently changing PBS regulations. Aspects of those regulations have a direct impact on admissions to universities and to preparatory EAP programmes, particularly regarding language qualifications. A brief summary of this context will illustrate some of the challenges for EAP management.

When the PBS was first introduced, no specific language standards were required. Following concerns that the visa system was being misused, restrictions were imposed. The level required for degree study was set at Common European Framework of Reference (CEFR) level B2 in all components (listening, reading, speaking and writing).

A range of commercially available language tests was sanctioned as acceptable indicators of the requisite CEFR level. The UKBA's Approved English Language Tests (UK Borders Agency, 2013) detailed the tests which could be used for different levels of various tiers and specified the minimum scores required for each skill component. Among the largest and best known of these were the IELTS, the Test of English as a Foreign Language (TOEFL) and the suite of examinations offered by Cambridge University Exams Syndicate.

Although the UKBA's approved list specified the acceptable tests, levels and component scores for a visa application, it was the test providers, not the UKBA, who 'mapped' their tests to the different levels of the CEFR. This process caused some considerable confusion and consternation at the time.

The IELTS level which was declared (by IELTS) as equivalent to CEFR B2 was IELTS 5.5 in each component. This is notable because for several years IELTS had published (and still publishes) advice to institutions recommending IELTS 6.5 for 'linguistically less demanding' academic courses and IELTS 7.0 for degree-level study (IELTS, 2013: 15). The same document states that IELTS 5.5 is 'probably acceptable … [for] linguistically less demanding training courses'.

There is an apparent misalignment between the IELTS score recommended for degree-level study and the IELTS score required to obtain a student visa to study for a degree. However, in a recent survey of institutions' entry requirements (Simpson, forthcoming), I found just two out of a sample of twenty-five institutions set their language entry requirement at IELTS 5.5. The same research found that most institutions' pre-sessional provision is broadly similar in terms of the length and level of the programmes, as summarized in Table 8.1.

A feature of the PBS which can be a source of frustration for EAP providers is the requirement for pre-sessional students to demonstrate their CEFR B2 level by taking a Secure English Language Test (SELT). It is not uncommon

Table 8.1 Pre-sessional Programme Durations

Pre-sessional programme durations (sample n=15)		
Course duration	IELTS deficit allowed	Number of institutions
5 or 6 weeks	½ a band	13
10 weeks	1 band	1
10 or 11 weeks	1 band	9
No programme	n/a	1

Source: Simpson (forthcoming), 'Academic Language & Literacy: Who Says What Goes?', EdD thesis, University of Sheffield.

for candidates to take their test multiple times and to achieve varying scores within a short time span. This experience may add to the attractiveness of a pre-sessional course which means another test is not needed.

Many institutions responded to the lockdown enforced by the Covid-19 pandemic by switching to online provision, for pre-sessional courses and subsequently for the degrees themselves. The fact that prospective pre-sessional students did not now need a visa raised a new dilemma for EAP managers: which language assessments to accept for pre-sessional entry. Discussion between the peer network of directors was not so much about the merits of individual tests but rather was centred on how much influence the director had in their institution's decision-making process.

In many cases the decision was taken at a higher – or different – level; in a number of these the centre director was overruled. Rather than the subject matter specialists, those responsible for delivering a programme of the requisite quality, having the power to decide which entry tests they could endorse, it was the sales and marketing executives, driven by 'market forces' and 'competitor intelligence', that had the final say. In responding to Covid-19, HEI were, unsurprisingly, concerned with protecting their very viability. Nonetheless, the experience of centre directors being overruled by market forces is not limited to extreme circumstances.

Strategies which might help the EAP sector to assert more influence include lobbying within institutions, participation in membership organizations such as BALEAP and English UK, informal peer networking and publications such as this one! These can all contribute to the professional standing of our field.

This section has given a sketch of some of the management issues and challenges associated with pre-sessional provision. The next section will consider a different route into degree programmes, which is also available to international students.

Pathway Provision

The explanatory notes published together with the Higher Education and Research Act 2017 (HERA) (United Kingdom, 2017a) make clear the government's desire to increase competition within the HE sector and to encourage 'new providers': 'Other providers offering accredited higher education courses can apply to join the register on a voluntary basis in return for compliance with the student complaints scheme of the Office of the Independent Adjudicator for Higher Education (OIA) but will not receive access to Office for Students (OfS) funding and/or student support' (United Kingdom, 2017b: p. 9).

Matthews (2014) gives an overview of the growth of for-profit pathway providers operating in the UK HE sector. He points to the growth in international student numbers from 2005 onwards and the related growth in the number of UK HEI entering pathway partnerships. The term *International Pathway College* (IPC) (Smith, 2014) is used to describe an institution established as a collaboration between a HEI and a private sector pathway provider. Smith states that between 2005 and 2014 the number of UK IPCs grew from three to more than forty (2014: 9).

According to a briefing document published by CIL Management Consultants, five providers account for more than 50 per cent of the pathway sector in the UK (CIL Management Consultants, 2018: 8). The five providers, Cambridge Education Group, INTO, Kaplan International, Navitas and Study Group, currently have sixty-two IPCs between them. The briefing paper suggests there is still space in the market for expansion.

The programmes offered by pathway providers include preparatory courses (pre-undergraduate and pre-masters courses) and International Year 1 courses. The key difference between the pathway preparatory courses and EAP pre-sessional courses is that the former address an 'academic gap' as well as any 'language gap' (Smith, 2014). International Year 1 courses cover the syllabus of the first year of a degree programme at the same time as raising the students' English to the entry level, preparing them for progression to Year 2 of the HEI's degree programme.

At undergraduate level, the academic gap may be due to the fact that the education system in the prospective student's home country is perceived as not achieving the same educational level as the UK system. China, the country of origin of the majority of UK pathway students, generally has twelve years of compulsory schooling, compared with thirteen years in the UK. Pathway providers claim that they address this gap: 'In essence, there continues to be a substantial mismatch in the schooling that is provided by the education systems of the c140 countries that we recruit students from, and the entry requirements to top universities in the UK – Managing Director UK & Europe, Study Group' (CIL Management Consultants, 2018: 4).

At postgraduate level, the academic gap is not as easily explained. The academic entry requirement for a master's degree in UK HE is usually completion of an undergraduate degree. Many international university graduates qualify for entry to postgraduate courses without the need for a preparatory programme. The gap which the IPC course seeks to bridge may be due to a shortfall in a candidate's degree classification or grade point average (GPA). In addition, some HEI take into consideration the institution which awarded the undergraduate degree. Some institutions refer to classifications such as the Chinese government's university development schemes: Double First Class University Project, Project 985 or Project 211 (Wu, 2020).

Several different collaboration models can be found within the sector. Some universities have an IPC and an in-house EAP provider which operate entirely separately. Others outsource their EAP provision to the pathway provider and retain very limited or no in-house provision. In some larger cities, there are IPCs which feed students to more than one university. Whatever model is in place, the students undertaking a pathway programme are very likely to undertake some EAP classes or modules. Their teachers are very much part of the UK EAP community.

In my own institution we have an unusual relationship with our pathway provider. The pathway provider is responsible for the academic teaching while my department, the university's English Language Teaching Centre (ELTC) teaches the language modules. Furthermore, students needing a course of English before studying at the IPC attend this at ELTC. This symbiotic relationship has worked well for over a decade and has survived a change in provider at the IPC.

Matthews (2014) raises the question as to whether the pressure to perform financially is compatible with the responsibility for progressing students to university. As well as receiving income from teaching the pathway students, the providers may receive a percentage of the fees their recruits pay to the university for their degree programmes. The pathway providers have very large marketing power in many of the countries from which students come to study in UK HEI. Their reach is far greater than an individual university could afford on their own. The pathway providers have very large networks of agents in many of the countries they operate in and those agents receive commission for recruiting students (Hulme et al., 2014).

According to the business-to-business company International Consultants for Education and Fairs [ICEF], the benchmark for commission paid by universities to recruitment agencies is 10 per cent of a student's first year fees; commission on shorter courses, such as pre-sessionals, varies between 15 per cent and 25 per cent of fees (ICEF, 2019: 8). The rates that pathway providers pay to their agents is not easily accessible in the public domain. However, personal communications from associates working in two of the larger UK pathway providers suggest rates of 15 per cent are common in the sector, supplemented by bonuses for achieving volume targets and a range of other incentives. Despite their collaboration in lobbying for the sector, the pathway providers are in direct commercial competition and consequently they seek to match each other in their offerings to students and incentives to agents.

Incentives mentioned by one of the associates in the field (anonymity necessary) include lavish hospitality and the gift of equipment such as laptops, iPads and mobile telephones to 'assist agents in productivity'. In making this confidential disclosure the informant was clear that if some of these practices took place within the UK they would be illegal under the Bribery Act 2010 (United Kingdom, 2010).

Discussions with peers in the sector have brought to light other practices which are of concern and where financial imperatives appear to have taken precedence. These must also remain anonymous.

A Japanese MSc candidate who had already completed a master's course at a prestigious Japanese university, had an offer for an MSc conditional only on English and had an IELTS score just half a band below the standard required by the local department. Had this candidate applied directly they would have been offered a six or ten-week pre-sessional course as described above. The pathway provider's agent sold them a one-year pre-masters course, at a cost of £14,000, despite there being no academic gap and a minimal language gap.

Other issues relate to language standards at the point of transition from IPC to HEI. Two cases focused on inappropriate and inconsistent 'scaling' of language test scores. One example related to uplifting scores to achieve a better pass rate; this scaling took place after the exam board had sat; the second example concerned a failure to scale down excessively high examination scores, awarding a whole cohort an 'IELTS equivalent score' in one component which was up to three bands higher than the average scores on the exam. In both cases, the suggestion was made that commercial interests took precedence over standard exam practice.

The previous section closed with concerns regarding the influence of sales and marketing colleagues within universities; this section concludes with similar discomfort regarding IPCs. Although the number of negative stories is low, the peer group which highlighted them is small. As the pathway providers register with the OfS, they will be subject to greater regulation and scrutiny.

The following section will focus on EAP provision for students who have successfully negotiated the various hurdles and have joined a degree programme.

In-sessional Provision

Most UK HEI offer some level of continuing academic language and literacy development for students after they begin their degree studies. Within our own institution there has been a move away from the more generic English for General Academic Purposes (EGAP) provision towards a greater level of English for Specific Academic Purposes (ESAP) (Blue, 2012; Hyland and Shaw, 2016).

Wingate (2015) presents an extensive *Case for Inclusive Practice* which challenges common denunciations of (falling) standards in HE. The 'discourse of deficiency and remediation' is frequently reduced to a focus on structural issues of grammar and vocabulary (2015: 1) rather than an understanding that the expansion of student numbers and the diversity of the student population mean there is an increased need for support for students. Many similar arguments have been proposed (Feak, 2016; Hyland, 2015; Pennycook, 1999) particularly noting that the deficit models tend to focus mostly or entirely on certain subgroups, usually non-native speakers of English.

The survey of provision in Wingate's (2015) study is based on thirty-one UK HEI. She presents a useful table showing a variety of types of academic literacy provision, organized to show increasing degrees of discipline specificity (60), the weakest being 'extra-curricular', followed by 'additional', 'curriculum-linked' and with 'curriculum-integrated' as the strongest.

Extra-curricular provision is characterized as remedial teaching of general or pseudo-academic materials focused on grammar/lexis by EAP teachers situated outside of the students' department, with which there is no collaboration (60),table 4.1, column 1). At the other extreme curriculum-integrated provision is timetabled, fully inclusive, credit-bearing teaching of subject-specific literacy conventions, genres and language provided with collaboration between EAP and subject specialists (60, table 4.1, column 4). There is no doubt that Wingate is proposing the latter as the preferable model.

At a BALEAP professional issues meeting (PIM) at the London School of Economics (LSE) in 2016, Wingate gave the plenary speech on 'Embedding academic literacy instruction in the curriculum: The role of EAP specialists' (2016). The presentation covered the key arguments from Wingate's (2015) book and included the table of types of academic literacy provision. Feedback from the audience suggested that within that professional grouping there was already a significant move towards the integrated approach.

Wingate is careful to note (46) that her searches may not have returned a complete picture of the provision available within the institutions sampled. Indeed, in my department's provision of embedded EAP the content description would not be easily accessible to browsers from outside the departments involved, and even less so for an external visitor. This might go some way to explaining why Wingate's survey found twenty-eight out of thirty-one HEI offering generic content while the BALEAP audience indicated considerably more discipline-specific provision.

The pragmatic reality of in-sessional EAP provision within a large university setting is that most or all of the range Wingate describes can be present within one institution. Some programmes are structured around relatively limited contact hours for students which makes timetabling of curriculum-integrated provision easy to achieve; other programmes have such full schedules that finding a timeslot for such provision is almost impossible. The collaboration required to achieve the ideal is considerable and many academic colleagues are pulled in so many directions that they may not be able to dedicate the time required. Departmental and faculty recognition of the value of such provision is needed to ensure the necessary staff resources are made available. While we have increased the proportion of curriculum-linked and curriculum-integrated provision to include most departments, we continue to offer more generic workshops for students who do not have access to the specialized provision.

Wingate's (2015) typology, framed around level of integration, includes an examination of the location of the provision. In a plenary for an earlier BALEAP PIM, David Hyatt (2015) focused on the location of the hosting department, geographically and within the institutional structure, arguing that both were evidence of the marginalization of EAP. In the following BALEAP PIM at the LSE, I offered something of a rejoinder to Hyatt's perceptions of our marginalization (Simpson, 2016: 117–18).

The thrust of my argument at the event was that EAP units which are not located within any one department or faculty may have better control of the resources available for the provision of EAP across their institution. In this respect they may, in fact, be less marginalized than those units which are within departments but are seen as inferior to their academic colleagues.

Ding and Bruce (2017) present a thorough overview of the EAP profession with a particular perspective on practitioners who, their subtitle suggests, are *Operating on the Edge of Academia*. An early consideration is whether EAP within universities is a support service, similar to housing or counselling, or an academic field in its own right. The position they take is 'that EAP is a research-informed *academic field of study*' (2017: 4; orginal emphasis). They also highlight the position of EAP within the marketized and massified UK HE context and the way in which this can affect the EAP practitioner: 'Where institutions take a "support service" view of EAP, practitioners are largely positioned as general or support staff within the university, … but not essentially belonging to the knowledge-building, knowledge-communicating body of academic staff of the university' (Ding and Bruce, 2017: 199).

Although I have a degree of sympathy with this view, it does appear to be somewhat overgeneralized. As mentioned above, a variety of modes of delivery and collaboration may be found within a single institution. It seems highly unlikely that the number of teaching staff required to deliver effective EAP provision of the model preferred by Wingate above could be realized with the professional model Ding and Bruce appear to champion.

Within my department there are currently 120 EAP tutors, all of whom are on open-ended contracts. Approximately one third of our work is in-sessional provision, one third is teaching at the IPC and the other third is on longer term pre-sessionals, visiting student programmes, teacher training programmes, community work and developmental work. There is no doubt that EAP is a valid field of academic study, but it is doubtful that 120 academic posts would ever be dedicated to that field.

A major challenge for EAP managers is to resist marginalization and to facilitate inclusion of EAP practitioners within the academy. In seeking to do so, we aim to achieve the professional relationship which Bond argues for: 'language should be embedded within the taught curriculum through collaborative working practices between students, EAP and disciplinary teachers' (Bond, 2020: 176).

Post-Covid EAP

During the Covid-19 pandemic most HEI switched their EAP provision online. At the outset it was hoped that the students we prepared for entry to university in autumn 2020 would be able to travel and take up their places. In practice, most of them studied the whole year online; a second summer of online pre-sessionals followed. EAP managers are now faced with the dilemma of how the future provision should be configured: in-person, online, blended and hybrid are the new possibilities we will need to balance.

A longer-term challenge from the pandemic is also likely to have a significant impact on EAP centres. Some institutions have had a rude awakening with regards to their reliance on overseas student fee income. That reliance came about in part due to the demographic dip in the number of 'home' students. With uncertainty over when and whether students will want to and be able to resume travelling to study, institutions are seeking to mitigate their risk. With the population of eighteen-year olds now rising, demand for university places is projected to increase and exceed the peak that was seen in 2009 (Bekhradnia and Bailey, 2018). There is a clear opportunity for institutions to reconsider the balance between home and international students, but this is a potential threat to EAP providers, particularly if they are reliant on income generation.

Conclusion

This brief sketch of the field has sought to offer a grounded view from the practical perspective of the local management. In many institutions the position of the teaching staff is very precarious. Hourly paid work, zero hours contracts and fixed term contracts are commonplace; the immediate future is fraught with uncertainty and the level of precarity across the sector seems likely to increase. It is very possible that the size of the HE EAP sector will decrease over the coming five years. It is also likely that the private providers will continue to seek a greater share of the market.

While the challenges of managing EAP show no sign of easing, there are strategies we can adopt to address them. Most HEI publicly commit to making a civic and/or regional contribution to their communities; EAP providers can help by offering language courses for refugees and asylum seekers and by training community volunteers. In addition, we can diversify our portfolio to include a range of delivery modes, building on some of the lessons learned during Covid-19. If we can win the argument for collaboration proposed by Bond (above) this will help consolidate our position and reduce precarity for EAP teachers.

References

Bekhradnia, B., and N. Bailey (2018). 'Demand for Higher Education to 2030', Higher Education Policy Institute. Available online: https://www.hepi.ac.uk/wp-content/uploads/2018/03/HEPI-Demand-for-Higher-Education-to-2030-Report-105-FINAL.pdf (accessed 3 October 2021).

Blue, G. (2012). 'The Specificity of English for Academic Purposes: EGAP/ESAP Revisited'. Available online: http://www.baleap.org.uk/baleap/conference-events/pims/pim-reports/baleap-pimiatefl-esp-sig-meeting/baleap-pimiatefl-esp-sig/george-blue-report (accessed 18 May 2014).

Bond, B. (2020). *Making Language Visible in the University: English for Academic Purposes and Internationalisation*, Bristol: Multilingual Matters.

CIL Management Consultants (2018), 'Opportunities in the Market for University Pathway Programmes'. Available online: https://cilconsultants.com/insight/international-education-opportunities-in-the-market-for-university-pathway-programmes (accessed 27 August 2020).

Conservative Party (2009), 'David Cameron's Contract with You'. Available online: http://conservativehome.blogs.com/files/ge_4pg-newspaper.pdf (accessed 20 December 2014).

Ding, A., and I. Bruce (2017), *The English for Academic Purposes Practitioner: Operating on the Edge of Academia*, Cham, Switzerland: Palgrave Macmillan.

Feak, C. B. (2016), 'EAP Support for Post-Graduate Students', in K. Hyland and P. Shaw (eds), *The Routledge Handbook of English for Academic Purposes*, 489–501, Abingdon: Routledge. http://doi.org/10.4324/9781315657455.

Hamid, M. O. (2016), 'Policies of Global English Tests: Test-takers' Perspectives on the IELTS Retake Policy', *Discourse: Studies in the Cultural Politics of Education*, 37 (3), 472–87. http://doi.org/10.1080/01596306.2015.1061978.

Home Office (2019), 'Document 1: Applying for a Tier 4 Licence Version 01/2019'. https://www.gov.uk/government/publications/student-sponsor-guidance (accessed 6 September 2019).

Hulme, M., A. Thomson, R. Hulme and G. Doughty (2014), 'Trading Places: The Role of Agents in International Student Recruitment from Africa', *Journal of Further and Higher Education*, 38 (5): 674–89. http://doi.org/10.1080/0309877X.2013.778965.

Hyatt, D. (2013), 'Stakeholders' Perceptions of IELTS as an Entry Requirement for Higher Education in the UK', *Journal of Further and Higher Education*, 37 (6): 844–63. http://doi.org/10.1080/0309877X.2012.684043.

Hyatt, D. (2015), 'Reconceptualising EAP as Academic Repertoire'. Available online: https://www.youtube.com/watch?v=HZLfgu9ySzg&t=1s (accessed 2 March 2022).

Hyland, K. (2009), *Academic Discourse*, London: Continuum.

Hyland, K. (2015), 'Prof Ken Hyland at the BALEAP 2015 Conference – Closing Plenary'. Available online: https://www.youtube.com/watch?t=2821&v=n-7dJ0VT SnM (accessed 5 August 2015).

Hyland, K. (2018), 'Sympathy for the Devil? A Defence of EAP', *Language Teaching*, 51 (3): 383–99. http://doi.org/10.1017/S0261444818000101.

Hyland, K., and P. Shaw (eds) (2016), *The Routledge Handbook of English for Academic Purposes*, London: Routledge.

ICEF (2019).,'Working with Agents'. Available online: http://marketing.icef.com/acton/attachment/18128/f-9a3bcc41-94f2-4836-9101-ae570699ac64/1/-/-/-/-/EN - 2019 Working with Agents Brochure.pdf (accessed 27 August 2020).

IELTS (2013), 'Guide for Educational Institutions, Governments, Professional Bodies and Commercial Organisations'. Available online: https://www.ielts.org/PDF/Guide_Edu- Inst_Gov_2013.pdf (accessed 18 April 2014).

Lomer, S. (2016), 'International Students in UK Policy from 1999 to 2013: Rationales for Recruitment and Representations of Students', EdD thesis, University of Sheffield.

Matthews, D. (2014), 'Pathways to Profit'. Available online: https://www.timeshighereducation.com/features/pathways-to-profit/2012075.article (accessed 25 March 2019).

Murray, N. (2016), *Standards of English in Higher Education: Issues, Challenges and Strategies*, Cambridge: Cambridge University Press.

National Audit Office (2012), *Immigration: The Points Based System – Student Route*, London: TSO.

Pennycook, A. (1999), 'Introduction: Critical Approaches to TESOL', *TESOL Quarterly*, 33 (3): 329–48.

Simpson, R. (2016), 'Funding In-sessional', in S. Brewer, A. Standring and G. Stansfield (eds), *Papers from the Professional Issues Meeting (PIM) on In-sessional English for Academic Purposes held at London School of Economics*, 19 March 2016, Renfrew: BALEAP. Available online: https://www.baleap.org/wp-content/uploads/2019/10/Baleap_Book_Interactive.pdf (accessed 25 February 2019).

Simpson, R. (forthcoming), 'Academic Language & Literacy: Who Says What Goes?', EdD thesis, University of Sheffield.

Smith, K. (2014), 'What Kind of Space Does Sheffield International College Provide for Its Students and Principal Stakeholders?', EdD thesis, University of Hull. Available online: https://ethos.bl.uk/OrderDetails.do?uin=uk.bl.ethos.676685 (accessed 26 August 2020).

Sweeney, S. (2012), 'Going Mobile: Internationalisation, Mobility and the European Higher Education Area'. Available onlne: https://www.heacademy.ac.uk/knowledge-hub/going-mobile-internationalisation-mobility-and-european-higher-education-area-0 (accessed 3 March 2019).

UK Borders Agency (2013), 'List of Approved English Language Tests'. Available online: https://webarchive.nationalarchives.gov.uk/ukgwa/20130103133413/http://www.ukba.homeoffice.gov.uk/sitecontent/applicationforms/new-approved-english-tests.pdf (accessed 17 March 2019).

United Kingdom (2010), *Bribery Act 2010*, c 23, London: HMSO.

United Kingdom (2017a), *Higher Education and Research Act 2017*, c 29, London: HMSO.

United Kingdom (2017b), *Higher Education and Research Act 2017 Explanatory Notes*, London: HMSO.

Wingate, U. (2015), *Academic Literacy and Student Diversity*, Bristol: Multilingual Matters.

Wingate, U. (2016), 'Embedding Academic Literacy Instruction in the Curriculum: The Role of EAP Specialists'. Available online: https://www.baleap.org/event/insessional-eap (accessed 9 February 2019).

Wu, Z. (2020), 'A Renewed Double-First Class Initiative Will Help Chinese Universities Better Engage with Global Challenges', *Times Higher Education*, 5 May. Available online: https://www.timeshighereducation.com/opinion/renewed-double-first-class-initiative-will-help-chinese-universities-better-engage-global (accessed 27 August 2020).

9

The Predicament of PEAPPs: Practitioners of EAP in Precarity

Michèle le Roux

Overview

The spread of the canker of precarious employment through the body of Higher Education (HE) has been documented in many countries around the world (Courtois and O'Keefe, 2015; De Angelis and Grüning, 2020; Horgan, 2021; UCU, 2020; Walsh, 2019). Precarity has become a focus of academic debate in the UK, not just within economics or politics departments, but also in fields such as history (Careering, 2017), philosophy (Precarity and Precariousness, 2019) and education (Precarious Work, 2019; Sarrico, 2021). The scandal of precarity in English for Academic Purposes (EAP), specifically, was addressed at the Practitioner Precarity (2020) event hosted by the Centre for English Language Teaching (CELT) at the University of Leeds. Attention has also been given to the intersectional nature of disadvantaging in precarity, which manifests in racialized and gendered inequalities (Kınıoğlu and Can, 2021; Murgia and Poggio, 2019; Navarro, 2017; Turner, 2002). Within EAP, 'nativespeakerism' adds a further dimension to this perfect storm of marginalization, as does the position of the entire field of EAP on the borders of academia. The gendering of work around student writing as care-work or domestic, reproductive labour (Blythman and Orr, 2006; Tuck, 2018) also serves to situate practitioners of EAP in precarity (PEAPPs) at the bottom of the academic pyramid.

It is notable that much of the discourse around precarity is embodied in forums and symposia, reading and discussion groups, videos, blog posts and email contributions to JiscMail lists: knowledge artefacts that are less valued by academia and do not contribute to Research Excellence Framework (REF) rankings. These artefacts are ephemeral and leave little trace: they are graffiti on the edifice of the neoliberal academy. Contributors to the discussion often choose to remain anonymous (*The Guardian*'s Academics Anonymous series; Honi Soit, 2021; Delivery or Deliveroo, 2021), presumably through fear of reprisals from employers. The lack of a safe space for PEAPPs to share their experience emerged as a key theme in the Leeds Practitioner Precarity event (2020). When I have contributed to the Global Forum for EAP Professionals (BALEAP) JiscMail forum on areas of concern for PEAPPs (the use of 'us' and 'them' language; contract-breaking by management during the Covid-19 pandemic; gaslighting/blaming PEAPPs for accepting atrocious employment terms and conditions), I have received numerous responses off-list from PEAPPs; typically, only managers and those in secure employment respond publicly. The voicing of the experience of the Precariat and of PEAPPs in particular, albeit muffled and marginalized, is the cry of the dispossessed for justice.

My own experience of the trauma of precarity informs the writing of this chapter, and my focus is both on the objective, material, practical and legal aspects of PEAPPs' predicament and on the psychological and spiritual impacts of precarity. I take it as axiomatic that, on issues of social justice, the perspective of the disadvantaged is more worthy of attention than that of the privileged (Wolff, 2021). Although I have recently, after eight years in precarious employment in EAP, secured a permanent post, I consciously resist positioning myself as poacher turned gamekeeper, fag turned prefect, or, as one participant, Bruno, in Mason and Megoran's (2021) study framed it, 'drug-seller' turned 'big narco'. Bruno goes on to say: 'If I get to the top of the academic pyramid, I will take advantage of post-docs too, there is no way out ... it is structural' (51).

I hope always to be mindful that I and all those higher up the academic hierarchy are sustained in their secure jobs and their privileged position by an army of casualized labour. The relationship between staff on precarious contracts and those in secure work is characterized by O'Keefe and Courtois (2019) as analogous to that between citizens and non-citizens. 'With the casualization of labour, the university institutionalizes and reinforces inequality through citizenship and non-citizenship status ... similar to the family employing foreign domestic workers, the citizenship and non-citizenship dichotomy in academia reinforces gender, economic and racial inequalities' (467). The authors go on to make this relationship explicit: employees on precarious contracts are the 'domestic workers whose labour frees up the time of more secure academics to pursue their career goals' (467). The same analogy can be applied to the teaching versus research dichotomy: '[Academic casualization] reconstructs teaching as "poorly paid housework in the marketplace", where some tend to the (college) kids and maintain the (departmental or campus) home, while others engage in more productive [research] work that circulates on the market' (Cardozo, 2017: 5, cited in Zheng, 2018: 243). This relationship of direct dependency can be seen very clearly in EAP departments because they tend to be small, with a fairly simple hierarchy and a limited range of roles. Were it not for summer pre-sessional courses for international students, the huge fees these students pay and the casualized labour of the PEAPPs who teach them, there would be no permanent year-round posts. I do not want to forget that my new-found security *depends upon* the insecurity and the labour of PEAPPs. I choose to use my now less vulnerable position to speak on behalf of PEAPPs and to speak truth to power.

In this chapter, I use examples from my personal experience, which has, I believe, been typical of the PEAPP predicament. I frequently use 'we' and 'our' when I articulate the PEAPP experience, partly from force of habit and partly because I believe that articulating the collective realities of lives shaped by precarity – telling our truth – is an essential step towards clarity and understanding. In particular, such a community of truth can help to develop a right interpretation of precarity not as individual failure but as a structural power dynamic of domination and exploitation. My analysis is based on my knowledge of the UK wasteland of precarity, and I mostly refer to 'universities'. Of course, many PEAPPs work for education businesses such as INTO, Kaplan and Study Group, where pay and conditions are often even worse than in universities. My arguments are equally relevant to both work contexts.

The conditions and demands of precarious employment have limited my capacity to conduct empirical research into PEAPPs' experience: I have had no time, funding or institutional support to do so. I draw therefore on the rich data obtained from participants in recent studies of precarity in HE in general (Courtois and O'Keefe, 2015; De Angelis and Grüning, 2020; Mason and Megoran, 2021; O'Keefe and Courtois, 2019), all of which paint a picture which will be familiar to PEAPPs. My analysis is also informed by the 'graffiti' discourses mentioned above, but I have chosen not to cite others' experiences or to quote, with one exception, from emails sent to the BALEAP JiscMail list. I am mindful of the risks PEAPPs take in voicing their experiences of exploitation and trauma, and of the need to honour confidentiality and to protect what little safe space remains available for PEAPPs to speak their truth.

The Logic of Precarity

Precarity designates the politically induced condition in which certain populations suffer from failing social and economic networks of support and become differentially exposed to injury, violence and death.

Butler (2010)

Precarity, as defined by the International Labour Organization, has both an objective and a subjective aspect. It can be understood in socio-economic terms as an employment regime which arises from deregulated labour markets within the capitalist system: a precarious job is characterized by 'uncertainty as to the duration of employment, multiple possible employers or a disguised or ambiguous employment relationship' as well as 'low pay, and substantial legal and practical obstacles to joining a trade union and bargaining collectively' (ILO, 2011: 5). Neoliberal ideology normalizes the exploitation of workers, who are seen as a 'cheap, flexible and disposable' resource (Zheng, 2018); precarious work is used as 'a means for employers to shift risks and responsibilities onto workers' (ILO, 2011: 5).

It is important to understand that precarity is not a by-product of the current economic climate; it is the logical and inevitable consequence of capitalism's neoliberal turn. Lordon articulates the 'original truth about the employment relation: that is it is a relation of dependence, a relation between agents in which one holds the condition for the material reproduction of the other' (2014: 7). The employment relation has always been a relation of domination, though this has sometimes been obscured by the allures that capitalism has 'put on stage to enrich its scenery and elicit more refined interests in the workplace – interests such as advancement, socialising, "fulfilment"' (8). Precarity is not, in truth, new; it is 'the stark backdrop of menace hanging over life *newly made bare*' (8; my emphasis). The current incarnation of capitalism 'mistreats employees at levels and intensities that have been unheard-of for decades' (150). Neoliberalism requires a work force that, like money, is liquid and undifferentiated. 'What the capitalist master-desire in the neoliberal era seeks is nothing less than the liquefaction of labour-power, making the overall size of the workforce into something fluid, reversible and … adjustable' (47); 'the employer needs *indefinite* labour-power … *this one* will do as well as *that one*' (18). These structures of exploitation and violence reveal themselves stark naked in the summer pre-sessional PEAPP labour market: the supply of fungible PEAPP labour is turned on and off, like water from a tap.

Precarity, then, is structurally necessary to neoliberal capitalism: this is the objective reality. The lures dangled by employers – of advancement through self-improvement, of more secure employment, of renewal of contracts – will, for most workers in precarity, never materialize. These false hopes are cynically leveraged in order to manipulate our desires and to make us complicit in our own exploitation. PEAPPs are persuaded that if they only work hard, do more Continuing Professional Development (CPD) or get more qualifications, they will enhance their job prospects. Standing (2011: 23) calls such activities 'self-exploitation': the work is done in the, usually deluded, hope of career progression, and it is often only the employer who profits (directly so, in the case of EAP-specific qualifications). For PEAPPs, this self-exploitation includes, potentially, taking on unpaid work or work that is 'downward' in terms of status or income, self-funded participation in conferences, paying for courses which lead to further academic or professional qualifications and engaging in Teaching English for Academic Purposes (TEAP) or Higher Education Authority (HEA) fellowship schemes.

The opportunity to escape from the precariat in our field is offered only on condition that we 'professionalize' ourselves, while the very conditions of our employment align us more with non-professional workers, such as Uber driver or migrant fruit-pickers. Furthermore, as EAP work is so seasonal, many PEAPPs will spend the other nine months of the year in work that marks them as 'not EAP professionals': teaching in language schools, doing private tuition, freelance editing and proofreading, teaching children or doing work that is unconnected with education. Other material labour which might serve to distinguish us as professionals or academics, such as research, scholarship or writing for publication, must, of course, be done in our own time and at our own expense, if it can be done at all.

Both EAP practitioners in secure employment and BALEAP, the body which supposedly represents those who work in EAP, are heavily invested in the need to 'professionalize' and to legitimize EAP as a field of academic endeavour – to bring EAP in from the margins of academia. BALEAP is primarily concerned with gatekeeping, through both individual and institutional accreditation schemes; like a mediaeval guild, it defends the privileges of those deemed to be 'EAP professionals', a status which is most usually accorded to those who are already in secure, permanent employment. There is a cruel circularity to this. The EAP establishment neither represents nor supports PEAPPs, who are, of course, an embarrassment. PEAPPs' very existence undermines the establishment's claims that EAP as a field is 'professional'. The myth of meritocracy (Zheng, 2018) serves to legitimize both the position of the privileged within the guild and the exclusion of those in the wilderness of precarity. PEAPPs, by being overworked, exploited and marginalized, are ipso facto not sufficiently 'professional' or deserving of admission to the academy.

PEAPPs, then, will need to look elsewhere for representation and for loyalty. However, their status as both seasonal, migrant labour and as would-be 'professionals' presents challenges in terms of collective, unionized representation and action. As PEAPPs, we spend our working lives within institutions which show no loyalty to us, and towards which we can therefore feel no loyalty. The same can be said of our relationship to BALEAP. The PEAPPrecariat, being as yet part of what Standing calls a 'class in the making', is not instinctively motivated to unionize. It has no traditions in which to take pride, no narrative or social memory of fraternity, or of solidarity or of loyalty even to itself.

The Trauma of Precarity

Everything is stamped with precariousness. No regular timetable, no fixed place of work; the same discontinuity in time and space. The search for work is the one constant factor in an existence swept to and fro by the whim of accident. … The whole of life is lived under the sign of the provisional.
Bourdieu ([1963]1979)

Subjectively, precarity is experienced as a trap from which it is hard to escape (O'Keefe and Courtois, 2019: 469; Standing, 2011: 17). Over time, the strain of living in poverty and insecurity manifests subjectively as vulnerability, anxiety, hopelessness and lack of self-worth. In Standing's analysis, the experience of the precariat is characterized by the 'four As': anger, anomie, anxiety and alienation (2011: 22). He expands on the 'frustration at the seemingly blocked avenues for advancing a meaningful life', the 'passivity born of despair', 'a listlessness associated with sustained defeat' and the alienation that 'arises from knowing that what one is doing is not for one's own purpose or for what one could respect or appreciate; it is simply done for others, at their behest'" (22-4). In her reflection in the *THES*, Rachel Moss (2020) shares her own and others' experience of the lasting toll that precarity takes on the psyche, even for those who do eventually find more secure employment in higher education. She suggests that 'precarity … [is] as much a state of mind as a state of employment'.

The common features of the experience of precarity are summarized by Mason and Megoran (2021) as: invisibility within the 'family' of the institution, resulting in feeling lonely and isolated; vulnerability to pressure to accept unfair and exploitative work practices, for fear of reprisals; a lack of agency to set one's own teaching and research goals; and the inability to project into the future and to make life or career plans. For PEAPPs, the vaunted internationalization of HE is often experienced as recurrent forced migration across regional or national borders (O'Keefe and Courtois, 2019: 469). This further ruptures PEAPPs' social and professional networks of support and can compound the loneliness and isolation of precarity (Ivancheva, 2015: 42). These deprivations can also be conceptualized as combinations of 'non-status' (O'Keefe and Courtois, 2019), the most egregious being legal non-status. Hourly paid and temporary workers do not benefit from the protections of labour law, such as entitlement to sick pay, maternity leave or the right to claim unfair dismissal. However, other aspects of non-status – social non-status, work/staff non-status and decision-making non-status – can be more corrosive to self-esteem.

The trauma of precarity is often internalized as a sense of shame. The lifestyle of PEAPPs is one of isolation, struggle and disappointment, and this can 'prevent them from formulating the issues affecting them as structural rather than the product of individual failures or weaknesses' (Courtois and O'Keefe, 2015: 44). This identification of structural disadvantaging as personal failure is not only something that PEAPPs internalize; it is also projected onto them by potential employers. Precarity is self-perpetuating; as one of Mason and Megoran's respondents says, 'you start to look unemployable' if you have been in a series of short-term jobs (2021: 50). I have often been interrogated at interview as to why I have had so many short-term jobs, the implication being that I am incapable of holding down any job for long. In one case, my history of precarious employment was the main reason given for not appointing me to a permanent position. Writ large, this scapegoating or gaslighting manoeuvre manifests as attributing the preponderance of low-paid exploitative jobs to the willingness of PEAPPs to accept them. In the context of writing centres in the United States, Fels et al. comment: 'contingent faculty are often blamed for their own "willingness" to take a low-paying job' (2016: 14). The advertising of a particularly exploitative job on the BALEAP website sometimes causes a temporary flurry of faux-naive outrage, most recently in March 2021, when one contributor wrote: 'These poor hourly salaries for highly qualified professionals will continue to be paid while teachers continue to accept them.' My response was: 'What choice do PEAPPs have but to accept any poorly-paid scraps of work that can be found? I do not think it is reasonable to hold PEAPPs responsible for the continuing deterioration of their socio-economic position in the job market, nor to blame them for employers' continued tightening of the thumbscrews.'

Lacking a secure work-based identity, PEAPPs are forced to take a series of career-less jobs. The work is often instrumental (done in order to live) and opportunistic (we take what we can get). The jobs we get do not allow us to fulfil our potential or to use our skills creatively. Summer pre-sessional curricula are increasingly designed to be prescriptive and 'fool-proof' (do our employers think we are fools?); PEAPPs' function is to 'deliver the syllabus'. Outwith the summer period, marking-only contracts or piece work are becoming increasingly common. PEAPPs are systematically deskilled and demoted from teaching professionals to postal workers and marking machines, in a process I term 'vocational deprivation'. Where work more suited to our skills, such as module and materials design, is available, the fruits of our labour and creative energy are appropriated by the employer to increase their capital, in the form of future iterations of the course sold to fee-paying students.

I believe that the experience of precarity in general and of vocational deprivation in particular is not only a matter of mental ill health; it is also a spiritual malaise – spiritual suffering. PEAPPs' souls are parched: cut off from the wellsprings of vitality, creativity and inspiration, the playfulness of experimentation, the desire to make a difference in the lives of young adults – all the energies which originally nourished our vocation to teach. In bringing this vocational deprivation to consciousness, I am resourced by the framework of Non-violent Communication (NVC) (Rosenberg, 2015). The intention of NVC work is to free us to speak our truth in ways which fulfil our 'nature to enjoy giving and receiving in a compassionate manner' (1). At the heart of the practice is learning to name and to take responsibility for our emotions, and to recognize that many 'negative' emotions are an expression of universal human needs which are not being met. As PEAPPs we are likely to feel, among other things: afraid, angry, anxious, bewildered, despondent, disaffected, discouraged, edgy, embittered, frustrated, helpless, hostile, jealous, overwhelmed, pessimistic, rancorous, resentful, sceptical, spiritless, suspicious and weary. Most prominent among the many needs which are unmet in precarity are Autonomy needs (choice, ease, independence), Meaning needs (authenticity, competence, creativity, dignity, honesty, integrity, trust, to matter to myself) and the Need to Matter (appreciation, consideration, respect, recognition, to be heard/seen, to be trusted). If, as a PEAPP, you recognize these emotions and these unmet needs in yourself, you may be feeling some liberation or lightening of the spirit in naming and claiming them as your own; it is also very likely that you will feel a sadness, a poignancy or a deep sense of mourning as you recognize and embrace heartfelt needs which are not being met.

I will argue that it is, paradoxically, when PEAPPs' material/survival needs are being most fully met – in the summer pre-sessional season – that the failure to meet their other needs becomes most visible. In other words, it is then that the structural violence of neoliberal capitalism reveals itself most clearly as the 'skull beneath the skin'. This begins with the elaborate rituals of recruitment and selection of PEAPPs, the principal function of which is to bolster management's apotropaic mythologizing of meritocracy. The 'resource leaching' (see Hadley, 2015) of human resources (HR) material labour onto PEAPPs press-gangs them into an endless filling-in of application forms, preparation of interview tasks, writing of tailored responses to lengthy lists of 'competency questions' – each one slightly different, each one taking hours of unpaid labour to complete. Rejections keep us asking: 'What is it these employers want?' We will never know the answer, as it is standard practice not to give feedback even to shortlisted unsuccessful candidates. Although the triaging of applicants may be carried out by computer algorithms, the disingenuous pretence of 'careful consideration' is maintained. The anger and frustration that PEAPPs experience arises from the knowledge, fully conscious or not, that these rituals are a fig leaf to cover the naked truth that *PEAPPs are a fungible, liquid resource*.

If we get a job, the next lie we are asked to swallow is that we are a valued member of the team. While for non-EAP precarious academics, the reality that they are 'not one of the family' tends to be unconcealed (O'Keefe and Courtois, 2019), PEAPPs on pre-sessionals are expected to be good team players and are fed a diet of departmental 'Values and Behaviours' – we are exhorted to go the extra mile, to do our best for our students, to whistle-blow on shirkers, to have a 'can do' attitude, to develop and improve ourselves and our performance, to 'enhance' everything and anything – in short, to conform to what Standing calls the 'alienating twaddle' (2011: 24) that is a calculated denial of the realities of our predicament. The terrible irony of this is that the very conditions of our precarity deter us from acts of solidarity with our *real team*: fellow PEAPPs. It is hard to form trusting, collegial relationships with other PEAPPs, trapped as we are in fierce competition for the same jobs, vying to comply with and to please management, struggling to sustain unmanageable workloads, all in the empty hope of being rehired. Knowing that we are all dispensable and replaceable is not conducive to fostering respect for ourselves or for each other.

I have had the experience of speaking up at a pre-sessional staff meeting to protest about the unreasonable workloads and deadlines which had kept me and fellow PEAPPs working long hours of unpaid overtime, and sometimes through the night, only to have my colleagues all stare at the floor and stay silent. I then received a formal email from management saying it had been noted that 'I could not manage my workload'. At the end of that summer, some PEAPPs were called in to meet with management one by one and were 'encouraged' to criticize those members of staff whom management had already decided to get rid of. With these delations, some PEAPPs bought themselves a few hours of in-sessional teaching until Christmas. I was not offered any follow-on work in the autumn (but at least I could look at myself in the mirror every morning). After repeated requests to management for feedback on their decision not to rehire me, the only reason I was given was that I was 'not as good a team player' as others.

PEAPPs can suffer further loss of dignity on pre-sessional contracts in being line-managed by permanent staff, who most probably have been promoted from the teaching ranks, who may have no aptitude for training or leadership and who, lacking a vocation for teaching, may be delighted to have escaped the classroom (see Greg Hadley's 2015 incisive and entertaining dissection of 'Blended EAP Professionals' (BLEAPS)). The PEAPP may be more experienced and better qualified than the BLEAP. The fallacy that workers in precarity are characterized by youth and inexperience is refuted by the research of Courtois and O'Keefe (2015: 56). This is an ideal breeding ground for envy and resentment – a toxic cocktail of emotions. Again, it is important to understand that this spiritual poisoning is the product of our predicament, not the effluent of some inner maladjustment or defect of character. In the language of NVC, this is to be recognized and accepted as the tragedy of unmet needs.

I do not, of course, dispute that, within neoliberal capitalism, managers are subject to the same domination and exploitation as other workers and are more vulnerable to the pressure to identify with their oppressors: having, or having the capacity to develop, Stockholm Syndrome should be part of their job description. The concomitant need to inflict the violence they experience on their subordinates is embraced by managers with varying degrees of enthusiasm, and not all organizational cultures are as toxic and corrupt as the one described above. However, the lack of scrutiny and oversight that is common within EAP departments, particularly around rehiring at the end of summer, is, for some, a license for nepotism and victimization. While my analysis in this chapter is informed by Bourdieu's (1992) conceptualization of 'symbolic violence', I have preferred the term 'structural violence', as, in my experience, this violence has often been far from symbolic. Bosses I have worked under have: ripped up my legal contract of employment and replaced it with a less advantageous one, softening the blow by telling me I should be 'grateful to have a job at all'; sent me to work in China with the wrong visa, putting me at risk of arrest and imprisonment; and refused to reschedule a job interview which I did not attend because, two hours earlier, I had learnt that my mother had died.

The final area of pre-sessional work that I want to address is professional development. The induction of PEAPPs to pre-sessional programmes has been successfully re-branded as 'CPD'. One anonymous manger contributed thus to the Practitioner Precarity blog (2020): 'We [sic] invest proportionately less time in their [sic] CPD. They [sic] all have at least two days' induction.' Admittedly, teacher inductions may include elements of CPD, although in my experience over the past eight years, this is becoming less common. Induction tends to focus on training teachers in the use of the institution's IT systems, procedures for taking attendance, the department's assessment criteria and other logistical processes. When PEAPPs express their disappointment at not being able to participate in CPD because they don't have the time or the money to do so, they are not lamenting their exclusion from yet another teacher induction session.

When I talk about 'CPD', what I mean is workshops, conferences, symposiums, Special Interest Group (SIG) events, webinars and massive open online courses (MOOCs) which enable me to learn from and to exchange ideas with the wider community of practice. CPD is also conversations with colleagues and with learners; it is having the opportunity to observe other practitioners at work and it is sharing my practice with others. It is not so much the form that makes it CPD for me, as the fact that I have chosen to engage with it, following my own interests, in order to foster my own professional and personal growth. CPD supports my autonomy and my authenticity as a practitioner, and commits and connects me to a mutually supportive network of other practitioners. Teacher inductions, I would argue, are aimed primarily at promoting conformity, compliance and parity across cohorts of teachers. Of course, consistency and parity and quality control are not unimportant. I just don't think they are 'CPD'.

Taking that metaphor of growth a little further, if I the practitioner am the plant, then CPD is the water and the manure which resources me to grow and flourish; it is the trellis which supports me to extend myself and to send out tendrils in new directions; sometimes it is the secateurs which lop and prune the parts of my practice which no longer serve me or my students, in order that new green shoots may emerge; and sometimes it is an uprooting and a replanting in different soil (though PEAPPs, like any plant, tend to suffer if they are too frequently repotted, especially if the new pot is smaller than the old one). Being 'inducted', by contrast, feels too often like being a piece of wood – a resource – turned on a lathe to shape me to function, like all the other cogs, in my allotted place in the system, until I am no longer useful.

Reclaiming Authenticity

Man is not a thing. He must be dealt with not as an "animated tool", but as a person sacred in himself. To do otherwise is to depersonalise the potential person and desecrate what he is.

King Jr (1965)

The experience of precarity is, as Mason and Megoran's (2021) analysis reveals, one of dehumanization. For me, the aspect of precarity that has been most corrosive to the spirit is alienation from my work – from the facet of my humanity that is my vocation to teach. Although, as I have argued, the framing of EAP as 'professional' is, for PEAPPs, problematic, I believe it is essential that we reclaim our work as profession, practice and vocation (Calderhead, 1988; Palmer, 1998; Palmer and Zajonc, 2010; Wallace 1991). It is because we have a vocation to teach that we find the work we are given (as syllabus-deliverers and markers) intolerable: this is the suffering of vocational deprivation. Our longing to live out our vocation is both thwarted and exploited/weaponized in the vice of neoliberal precarity. At the same time as our work becomes increasingly 'unlovable', the myth of teaching/academic work as inherently 'lovable' is used, as Zheng (2018) argues, to justify low wages and poor conditions – if we have a vocation to this work, we should be glad to do it for nothing. To speak of 'vocation', then, is to wield a double-edged sword.

The neoliberal marketization of higher education prioritizes that which can be quantified over quality. I don't just mean quality in the sense of 'excellence' (which has now also been reduced to metrics). The teaching of each skilled practitioner has its own quality – its texture, its rhythm, its flavour, its mood, its individuality. Growing into ourselves, exploring who we are as teachers, experimenting, taking risks, failing, creating, becoming, these are the things that are most fulfilling about being a practitioner, about living out our vocation. For PEAPPs, such self-actualization is almost impossible. If we are to reclaim our humanity and our vocation, I believe we need to reframe the discourse around precarity in ways that challenge the hegemony of neoliberalism's market economy and managerial models. We need to think outside that prison-box. While I have, in this chapter, used the Marxist lens of Lordon and Standing to reveal the ugliness and violence of precarity, this framing alone is not sufficient to accommodate a re-envisaging of 'vocation' as human flourishing. In Lordon's terms, this re-envisaging would mean to pursue our longings by 'becoming-orthogonal', which is to resist the hijacking manoeuvres (e.g. of 'vocation') of neoliberalism and to 'step into a life *determined in another way*' (2014: 141–2). Other lenses and other language are needed.

I will close this chapter by suggesting some of the wellsprings which have resourced me in this process of enquiry into 'becoming-orthogonal' (le Roux, 2021). Mason and Megoran (2021) use the lens of African American theological anthropology to interpret casualization and precarity as 'not simply the product of a reprehensible political economy', but as 'an affront to the very meaning and dignity of being human' (35). The discourses of social justice can also be invoked. Rawls's (1971) conceptualization of justice as equity, magisterial though it is, does not entirely escape the quantifying and scarcity mindset of utilitarianism. I prefer Nussbaum's (2011) framing of justice as the actualization of human capabilities, with its focus on fulfilment and flourishing, on the *quality* of individual human lives. Other discourses which take human flourishing seriously include Rosenberg's Non-violent Communication, which I have already referenced in this chapter. NVC aims to enable us to show up in the world in integrity and authenticity. The work of Kreber (2013) within the field of SoTL also foregrounds authenticity and speaks to our 'shared sense that aspects of our professional lives have become increasingly separated from this core characteristic [authenticity] of what it means to be truly human' (7–8). Kreber's analysis serves to reveal how the predicament of PEAPs in the neoliberal academy is characterized not only by precarity and marginalization, but by a profound cognitive dissonance: the 'disjuncture between what we ourselves regard as meaningful practice and what we are instead expected to comply with' (13). I believe that resources and discourses such as these can reveal new ways to reclaim and re-member vocation, both individually and collectively; to create an alternative community of truth; to build collegial solidarity that is strong enough to overcome self-interest;and to foster a fidelity to knowledge, to education and to learners that can withstand the betrayal and violence of neoliberalism.

References

Academics Anonymous, various dates, *The Guardian*. Available online: https://www.theguardian.com/education/series/academics-anonymous (25 September 2021).

Blythman, M., and S. Orr (2006), 'Mrs Mop Does Magic', *Zeitschrift Schreiben: Schreiben in Schule, Hochschule und Beruf*. Available online: https://zeitschrift-schreiben.ch/

globalassets/zeitschrift-schreiben.eu/2006/blythman_orr_mrsmop.pdf (accessed 20 September 2021).

Bourdieu, P. ([1963]1979), *Travail et travailleurs en Algérie*, Paris: Mouton. Translated in an adapted version by R. Nice as *Algeria 1960: The Disenchantment of the World*, New York: Cambridge University Press.

Bourdieu, P. (1992), *Language and Symbolic Power*, London: Polity Pres.

Butler, J. (2010), *Frames of War: When is Life Grievable?* Cambridge: Cambridge University Press.

Calderhead, J. (ed.) (1988), *Teachers' Professional Learning*, London: Falmer Press.

Cardozo, K. (2017), 'Academic Labor: Who Cares?', *Critical Sociology*, 43 (3): 405–28.

Careering: Precarity and Solidarity in Higher Education (2017), 'Forum Event at the University of Birmingham Department of History', report by T. Cutterham. Available online: https://moderncontemporarybham.wordpress.com/2017/03/17/careering-precarity-solidarity-in-higher-education/ (accessed 18 September 2021).

Courtois, A., and T. O'Keefe (2015) 'Precarity in the Ivory Cage: Neoliberalism and Casualisation of Work in the Irish Higher Education Sector', *Journal of Critical Education Policy Studies*, 13 (1): 43–65.

De Angelis, G., and B. Grüning (2020), 'Gender Inequality in Precarious Academic Work: Female Adjunct Professors in Italy', *Frontiers in Sociology*, 4: 1–18.

Delivery or Deliveroo (2021), 'EAP for Social Justice Anonymous Blog'. Available online: https://eap4socialjustice.net/2021/07/02/delivery-or-deliveroo-rethinking-the-summer-pre-sessional/ (accessed 23 September 2021).

Fels, D., C. Gardner, M. M. Herb and L. M. Naydan (2016), 'Toward an Investigation into the Working Conditions of Non-Tenure Line, Contingent Writing Center Workers', *College Composition and Communication*, 68 (1): A10–A16.

Hadley, G. (2015), *English for Academic Purposes in Neo-liberal Universities: A Critical Grounded Theory*, New York: Springer.

Honi Soit (2021), 'University of Sydney Student Forum Blog'. Available online: https://honisoit.com/2021/08/academic-housework-the-gendered-effects-of-precarity/ (accessed 21 September 2021).

Horgan, A. (2021), *Lost in Work: Escaping Capitalism*, London: Pluto Press.

International Labour Organization (2011), 'Policies and Regulations to Combat Precarious Employment', Geneva: International Labour Organization. Available online: https://www.ilo.org/wcmsp5/groups/public/@ed_dialogue/@actrav/documents/meetingdocument/wcms_164286.pdf (accessed 23 September 2021).

Ivancheva, M. P. (2015), 'The Age of Precarity and the New Challenges to the Academic Profession', *Studia Ubb. Europaea*, LX (1): 39–47.

King, M. L., Jr (1965), 'Man in a Revolutionary World', speech at the United Church of Christ, Chicago, 6 July, The University of Memphis Libraries. Available online: https://www.memphis.edu/libraries/mlk50/speech.php (accessed 22 September 2021).

Kınıoğlu, C. N., and A. Can (2021), 'Negotiating the Different Degrees of Precarity in the UK Academia during the Covid-19 Pandemic', *European Societies*, 23 (S1): S818–S830.

Kreber, C. (2013), *Authenticity in and through Teaching in Higher Education: The Transformative Potential of the Scholarship of Teaching*, Abingdon: Routledge.

le Roux, M. (2021), 'Using Circles of Trust to Explore EAP Practitioner Agency & Identity', presentation at the *Norwegian Forum for English for Academic Purposes* (NFEAP) conference, Oslo, 4 June (online).

Lordon, F. (2014), *Willing Slaves of Capital: Spinoza and Marx on Desire*, London: Verso.

Mason, O., and N. Megoran (2021), 'Precarity and Dehumanisation in Higher Education', *Learning and Teaching: The International Journal of Higher Education in the Social Sciences*, 14 (1): 35–59.

Moss, R. (2020), 'Precarity Has a Long Hangover', *THES*, 12 February. Available online: https://www.timeshighereducation.com/opinion/precarity-has-long-hangover?utm_source=THE+Website+Users&utm_campaign=8e74a38aa5-EMAIL_CAMPAIGN_2020_02_11_02_57&utm_medium=email&utm_term=0_daa7e51487-8e74a38aa5-74879469 (accessed 15 September 2021).

Murgia, A., and B. Poggio (eds) (2019) *Gender and Precarious Research Careers: A Comparative Analysis*, London: Routledge.

Navarro, T. (2017), 'But Some of Us Are Broke: Race, Gender and the Neoliberalization of the Academy', *American Anthropologist*, 119 (3): 506–17.

Nussbaum, M. C. (2011), *Creating Capabilities: The Human Development Approach*, Cambridge, MA: Belknap Press of Harvard University Press.

O'Keefe, T., and A. Courtois (2019), '"Not One of the Family": Gender and Precarious Work in the Neoliberal University', *Gender Work Organ*, 26: 463–79.

Palmer, P. J. (1998), *The Courage to Teach: Exploring the Inner Landscape of a Teacher's Life*, San Francisco, CA: Jossey-Bass.

Palmer, P. J., and A. Zajonc (2010), *The Heart of Higher Education: A Call to Renewal*, San Francisco, CA: Jossey-Bass.

Practitioner Precarity and the Coronavirus (2020), Centre for Excellence in Language Teaching, University of Leeds. Available online: https://celt.leeds.ac.uk/practitioner-precarity-and-the-coronavirus-introduction/ (accessed 13 September 2021).

Precarity and Precariousness (2019), University of Warwick Department of Philosophy. Available online: https://warwick.ac.uk/fac/soc/philosophy/news/conference/precarityandprecariousness/ (accessed 15 September 2021).

Precarious Work and Gender Inequality in Higher Education: Researching for Change (2019), Research Symposium at the University of Bath Department of Education. Available online: https://researchportal.bath.ac.uk/en/publications/precarious-work-amp-gender-inequality-in-higher-education-researc (accessed 15 September 2021).

Rawls, J. (1971), *A Theory of Justice*, Cambridge, MA: Harvard University Press.

Rosenberg, M. B. (2015), *Nonviolent Communication: A Language of Life*, 3rd edn, California: PuddleDancer Press.

Sarrico, C. L. (2021), 'Addressing the Precarity of Research Careers', presentation at UCL Institute of Education webinar, 15 December. Available online: https://www.ucl.ac.uk/ioe/events/2021/dec/virtual-event-addressing-precarity-research-careers (accessed 15 December 2021).

Standing, G. (2011), *The Precariat: The New Dangerous Class*, London: Bloomsbury.

Tuck, J. (2018), ' "I'm Nobody's Mum in This University": The Gendering of Work around Student Writing in UK Higher Education', *Journal of English for Academic Purposes*, 32: 32–41.

Turner, C. (2002), 'Women of Colour in Academe: Living with Multiple Marginality', *Journal of Higher Education*, 73 (1): 74–93.

UCU (2020), *Precarious Work in Higher Education: Insecure Contracts and How They Have Changed Over Time*, a report by University and College Union. Available online: https://www.ucu.org.uk/media/10899/Precarious-work-in-higher-education-May-20/pdf/ucu_he-precarity-report_may20.pdf (accessed 21 September 2021).

Wallace, M. J. (1991), *Training Foreign Language Teachers: A Reflective Approach*, Cambridge: Cambridge University Press.

Walsh, P. (2019), 'Precarity', *ELT Journal*, 73 (4): 459–62.

Wolff, J. (2021), 'The Dudley Knowles Lecture in Political Philosophy: Injustice in the Real World', University of Glasgow Stevenson Trust for Citizenship Lecture, 1 February. Available online: https://www.gla.ac.uk/schools/socialpolitical/research/politics/stevensontrust/newsandevents/headline_769712_en.html (accessed 12 August 2021).

Zheng, R. (2018), 'Precarity Is a Feminist Issue: Gender and Contingent Labour in the Academy', *Hypatia*, 33 (2): 235–55.

Part 4

Collective Organization and Positioning of EAP and the Future

10

Association: Power, Politics and Policy

Alex Ding and Ian Bruce

Introduction

This chapter is a critical exploration of professional association and associations, and how this under-examined but essential facet of practitioners' lives intersects with issues of collective power within the domain of professional politics and policy. The chapter begins by considering the occlusion of English for Academic Purposes (EAP) practitioners in the research literature of the field. This is then followed by a review of the relatively small literature that has considered language teacher associations and their roles. Against this background, the chapter then considers EAP associations and the scope of their activities. The concluding section of the chapter makes the case for a more self-conscious, reflexive, critical and politically and publicly engaged understanding of association that sits better with historical practices reflecting the values and roles of professional bodies.

EAP Practitioners: Occluded Actors in the Field

Three very recent large-scale, systematic historical reviews of the EAP research literature (Hyland and Jiang, 2021; Liu and Hu, 2021; Raizi, Ghanbar and Fazel, 2020) collude to confirm Belcher's observation that the 'community that ESP professionals know the least about is their own' (2013: 544) where 'this lacuna is symptomatic of the continued marginalisation of practitioners both within their own discipline and beyond' (Ding and Bruce, 2017: 117). In Raizi, Ghanbar and Fazel (2020), the practitioner is only mentioned in relation to a recommendation for more research on the education of practitioners. Their research on publications in the *Journal of English for Academic Purposes*

(JEAP) reveals the top ten research foci for this journal and, unsurprisingly, the practitioner does not feature even when the equal tenth entries only account for 2.9 per cent each of research foci. A different methodological approach was adopted by Liu and Hu (2021) analysing JEAP and *English for Specific Purposes Journal* (ESPJ) articles to tease out landmark studies and research orientations in these journals but, as far as the practitioner is concerned, the conclusion is the same: the practitioner is absent. The third study by Hyland and Jiang (2021), broader in scope than the two other studies mentioned, presents data on the most frequently explored topics in EAP over a forty-year period (and within this, those topics moving in or out of fashion) with, again, no mention of the practitioner. However, and unlike the two other studies mentioned, Hyland and Jiang do emphasize the marginalization of the practitioner:

> EAP practitioners around the world thus struggle to find the time, the support and the advice to translate their interests and curiosity into publishable research. The absence of institutional incentives and lack of an established research culture in EAP acts as a brake on the advance of publishing and on the future development of the field. (2021: 10)

Despite their historical occlusion in EAP research literature, EAP practitioners are becoming more visible, and recent tropes in the literature 'reveal and shape concerns around status, recognition, role and position in the field' (Ding, 2019: 66). These concerns have persisted throughout the literature, initially visible only fleetingly and fragmentally, to become a focal point in the ideational domain. Early references highlight the marginalization and low status of the practitioner (cf. Hall, 2013; Hyland, 2012; Johns, 1981; Robinson, 1991; Strauss, 2012), with Johns (1981) concerned that the marginal position of the practitioner impacts on professional identity and Robinson (1991) linking this diminished professional identity to the need to fight for improved pay and conditions and challenging practitioners to assess the extent to which they can consider themselves professionals. Echoing many of Stevenson and Kokkinn's (2007) earlier concerns, this trope continued with Hamp-Lyons (2011a: 4) anxious about the trend to divorce practitioners from academic departments, to rename practitioners to emphasize their service or teaching-only status and, significantly, to outsource EAP to private providers.

These issues were more fully explored by Ding and Campion (2016) and Fulcher (2009), but the book length expositions by Hadley (2015) and Ding and Bruce (2017) signalled a significant shift from a fragmented to a concerted focus on the practitioner. Although both publications evoke neoliberalism as overarching structural and ideational forces that shape (and diminish) the identity, agency and status of practitioners, they do differ in approach. Hadley (2015) provides a rich empirical exposé of the professional and identity struggles of EAP managers in Japan, the UK and the United States. He provides the striking lens or trope of professional disarticulation through which much of the literature on the practitioner can be read. Disarticulation refers to a sense of divorce or disjointedness between an idea(l) of professional identity and practice. Hadley's book focuses on exposing the impact of neoliberalism on EAP and its practitioners. While Ding and Bruce (2017) also do this, they stress the agential practitioner and the ways in which practitioners can forge a stronger academic identity, obtaining the cultural capital needed – through undertaking scholarship and research – to exert influence and obtain recognition within universities and to fight back against increasing marginalization of the practitioner and increasing privatization of the profession. Alongside these publications, more recent doctoral theses (Bell, 2016; Jones, 2020; Taylor, 2020) and publications by MacDonald (2016), Flowerdew (2019) and Ding (2019) have added depth and diversity to discussions of EAP practitioners' professionalism, status and identity.

Early concerns also focused on the emotional effect of teaching EAP where novice practitioners were presented as 'reluctant dwellers in a strange and unchartered land' (Hutchinson and Waters, 1987: 152), entailing 'shock' (Strevens, 1988: 41) and 'fear' (Robinson, 1991: 79) and a reticence to engage with EAP (Alexander, 2012). While Hyland (2018) claims this has largely disappeared and been 'replaced by a more confident figure' (390), Bond's (2020) recent study suggests that Hyland's assertion is more aspirational than real and that there is still considerable doubt and confusion among practitioners regarding their teaching practices and educational purposes. However, it is true that this emotional trope has been superseded or sublimated by a focus on transitions into EAP. Practitioner education and development are a significant theme within the practitioner literature especially that of the 'novice' practitioner. This notion of transition to EAP (most often from what is labelled 'general English') expresses early concerns in the UK around the qualifications needed for EAP and their ability to prepare practitioners for the specific demands of teaching EAP (Errey and Ansell, 2001; Krzanowski, 2001; Roberts, 2001; Sharpling, 2002). Because of a lack of EAP specific qualifications (and lack of general agreement around those qualifications that do exist), entry to the profession is ad hoc (Ding, 2019; Ding and Bruce, 2017; Ding and Campion, 2016). This situation has led to a few UK-based studies exploring in situ, post hoc development and socialization of novice practitioners (cf. Alexander, 2010; Elsted, 2012; Martin, 2014; Post, 2010) and, much more recently, a growing literature, especially from Iran (cf. Bahrami, Hosseini and Atai, 2019; Kaivanpanah et al., 2021; Tavakol and Tavakol, 2018) and China (cf. Li and Wang, 2020) in this area. Aside from studies on initial transitions into EAP, the developmental needs of (more experienced) practitioners are even less of a focus, Campion's (2016) thoughtful study being a notable exception.

Ding and Bruce (2017) argue that, because socialization takes place in situ (unlike all established professions), it also means that it is post hoc and potentially ad hoc, and practitioners' development is then subject to the vagaries of the micro-politics of EAP centres where local politics (relationships, beliefs about EAP, power and ideologies) and the location and identity of EAP centres (in academic schools, independent units, in an administrative centre) within neoliberal universities impact opportunities to develop. This consequences of which are:

> Short-sighted managerial concerns for efficiency and profit will not see benefits in encouraging and financially supporting practitioners to develop an understanding of the knowledge base of EAP, to pursue research and scholarship interests, as well as gain specialist expert powerful knowledge. This places the burden on practitioners themselves to develop without the institutional support that would make this feasible. (Ding, 2019: 70)

Davis (2019) provides important empirical evidence to support this claim regarding the micro-politics of EAP centres where there is often considerable resistance from EAP directors to enabling and supporting practitioners to develop and increase their cultural capital in academia through scholarship and research. Davis (2019) reveals just one occluded facet of practitioners' lives and concerns. In the following section, we consider a further occluded element of any discussions of EAP – that of the role of associations

EAP Associations

The marginalization of association in analyses of the field of EAP is marked. For example, Hyland (2018) celebrates the establishment of *EAP as a discipline* by pointing to the 'paraphernalia of journals, monographs, conferences, and research centres: all the trappings, in fact, of a full-fledged educational practice' (389). Hamp-Lyons (2011b) sees the launch of the *Journal of English for*

Academic Purposes in 2002 as 'a clear indication that EAP had come of age as an independent academic field' (93). While Hyland and Hamp-Lyons identify (and celebrate) the key indicators that demonstrate the arrival of EAP as a legitimate academic field/discipline, they perhaps forget, ignore or consider irrelevant or marginal the role of associations in helping to establish academic capital and credentials for EAP. EAP associations, such as BALEAP, existed long before JEAP. Practitioners (and researchers) have exchanged ideas, research and praxis in and through association for more than forty years. The ideational domain, in other words, that shapes ideas, practices, concerns, interests and theories of practitioners *in association* has both preceded, continues alongside and is interwoven with the paraphernalia of accruing academic capital.

More significantly, the rise and celebration of EAP as a legitimate academic field reveals a rupture or lacunae with EAP *as a profession and professional endeavour*. Professional and academic endeavours, interests, questions, investments, goals, rewards, actors, professional and academic agency, capital, values, practices and loyalties (among others) are not synonymous. Although partially distinct, they overlap and are mutually dependent. They stem from different sources and hold differing degrees of power over their respective domains of activity and, importantly, over each other; they operate in different fields. As we and others have noted elsewhere, researchers and practitioners tend to be different people (Ding and Bruce, 2017; Hyland and Jiang, 2021) and, we would add, with different interests.

On the one hand, it would be easy to castigate the EAP research community. As we have already noted, the practitioner is largely ignored in the research literature especially in terms of the sociopolitical factors that shape their world (exceptions have been Flowerdew, 2019; Hyland, 2018; Hyland and Jiang, 2021). On the rare occasions when practitioners do feature, it is their apparent apolitical, accommodationist or collusional adoption of hegemonic norms that is highlighted (cf, Benesch, 2001; Morgan, 2009) without giving any serious consideration, again, to the sociopolitical factors shaping their agency (Ding, 2019). Bruce (2021), Swales (2019) and Cheng (2019) have all expressed criticism of an assumed link between theory and practice in research publications. Claims of pedagogical implications are often unjustified (Bruce, 2021: 26), too vague (Cheng, 2019) or articles 'fade way before articulating well-articulated pedagogical applications' (Swales, 2019: 78).

Not only is the practitioner largely absent – especially in prestigious journals – but they also have to work (too) hard to locate pedagogical relevance and applications in these sources. These factors feed into a growing divide between the researchers and practitioners of EAP (Ding and Bruce, 2017) and contribute to a more fractured, siloed field. This is combined with a narrowing of foci within journals with resultant doxas established and an increasingly limiting/limited coverage of EAP (Bruce, 2021). This lack of 'synergy' was a concern to the then editors of JEAP (Hamp-Lyons and Hyland) in 2005. In brief, we would argue that the practitioner is poorly served by the EAP literature and especially by prestigious journals.

On the other hand, the demands on EAP researchers are 'to specialise narrowly and publish prodigiously and prestigiously' (Ding, 2019: 73), and given that EAP researchers are subject to the same neoliberal imperatives of performativity, metrics and overwork as in any other academic discipline, it should come as little surprise that broader material and political concerns about the field are absent. It should be even less of a surprise that associations and association simply do not feature in the research and ideational domains. Associations seemingly simply exist; transparent and obvious in their purposes and functions, unworthy of examination or a reflexive, sociological account of the roles, power and potential of associations to contributing to practitioners' agency, knowledge and values. Focusing on associations reveals the fractures not only between research and practice orientations but also between the academic and professional concerns within EAP.

Turning to, firstly, the fragmented and sparce literature on EAP associations and then, more broadly, to the equally sparce literature on language teacher associations (LTAs) and English language teacher associations (ELTAs) reveals as much, if not more, about what remains hidden and unexamined about associations as it does about facets of associations.

There is a small cluster of publications within EAP that mention or focus on associations, especially BALEAP. Ding and Campion (2016) in their chapter on practitioner development and education critically assess BALEAP's teaching fellowship scheme with a focus on exploring the assimilative rather than transformative nature of the scheme for practice and practitioners. Ding and Bruce (2017) devote a chapter to mapping the contributions of BALEAP for practitioners drawing the conclusion that much has been achieved internally over the years in terms of practitioner development, standards and accreditation, but these developments have not been matched externally, and BALEAP 'has yet to take on a more public and possibly combative role in defending and supporting practitioners in their more worldly and material dimensions' (191). Bruce (2021) argues for a greater role for associations in developing practitioners' knowledge base, through scholarship and research, and developing a collective voice concerning issues affecting the community. Two empirical papers highlight different aspects of BALEAP. Charles (2021) examines BALEAP's contribution to research through a corpus analysis of the 1,310 papers presented at BALEAP's biennial conferences and professional issues meetings (PIMs) with the aim of revealing what practitioners discuss and research, where there are gaps or underexplored areas and to show research trends over the fifty years of BALEAP events. Although she comments favourably on practitioners' rootedness in the practicalities of EAP, she unfortunately does so by contrasting this orientation to a (welcome?) lack of theoretical discussion and, by doing so, reinforces anti-intellectualism in the field as if theory is not for, or of any use to, practitioners. Ding, Bond and Bruce (under review) trace the debates and discussions on the BALEAP mailing list from 1998 to 2021 with a particular focus on exploring issues of identity and agency of practitioners through discourse analysis of discussions on outsourcing/privatization of EAP provision in universities and analysis of periodic discussions of the renaming (and confusion) around BALEAP. One important finding was a significant reluctance within the association to collectively address the continuing menace and impact of privatization. This, in sum, is the literature on EAP and associations and amounts to a handful of publications with only a few contributors to public scholarship on associations. With the special issue of JEAP on BALEAP due to be published in 2022, we can look forward to a wider range of research on BALEAP, more perspectives on BALEAP and, most of all, stimulation for practitioners to develop their scholarship and research on associations.

Clearly much is missing from the existent literature on EAP associations and turning to the wider fields of LTAs and especially ELTAs would, in theory, help supplement the scant research on EAP. Unfortunately, there is little research to draw on. A handful of ELTA publications, one an edited book (Elsheikh and Effiong, 2018) a special edition of ELT-J (2016) alongside Rimmer and Floyd's (2020) recent study on professionalism is the sum of research, although Lamb's (2012) study on LTAs is also highly relevant in many ways. In sum, the limitations of current ELTA research are the inward facing and apolitical orientation of the studies and a disproportionate emphasis on leadership of associations. Elsheikh and Effiong provide a salient example of both these points when in their introduction they write that the 'core of this book is the inward look at the work and impact of LTAs' (2018: xxiv), and they then dedicate nine of the twenty-two chapters to aspects of association leadership. Although research points to the challenges facing associations, there is a strong emphasis on positive aspects such as professional identity, belonging, instrumental motivations and knowledge-building as being key to association members (Ding and Bruce, 2017). For example, community and belonging (Abatayo, 2018; Motteram, 2016; Paran, 2016): networking (Motteram, 2016); developing new ideas and engaging in debates (Lamb, 2012; Paran, 2016); keeping up to date (Motteram, 2016); evidencing professionalism (Motteram, 2016) and enhancing professional status and reputation, all feature as strong motivations for practitioners to engage with, and in, associations (Rimmer and Floyd, 2020). Very few of the studies use large scale data, the exceptions being Lamb (2012), Smith and Kuchah (2016) and Motteram (2016), who use surveys and questionnaires of association members and/or association leaders. Shamin and Sarawar (2018) and Elsheik and Effiong (2018) conducted interviews with very small numbers of association members, while Rimmer and Floyd (2020) are unique in seeking the views of a small number of practitioners who are not members of ELTAs. Many accounts are descriptive, reflective, narrative, anecdotal or auto ethnographical. None of the studies seem to be guided or grounded in a theoretical framework. Theory, when theory does appear, is largely incidental to the focus of the studies.

Lamb's study of LTAs provides a clear idea of the roles of LTAs:

> Networks of professionals, run by and for professionals, focused mainly on support for members, with knowledge exchange and development as well as representation of members' views as their defining functions. (2012: 295)

However, Paran (2016) noted:

> The external advocacy element which is so important for subject associations as well as professional associations is positioned as the last element for LTAs, as an addition to their core activities. (128)

Representation of members' views in the form of public advocacy and policy in the political and social arena is a core feature of professional associations. However, Paran notes that this comes almost as an afterthought and is of much less significance than the inward looking association activities for ELTAs. IATEFL and BALEAP, for example, have consistently refused or been unable to undertake this core feature of associations (Ding and Bruce, 2017). A hint of this reticence from association members to engage in or wish for association advocacy is evident in Rimmer and Floyd's (2020) very small-scale study, which suggests that advocacy 'tended to polarise teachers based on their personal values and experiences' (134).

If a key feature of professions and, therefore, associations is advocacy and engaging in the sociopolitical world, then it follows that ethics should be at heart of associations. Sarfatti Larson (1977/2013) and Archer (2000) both stress the importance of ethics for professions. Archer comments as follows: 'The typical defining feature of the professions, their possession of an ethical standard, is not just a guide to professional conduct but also a moral raison d'être for the profession itself' (2000: 291). The ethics of LTAs, along with other outward facing roles of LTAs such as employment, work conditions and precarity, are absent from much of the literature. It is as if, not only are the workings, power and functions of professions such as EAP entirely transparent or unworthy of investigation, associations exist in a sociopolitical vacuum without a history and with a narrow set of professional concerns and interests.

EAP Associations and the Scope of Their Activities

While the earlier sections of this chapter have identified the lack of a research or publication focus on EAP practitioners individually (and on their associations as collective groups), this situation does not negate the fact that worldwide there is, in fact, a considerable number of EAP/ESP practitioner associations, and that these organizations undertake a range of activities on behalf of their members. In the United States, EAP practitioners may participate in the Symposium of Second Language Writing (SSLW), the second language writing section of the CCCC organization and in the TESOL second language writing interest group. In Australasia, EAP practitioners may be found among members of the Australian Association of Writing Programmes (AAWP) and the Tertiary Writing Network (TWN) in New Zealand. In Europe, there are several organizations. These include BALEAP in the UK, AELFE in Spain and GERAS in France (both with more of a focus on ESP), the European Association for the teaching of Academic Writing (EATAW) and the Norwegian Forum of English for Academic Purposes (NFEAP) in Norway. In addition, there are now well-established practitioner organizations in several Asian countries, including Iran's ESP Association, the China EAP Association (CEAPA), the China ESP Association, the newly formed, China-based Asia Pacific EAP Association and the Hong Kong-based Language for Specific Purposes and Professional Communication Association (LSPCA).

The contributions of all of these practitioner organizations include organized gatherings, such as conferences, symposia and professional development workshops, which provide opportunities for networking and engagement. Through face-to-face (and online) events, practitioners can interact with peers, senior colleagues and researchers in the field. Such events provide opportunities for mutual sharing of practice, scholarship and research, and they provide connections with publishers and technology providers. Beyond the larger conferences, such organizations also organize smaller events such as symposia, professional development workshops and working groups that address particular issues. For example, BALEAP, the UK EAP association has a long tradition of one-day events called PIMs, which address specific aspects of teacher knowledge and practice. Often these smaller events are organized regionally, with the aim of being accessible to those who are unable to attend larger conferences nationally or internationally. In addition to their organized meetings, practitioner associations are also involved in the dissemination of knowledge through the publication of conference proceedings, and some have their own journals. As well, several have their own online discussion lists and social media feeds. Therefore, in terms of supporting the field, these organizations make a considerable contribution through the events that they organize and their publications.

However, as previously noted in the three overview studies of EAP and ESP research, practitioners, and especially practitioner associations, have received little attention in the research literature. In addition, practitioner organizations have tended to have a relatively inward-facing focus in terms of the issues that they themselves address. Their events and publications are mostly concerned with EAP practice, such as the content of curriculum, pedagogy and to a lesser extent the needs of students. While they tend to be preoccupied with the practitioner-related elements of pedagogy, these associations seem to have less of a concern with practitioners themselves, such as their pre- and in-service training, knowledge development, professional identity or their employment conditions. Furthermore, these organizations have also tended to ignore larger, macro-level sociopolitical and economic issues that fundamentally shape the EAP field and practice within it. A major structural influence that has reconfigured universities over more than two decades (and EAP centres embedded within universities) is that of neoliberal economic ideology and its resultant effects of financialization, managerialism and marketization. In response to governments' policies, universities in many contexts operate as business enterprises, adopting the organizational and administrative practices of businesses (managerialism), undertaking decision making based primarily on financial concerns (financialization) and a shifting the focus on students from apprentice academics to fee-paying clients or customers (marketization). In this wider socio-economic context, there is little or no research focus on (or body of literature relating to) EAP as an entrepreneurial activity of the university and the implications that this has for the organizational practices of EAP centres and the employment conditions, professional practice and identities of practitioners themselves.

A particularly concerning consequence of this increasing business focus of universities has been the privatization or outsourcing of their EAP provision to private companies and the resulting commodification of courses in terms of their content and delivery (Hadley, 2015). The consequences of this trend have been changes in the employment and academic conditions of staff, the recruitment and treatment of international students and related issues. In such contexts, EAP tends to be delivered as a commodified, TESOL-style offering with little or no focus on needs analysis, scholarship or research. Where privatizations and outsourcings have taken place, it often appears that increasing numbers of international students are admitted into academic courses who are not equipped with the necessary academic English competencies, a practice that can have serious effects on the mental health and well-being of such students. As Fleming (2021) notes, "some universities turn a blind eye to English language standards to get more through the door. Once in the classroom, learning becomes a painful and disorientating exercise" (30). Fleming goes on to document student suicides in Australia attributable to this international student exploitation issue. Although EAP units are central to the commercial activities and revenue-raising of corporatized and financialized universities, practitioner organizations have generally shied away from any type of critical analysis or position-taking in relation to these major structural issues, issues that fundamentally shape the organization and delivery of EAP in university contexts. These larger structural influences shape the working life and academic identity of EAP practitioners themselves, as well as affecting the welfare and well-being of international students.

Despite this lack of position-taking on larger structural issues at an organizational level, some ESP/EAP (and TESOL) organizations have *special interest groups* (SIGs), subgroups that are concerned with wider issues that relate directly or indirectly to the wider issues such as social justice, migrants and refugees, gender identity, curriculum decolonization and teacher education. The proliferation of such SIGs in recent years is a positive trend in that they allow interested practitioners a voice on issues of concern, and their organized activities constitute valuable consciousness-raising activities among practitioners. However, the work of these SIGs potentially has a limited effect in that they are additional, potentially peripheral activities, loosely related but not integral to the core concerns of the larger practitioner organizations. Their work exists at the level of defining issues where their concerns are framed as more personal, political or ethical judgements rather than embedded within a deeper explanation based on a consensus grounded in the ethics and ethos of the practitioner organization itself. While SIGs have important consciousness- (and conscience-) raising roles, the devolution of issues to such groups has two costs. The first is that the larger practitioner organization itself is able to section-off or sequester such issues (relegated to the concerns and activities of the members of the SIG) rather than addressing them more widely and taking a whole organization position. The second cost is that, as a result of this sequestration, the position-taking of the SIGS becomes a specialism; it is not part of a coherent overview of the field, based on the values and ethics of the organization. Consequently, practitioner organizations (with the exception of TESOL) tend to be silent on wider structural issues and are non-participant in larger national and international fora, where issues such as engagement with governments and ministries of education are addressed.

Concluding Remarks

Given how important associations are, or could be, for EAP practitioners, the field and discipline in terms of building a community, promoting scholarship and research, exchanging ideas and practices, ensuring courses and programmes meet standards, as well as their (largely unfulfilled) potential to act as *corporate agents* to engage in wider sociopolitical discussions that impact higher education (HE) and EAP, it is surprising just how little attention has been devoted to understanding and researching associations. It is as if, as we have argued above, associations are transparent and obvious in their purposes and functions, unworthy of examination or of a reflexive, sociological account of the roles, power and potential of associations to contribute to practitioners' agency, knowledge and values. The remainder of this chapter outlines some of major challenges that EAP associations, particularly BALEAP face, which, in turn point towards issues that require scholarship and research to enhance collective reflexivity and therefore the collective agency of associations and their members.

One noticeable feature of ELTA research is a strong orientation to discovering the interests of individual members when joining or participating in associations. This suggests one function of associations is, like any consumer offering, to satisfy individual needs and wants through, for example, offering networking opportunities, creating fora for new ideas and engaging in debates, evidencing professionalism for members and enhancing members' professional status and reputation. Clearly, none of these functions are invidious or unsurprising and associations need to be of use for members if they are to flourish. However, what is noticeable in the literature is an absence of altruism, collective political engagement or professional solidarity, with little intervention in the working conditions and lives of practitioners. Even in the chapters cited discussing leadership in associations they generally focus on professional benefits to those who undertake leadership (rather than for the association they lead) and this too skews the fact that many give up their free time and energy to support associations. The reason for this reticence to engage in the ethical and political dimensions of associations is unclear. The question of why this is the case is an important one to ask. Social justice issues are often discussed separately from the main association body and are treated as individual rather than connected or systematic structural issues; they are more visible in association discussions. Some political discussions seem to be acceptable to associations and its members but not all.

On a related theme, we have noted previously that BALEAP (and many if not all other LTA associations) are only weakly associative. By that we meant that

> there is no control over governance of EAP teaching and no control over entry to the profession, and it cannot dictate the training and education of practitioners or enforce terms and conditions of employment of practitioners. It is not international, it is not obligatory to join or conform and it has no formal authority over EAP; nor does it have a strong voice in the public domain of advocacy and policy. BALEAP and other language organisations simply do not pack a very strong punch. As a corporate agent, BALEAP cannot be considered effective. (Ding and Bruce, 2017: 187)

Perhaps as a corollary of this the number of HE EAP institutions that actively engage with BALEAP is smaller than one might imagine. For example, fewer than half of HE institutions had any attendees at the biennial BALEAP conference in Leeds in 2019 and some EAP centres seem to have little to no active involvement in BALEAP at all. The profession is weakened by this non-engagement and, again, reasons for this need exploring.

One clear example of where associations need to intervene is in relation to private providers. It should be clear from our chapter where we stand on this, but we would like to stress that private providers should have no place in an association such as BALEAP. More than sixty (and growing) universities have some relationship with Kaplan, INTO and other providers, and they threaten the existence of EAP as a legitimate academic endeavour, and, as such, they have no place or role in an association promoting EAP as a legitimate discipline and field. This does not preclude individual practitioners working in private providers engaging fully in BALEAP as they should be able to seek support, contribute and develop as practitioners, and they often have little choice but to work in these companies. However, any association endorsement of or collaboration with these companies, such as accrediting centres or allowing these companies to host BALEAP events, should be excluded. In addition, associations should also draw on their collective experience of private providers and privatization of EAP to share strategies and information to protect and support those centres threatened with privatization.

Finally, it is worth considering whether EAP is, in fact an ill-defined field of practice and, if so, what are the consequences for EAP associations. Ding (2022) draws on Bourdieu to map the field of EAP and in doing so draws on a comment from Bourdieu about agents in ill-defined fields:

> Because these posts ill-defined and ill-guaranteed but open and 'full of potential' as the phrase goes, leave their occupants the possibility of defining them by bringing the embodied necessity which is constitutive of their habitus, their future depends on what is made of them by their occupants, or at least those of them who, in the struggles with the 'profession' and in confrontations with neighbouring and rival professions, manage to impose the definition of the profession most favourable to what they are. (Bourdieu, 2000: 158)

This thought-provoking observation suggests that there is still much at stake in defining the field especially if that entails defining it in ways that suit those protagonists which are most active and powerful in the field. Firstly, associations are crucial to ensure that individuals and groups with significant symbolic and economic capital do not get to dominate the future of EAP through defining the field in ways that are advantageous to them. Associations can and should mediate different interests and agents in the field to ensure that EAP develops in the interests of all its practitioners. In Ding, Bond and Bruce (under review), we noted that more powerful and senior members of the community not only dominated discussions but also the nature and direction of discussions. This needs addressing to enable newer and more marginal members of the community to have a voice in field matters.

Finally, we have focussed on formal association and have said nothing about informal, ad hoc networks that do arise through shared interests and projects.

These are also very powerful ways to further collegiality, community and scholarship in the field and offer its participants powerful means to collectively achieve what would be impossible individually. These types of association are as crucial for the field as formal associations and, as such, also need to be understood much better than they are at present.

References

Abatayo, J. (2018), 'Developing Communities of Practice through Language Teacher Associations in Oman', in A. Elsheikh, C. Coombe and O. Effiong (eds), *The Role of Language Teacher Associations in Professional Development*, 105–16, Cham: Springer.

Alexander, O. (2010), 'The Leap into TEAP: The Role of the BALEAP Competency Framework in the Professional Development of New EAP Teachers', in IATEFL English for Specific Purposes SIG (Conference title: *English for Academic Purposes in University Settings: Teacher and Learner Competencies*), Ankara: Bilkent University.

Alexander, O. (2012), 'Exploring Teacher Beliefs in Teaching EAP at Low Proficiency Levels', *Journal of English for Academic Purposes*, 11 (2): 99–111.

Archer, M. S. (2000), *Being Human: The Problem of Agency*, Cambridge: Cambridge University Press.

Bahrami, V., M. Hosseini and M. R. Atai (2019), 'Exploring Research-Informed Practice in English for Academic Purposes: A Narrative Study', *English for Specific Purposes*, 54: 152–62.

Belcher, D. (2013), 'The Future of ESP Research: Resources and Access and Choice', in B. Paltridge and S. Starfield (eds), *Handbook of English for Specific Purposes*, 535–52, Boston, MA: Blackwell.

Bell, D. E. (2016), 'Practitioners, Pedagogies and Professionalism in English for Academic Purposes (EAP): The Development of a Contested Field', unpublished Ph.D. thesis, University of Nottingham, UK.

Benesch, S. (2001), *Critical English for Academic Purposes: Theory, Politics, and Practice*, Mahwah, NJ: Lawrence Erlbaum.

Bond, B. (2020), *Making Language Visible in the University*, Clevedon: Multilingual Matters.

Bourdieu, P. (2000), *Pascalian Meditations*, Cambridge, MA: Polity Press.

Bruce, I. (2021), 'Towards an EAP without Borders: Developing Knowledge, Practitioners, and Communities', *International Journal of English for Academic Purposes*, 1: 23–36.

Campion, G. C. (2016), 'The Learning Never Ends: Exploring Teachers' Views on the Transition from General English to EAP', *Journal of English for Academic Purposes*, 23: 59–70.

Charles, M. (2021), 'EAP Research in BALEAP 1975–2019: Past Issues and Future Directions', *Journal of English for Academic Purposes*. Available online: https://

www.sciencedirect.com/science/article/pii/S1475158521001041 (accessed 11 November 2021).

Cheng, A. (2019), 'Examining the "Applied Aspirations" in the ESP Genre Analysis of Published Journal Articles', *Journal of English for Academic Purposes*, 38: 36–47.

Davis, M. (2019), 'Publishing Research as an EAP Practitioner: Opportunities and Threats', *Journal of English for Academic Purposes*, 39: 72–86.

Ding, A. (2019), 'EAP Practitioner Identity', in K. Hyland and L. L. C. Wong (eds), *Specialised English: New Directions in ESP and EAP Research and Practice*, 63–76, Abingdon: Routledge.

Ding, A., and G. Campion (2016), 'EAP Teacher Development', in K. Hyland and P. Shaw (eds), *The Routledge Handbook of English for Academic Purposes*, 547–59, Abingdon: Routledge.

Ding, A., and I. Bruce (2017), *The English for Academic Purposes Practitioner: Operating on the Edge of Academia*, Basingstoke: Palgrave.

Ding, A., B. Bond and I. Bruce (2022). '"Clearly You Have Nothing Better to Do with Your Time Than This': A Critical Historical Exploration of Practitioners' Discussions on the BALEAP Mailing List', *Journal of English for Academic Purposes*.

Elsheikh, A., and O. Effiong (2018), 'Teacher Development through Language Teacher Associations: Lessons from Africa', in A. Elsheikh C. Coombe and O. Effiong (eds), *The Role of Language Teacher Associations in Professional Development*, 71–86, Cham: Springer.

A. Elsheikh, C. Coombe and O. Effiong (eds) (2018), *The Role of Language Teacher Associations in Professional Development*, Cham: Springer.

Elsted, F. J. (2012), 'An Investigation into the Attitudes and Attributes That can Support Teachers in Their Transition from General English to English for Academic Purposes', unpublished Masters thesis, The University of Essex, UK.

Errey, L., and M. A. Ansell (2001), 'The MA in EAP and ESP. BALEAP PIM Reports, 7'. Available online:http://www.uefap.com/baleap/pimreports/2001/bath/errey_ansel.htm (accessed 11 November 2021).

Fleming, P. (2021), *Dark Academia: How Universities Die*, London: Pluto Press.

Flowerdew, J. (2019), 'Power in English for Academic Purposes', in K. Hyland and L. L. C. Wong (eds), *Specialised English: New Directions in ESP and EAP Research and Practice*, 50–62, Abingdon: Routledge.

Fulcher, G. (2009), 'The Commercialisation of Language Provision at University', in J. C. Alderson (ed.), *The Politics of Language Education: Individuals and Institutions*, 125–46, Bristol: Multilingual Matters.

Hadley, G. (2015), *English for Academic Purposes in Neoliberal Universities: A Critical Grounded Theory*, Heidelberg: Springer.

Hall, D. R. (2013), 'Teacher Education for Languages for Specific Purposes', in C. A. Chapelle (ed.), *Encyclopedia of Applied Linguistics*, 5537–42, Oxford: Blackwell.

Hamp-Lyons, L. (2011a)., 'Editorial', *Journal of English for Academic Purposes*, 10 (1): 2–4.

Hamp-Lyons, L. (2011b), 'English for Academic Purposes', in E. Hinkel (ed.), *Handbook of Research in Second Language Teaching and Learning*, Vol. II, 89–105, New York: Routledge.

Hamp-Lyons, L., and K. Hyland (2005), 'Some Further Thoughts on EAP and JEAP', *Journal of English for Academic Purposes*, 4 (1): 1–4.

Hutchinson, T., and A. Waters (1987), *English for Specific Purposes: A Learning-Centred Approach*, Cambridge: Cambridge University Press.

Hyland, K. (2012), 'The Past Is the Future with the Lights On: Reflections on AELFEs 20th birthday', *Iberica*, 42: 29–42.

Hyland, K. (2018), 'Sympathy for the Devil? A Defence of EAP', *Language Teaching*, 51 (3): 383–99.

Hyland, K., and F. K. Jiang (2021), 'A Bibliometric Study of EAP Research: Who Is Doing What, Where and When?', *Journal of English for Academic Purposes*, 49: 16–22. https://doi.org/10.1016/j.jeap.2020.100929.

Johns, T. F. (1981), 'Some Problems of a World-wide Profession', in J. McDonough and T. French (eds), *The ESP Teacher: Role, Development and Prospects*, 16–22, London: British Council English Teaching Information Centre, ELT document 112.

Jones, C. T. (2020), 'The Position and Professional Status of the Tutor of English for Academic Purposes in Higher Education', unpublished Ph.D. thesis, University of Cardiff, UK.

Kaivanpanah, S., S. M. Alavi, I. Bruce and S. Y. Hejazi (2021), 'EAP in the Expanding Circle: Exploring the Knowledge Base, Practices, and Challenges of Iranian EAP Practitioners', *Journal of English for Academic Purposes*, 50. https://doi.org/10.1016/j.jeap.2021.100971.

Krzanowski, M. (2001), 'S/he Holds the Trinity/UCLES Dip: Are They Ready to Teach EAP', Conference *Teacher Training for EAP*, Bath: University of Bath.

Lamb, T. (2012), 'Language Associations and Collaborative Support: Language Teacher Associations as Empowering Spaces for Professional Networks', *Innovation in Language Learning and Teaching*, 6 (3): 287–308.

Li, Y., and L. Wang (2020), 'Chinese Teachers' Perception of How TESOL Differs from Teaching EAP', *Indonesian Journal of Applied Linguistics*, 10 (2): 562–70. https://doi.org/10.17509/ijal.v10i2.28609.

Liu, Y., and G. Hu (2021), 'Mapping the Field of English for Specific Purposes (1980–2018): A Co-Citation Analysis', *English for Specific Purposes*, 61: 97–116.

MacDonald, J. (2016), 'The Margins as Third Space: EAP Teacher Professionalism in Canadian Universities', *TESL Canada Journal*, 34 (11): 106–16.

Martin, P. (2014), 'Teachers in Transition: The Road to EAP', in P. Breen (ed.), *Cases on Teacher Identity, Diversity, and Cognition in Higher Education*, 287–315, Hershey, PA: Information Science Reference.

Morgan, B. (2009), 'Fostering Transformative Practitioners for Critical EAP: Possibilities and Challenges', *Journal of English for Academic Purposes*, 8 (2): 86–99.

Motteram, G. (2016), 'Membership, Belonging, and Identity in the Twenty-First Century', *ELT Journal*, 70 (2): 150–9.

Paran, A. (2016), 'Language Teacher Associations: Key Themes and Future Directions', *ELT Journal*, 70 (2): 127–36.

Post, D. (2010), *The Transition from Teaching General English to English for Academic Purposes: An Investigation into the Challenges Encountered by Teachers*, Bath: University of Bath.

Riazi, A. M., H. Ghanbar and I. Fazel (2020), 'The Contexts, Theoretical and Methodological Orientation of EAP Research: Evidence from Empirical Articles Published in the Journal of English for Academic Purposes', *Journal of English for Academic Purposes*, 48. https://doi.org/10.1016/j.jeap.2020.100925.

Rimmer, W., and A. Floyd (2020), 'Teaching Associations and Professionalism', *ELT Journal*, 74 (2): 126–35.

Roberts, P. (2001), 'Teacher Training for EAP', BALEAP PIM Reports, 7. Available online: http://www.uefap.com/baleap/pimreports/2001/bath/roberts.htm (accessed 11 November 2021).

Robinson, P. C. (1991), *ESP Today: A Practitioner's Guide*, Hemel Hempstead: Phoenix.

Sarfatti Larson, M. (2013), *The Rise of Professionalism: Monopolies of Competence and Sheltered Markets*, New Brunswick, NJ: Transaction.

Shamim, F., and Z. Sarwar (2018), 'Killing Two Birds with One Stone: SPELT's Professional Development Programs', in A. Elsheikh, C. Coombe and O. Effiong (eds), *The Role Of Language Teacher Associations in Professional Development*, 87–104, Cham, Switzerland: Springer.

Sharpling, G. (2002), 'Learning to Teach English for Academic Purposes: Some Current Training and Development Issues', *English Language Teacher Education and Development*, 6: 82–94.

Smith, R., and K. Kuchah (2016), 'Researching Teacher Associations', *ELT Journal*, 70 (2): 212–21.

Strauss, P. (2012). '"The English Is Not the Same": Challenges in Thesis Writing for Second Language Speakers of English', *Teaching in Higher Education*, 17 (3): 283–93.

Strevens, P. (1988), 'The Learner and Teacher of ESP', in D. Chamberlain and R. J. Baumgardner (eds), *ESP in the Classroom: Practice and Evaluation*, 39–44, London: Modern English Publications in association with the British Council, ELT document 128.

Stevenson, M., and B. Kokkin (2007), 'Pinned to the Margins? The Contextual Shaping of Academic Language and Learning Practice', *Journal of Academic Language and Learning*, 1 (1): 44–54.

Swales, J. (2019), 'The Futures of EAP Genre Studies: A Personal Viewpoint', *Journal of English for Academic Purposes*, 38: 75–82.

Tavakoli, M., and M. Tavakol (2018), 'Problematizing EAP Education in Iran: A Critical Ethnographic Study of Educational, Political, and Sociocultural Roots', *Journal of English for Academic Purposes*, 31: 28–43.

Taylor, S. (2020), 'An Enquiry into How English for Academic Purposes Practitioners Construct their Professional Identities', unpublished EdD thesis, University of Roehampton, UK.

11

Final Reflections: Key Themes and Future Landscapes

Ian Bruce and Bee Bond

The contributors of the different chapters of this volume have addressed a wide variety of issues, providing an overview of the politics, policies and practices that relate to and shape English for Academic Purposes (EAP). Despite the diversity of the areas that they address, all support the overall idea that EAP is not an apolitical activity. EAP is not a detached academic activity practised in isolation from the influences of contemporary economic, political and social movements. Rather, it is subjected to and shaped by these influences, which are often embedded within the requirements of government and institutional policies. Taken together, the preceding chapters provide evidence for the argument that there needs to be a greater level of engagement by EAP practitioners and their organizations with the politics, policies and decision-making that shape both the field more widely as well as their individual practice.

While advancing this argument, we acknowledge that EAP practitioners and associations have always been active in constructing their field. Individual actions by practitioners in terms of their daily practice, scholarship, action research studies, critiques and involvement in associations have all helped make EAP what it is today. At a collective level, their frequent contributions to professional development sessions, symposia and conferences have been central to establishing the field and its literature. However, supported by the different chapter contributions to this volume, we are arguing here for a broadening of the focus and engagement of both individual EAP practitioners and their associations, an engagement that acknowledges (and responds to) the larger structural forces and influences (the politics, policies and practices) that shape the field of EAP within higher education (HE).

In setting out our ideas, we draw on the preceding chapters and focus specifically on issues in three broad areas: economic issues, language issues and positioning and delivery issues. In addressing these three areas, we propose that EAP engagement can take place at the micro-level (the individual practitioner), the meso-level (the language centre and the university) and the macro-level (policies of governments and international agencies).

Economic Issues

As the overarching economic issue, the financialization of universities has exercised a transformative influence on higher education for several decades. Important effects of this long-term process have been discussed in this volume. One such effect of the financialization of higher education is that of positioning students as clients and university staff as service providers. This changed staff–student relationship has influenced students' attitudes towards, and approaches to, university study, potentially resulting in a more limited, superficial engagement with knowledge and a diminution of the idea of the student as a novice academic working to be socialized into specialized knowledge areas. As noted by Jenna Mittelmeier and Bowen Zhang in Chapter 2, the financialization of HE is frequently dressed up in the ideology and rhetoric of internationalization, which claims to promote a broadening of institutional horizons through intercultural and international engagement. In reality, internationalization is often merely a justification for enhancing the financial base and revenue sources of universities through international student recruitment. Building on this discussion, the whole issue of international student recruitment is discussed by Sylvie Lomer and Ying Yang in Chapter 3, who note the dual financial role of EAP; it constitutes an important revenue-raising activity on its own, as well as being central to the assimilation of fee-paying international students into the programmes of the university, where they continue to be an ongoing revenue source.

Financialization, the overriding economic imperative that drives EAP and its downstream effects, potentially impacts negatively on students, on EAP practitioners and ultimately on the academic standards of universities themselves. The effects of the financialization imperative on EAP have long been noted, and this concern is encapsulated in Joan Turner's frequently quoted summary of the situation.

> From its outset, it [EAP] has accepted the role as an economic and intellectual short-cut … [i]t seems that maximum throughput of students with minimum

attainment levels in the language in the shortest possible time was the conceptual framework within which EAP was conceived. (2004: 96–7)

Furthermore, the ongoing problems stemming from lowering the quality (and length) of provision and weaker English language (EL) entry standards tend to be exacerbated when EAP units are privatized or EAP provision is outsourced to private companies, who, as part of their deal-making with universities, promise increased numbers of students as an enhanced revenue source.

Implications

Issues arising from the financialization of universities and its effects on EAP need to be addressed at a number of levels. At a macro-level, there is an urgent need for research to be undertaken (and publicized), which investigates the negative downstream effects of financialization on EAP, such as commodified courses, lack of needs analysis-informed programme development, diminution of scholarly activity and precarious employment practices. Also at a macro-level, EAP associations need to raise a voice with governments relating to policies around the recruitment of international, fee-paying students, internationalization and the activities of universities in this area.

At a meso-level (within institutions), addressing problems resulting from financialization requires input from EAP practitioners into all aspects of university policies and developments that involve EAP and international students, such as off-shoring, tailored courses, demands for 'language repair' and ad hoc insessional provision. Strong arguments should be advanced that experienced EAP practitioners (rather than sales and marketing staff alone) should have input into policies and practices relating to the recruitment of international students, the configuration of joint ventures with institutions in other countries or any other 'pipeline' or 'pathway' scheme aimed to increase the numbers of international students as a revenue source. However, we suggest that for practitioners to undertake this level of intra-institutional engagement requires the support of EAP associations and also the development of a code of ethical practice that can provide a solid basis for a practitioner voice and practitioner action within institutions.

Language Issues

While EAP centres and their practitioners are engaged in the development of their students' academic language competencies and skills, their work is largely framed by external policies and, generally agreed, 'industry-wide' practices over which they have no influence or control (e.g. the setting of International English Language Testing System [IELTS] proficiency levels for university entry). Policies and practices relating to international students' English language competencies and their language support are a central concern of three important chapters in this volume. Neil Murray in Chapter 4 outlines key issues relating to the predictive validity of the commonly used English language proficiency tests that provide a basis for international students' entry to universities. Specifically, Neil highlights the fact that these tests do not necessarily measure students' proficiency in the varieties of language and literacy practices that they will need when entering particular disciplines within universities. These are language and literacy practices that they often struggle to master after admission to degree courses. In addressing this issue, he then provides an account of a decentralized model for providing post-entry academic language support in the disciplines that meets these specialist language needs. In further developing this discussion about ongoing student issues related to language competency and skills needs, Chang Liu and Nigel Harwood in Chapter 5 report and comment on an empirical study that explores students' post-entry language needs in terms of their expectations of, and engagement with, university writing centres, and specifically the issue of such centres providing writing support but not providing proofreading services. Their study of the policies and practices that surround the proofreading issue in many ways provides evidence for the language struggles faced by students for whom English is an additional language (EAL) after university entry and their particular developmental needs. In further continuing this important discussion, Bee Bond in Chapter 6 draws these threads together with an apt characterization of this situation within universities, and proposes multi-level responses to language issues and students' ongoing need for academic language competency development, not just through EAP pre-sessional courses but through their subsequent years of study. Bee's nuanced discussion avoids simplistic answers and one-size-fits-all solutions to what are complex and entrenched problems. She suggests a multi-level approach by EAP centres and practitioners, based on her extensive experience of EAP practice and relevant scholarship activities undertaken at the University of Leeds.

These chapters raise issues relating to the ongoing academic language development of EAL students, addressing not only structural issues relating to these students, specifically their often-occluded, post-entry language needs, but also the structural issues relating to universities themselves in how these ongoing language needs are addressed, issues of responsibility and the various constraints that operate around offering support for students at this level. While entry tests and their predictive validity are wider systemic issues to be addressed by the whole universities sector and governments', in-sessional, post-entry academic language support is an issue that universities themselves have to address at the levels of faculties, schools, departments and programmes.

Implications

These chapters raise three important structural issues for EAP: what English language tests operationalize and measure (and what they don't), the resulting in-sessional (post-entry) student needs and the types of language support that can and can't be provided by writing centres and EAP units. Rather than being driven by conscious, articulated policies, it is probably more accurate to say that the constraints that give rise to these three issues are the result of conventionalized (and generally unchallenged) long-standing practices. Responses to each of these issues can potentially take place at the macro and the meso-levels.

At the macro-level, and in the longer term, assessment research that examines the predictive validity of proficiency tests in relation to academic language and literacy skills needs to be highlighted and further developed. However, because of the human and social issues involved (McNamara, 2001), publication and dissemination of the findings of such studies need to be extended beyond the usual journals on language testing to wider fora that include higher education publications, conferences and to administrative and managerial audiences. The negative 'business implications' of these structural issues around language needs could lead to publications in business and marketing so that the message can be communicated to as wide an audience as possible.

In terms of addressing the issue of in-sessional support for students to meet the requirements of academic study, it is important for EAP centres (and particularly those who lead centres) to be engaged and 'at the table' when it comes to policy formulation and scrutiny of institutional practices relating to language needs. At the micro-level, embedded local EAP initiatives within disciplinary contexts and the on-the-ground work of individual practitioners are probably the most important and effective responses to this area. However, as past experience has told us, embedded disciplinary actions need to be strongly supported by leadership and scholarship that constantly communicates to the wider university the fact that embedded support is not a luxury extra that can be discarded in times of restructuring and financial retrenchment, which has been the case in several contexts in the past. EAP leaders concurrently also need to be mindful that embedding EAP practitioners within schools may lead to a more dispersed and ultimately diffused identity, which, in itself, may lead to the erosion of any central status and power the language centre has developed. It is here that the importance of scholarship is again highlighted as a means of developing and maintaining a focus for EAP practitioner identity as distinct from other disciplines.

Beyond this, though, we would argue that those who work politically through their EAP practice need to go even further than addressing issues of language standards and access to in-sessional support, to a critical questioning of the power and position of English as an academic lingua franca. This is complex territory that in many ways feels counterproductive to attempts to move EAP out of the margins of the academic world as it would seem to undermine rather than highlight its purpose. However, if EAP aims to move towards a more ethical, socially just position, it is necessary to confront the uncomfortable truths behind the position of English in academic communication. This is where EAP practitioners should most obviously join forces with researchers, scholars and practitioners from Teaching English to Speakers of Other Languages (TESOL), English as a Foreign Language (EFL) and other languages – scrutinizing and questioning the continued power of the 'native speaker'; the colonial past and ongoing power structures that have led to English becoming the globally accepted world and academic language; the prejudices faced by teachers who do not conform to the standard expectations of white native speaker; the prejudices and deficit perceptions of students who do not use 'standard' English (see, e.g. Baker-Bell 2020; Cushing, 2020) or speak with the right accent (Ramjattan, 2020). The work of BALEAP's Special interest group, EAP for Social Justice, is already doing much to raise these questions and highlight where EAP practitioners can, and should, play a large role in university-wide discussions around decolonization and inclusion. However, it is important to guard against these issues being siloed as being 'dealt with' by a select group of people who have an expressed interest in social justice rather than it being an ethos woven into the ethics of a profession as a whole.

More specifically in tertiary education, we would argue that EAP practitioners need to work alongside other languages and agitate to position English as just one of many. While it is unlikely that the position and power of English as the global language of academia will diminish in the near future, this should not be at the cost of other languages. Swales (1997) raised the issues inherent in English becoming a tyrannosaurus rex in 1997; Canagarajah (2011), Garcia (2009), Li (2018) and others have suggested that a move towards translanguaging – accepting and enabling those who are able to draw on the resources of more than one language to do so – would allow for a richer form of communication. Empowering students, researchers and even established academics to draw on all their languages and linguistic resources should be viewed as a means of enriching rather than diminishing the position of EAP.

Concurrently, we would argue that, as part of the work of EAP practitioners is to enable intercultural communication between students from diverse backgrounds and contexts, another area for political and policy work would be through destabilizing the perception of English as the assumed norm for this communication. Again, this seems counterintuitive for EAP practice. However, in the context of English-speaking countries, the development of a language policy that places language learning as a core element of a tertiary education curriculum should help to shift the burden for making communication work away from 'international' students and onto all while continuing to emphasize the centrality of language to all aspects of academic work and communication.

Positioning and Delivery Issues

The relatively marginalized position of EAP, its practices and practitioners, previously highlighted by Ding and Bruce (2017), is further explored from a range of perspectives in the final four chapters of the volume. In Chapter 7, Jennifer MacDonald, through her analysis of universities' website materials and policy documents, uncovers the discursive marginalization of language instruction, international students and EAP practices. In these documents, international students are portrayed as a commodity and EAP as a facilitative service enabling university entry, which contrasts with EAP practitioners own view of the transformative role of their work. The institutional positioning and delivery of EAP is then ably presented in Chapter 8 by Richard Simpson in his discussion of the operational and ethical complexities inherent in directing and managing a large UK university language centre. In his chapter, Richard highlights the multiple areas of activity and the complex relationships involved in running a centre. He exemplifies how the economic, academic and linguistic considerations raised in earlier chapters relate to the multiple, day-to-day, operational decisions involved in building and maintaining a centre's position within a university. He also highlights some of the recurring threats to the status of EAP in higher education. The following chapter from

Michèle le Roux further demonstrates the powerful, negative impact that the neoliberal economic model within which EAP currently operates can have on EAP practitioners who are working in precarity. Precarity is an issue across higher education in general, and Michèle's highly personal account reveals it as endemic within EAP. The impact of working under such contracts is felt not only by the practitioners in question but also by students. In Chapter 10, Alex Ding and Ian Bruce focus on the need for practitioners to become more visible in the research and scholarship literature of EAP, and to develop a stronger collective voice through their associations to overcome their occlusion in the literature as a basis for addressing the wider political, social and ethical concerns that relate to their practice and their field. As part of this, it would seem important to consider the development of a code of ethics for EAP, which could address different aspects, including the recruitment and treatment of international students and key elements of EAP professional practice within universities. The development of a code of ethics by associations for the practice of EAP would provide a collective basis for a voice to universities and to governments that address the policies and practices that relate to this area of transnational education in which they are involved.

Implications

The final four chapters of the volume provide detailed views of the positioning, operation and staffing of EAP courses in higher education, focusing on a range of issues associated with these three areas. While EAP is not alone in being subject to the ideological and discursive forces that shape higher education, it is perhaps more centrally subject to those imperatives for the reason that the activity of EAP and the international students that enter tertiary study via EAP courses are seen as essential to the revenue-generating activities of universities. However, influencing and promoting change to the wider perceptions of EAP, the roles of EAP centres and their staff, like many of the other recommendations here, is a long-term enterprise.

To challenge the instrumental, financialized discursive construction of EAP at a macro-level (along with that of the roles of international students within universities), it is important that there are further, and ongoing, critical discourse analyses (following the example of Jennifer MacDonald) of the policy documents, marketing and discursive meaning-making of universities. This type of research also needs to be part of a larger critique of institutional portrayals of the whole 'business' of cross-border education, 'pipelines' of international students and the leveraging of economic advantage from English language and English-medium education by universities. A strong and consistent challenge to this type of discursive construction of international students and of EAP needs to be ongoing through research, its publication and other forms of communication, such as blogs and social media action.

Navigating the ongoing challenges of the delivery of EAP has been discussed in a number of chapters in this volume in the different sections. Issues relating to language proficiency standards for university entry and post-entry support and how to respond to them have been aired in relation to previous chapters. Also it has been reemphasized that there is not one homogeneous approach to EAP delivery, but that pathways, pre-sessional and in-sessional programmes address differing student needs, and themselves will have different configurations and require different resources. In particular, what emerges from the chapters is the importance of continuing to undertake research and scholarship, including studies of models of integration of discipline-specific, in-sessional EAP within academic programmes. However, in relation to in-sessional EAP, perhaps the greater, underlying issue (already aired in this chapter) will be work at consciousness-raising within universities that draws attention to, and highlights the post-entry academic language needs of students as well as the existing, institutional and organizational barriers to meeting those needs. This often-occluded issue of post-entry student needs that requires further development (through in-sessional EAP) needs to be rigorously researched and communicated vocally through different media to reach and penetrate the broader HE discourses.

Concerning the EAP practitioner and the politics, policies and practices that relate to their academic and employment status within universities, it seems that there is an ongoing need for collective and individual action. Precarity in employment conditions is an issue across HE as well as being a common practice in EAP. EAP practitioners in precarious employment are those who are least able to raise a voice to address the issue and challenge the policies and managerial practices that perpetuate its use. Therefore, it is essential that EAP organizations themselves (while they may have studiously avoided involvement in such 'industrial' matters hitherto) collectively develop and articulate a position on work conditions as part of professional standards, similar to the positions of other professional associations. Essentially, what is needed is the establishment of a collective voice that articulates values and standards relating to employment as part of EAP professional practice.

Final Thoughts

The chapters for this volume were written during the global Covid-19 pandemic, the consequences of which are already far-reaching. However, it is not yet clear what the long-term impact of the pandemic, the related lockdowns and restrictions on international travel will be for the future position of EAP practice and centres. What is clear is that a reliance on 'international' student fees to support all other university activity holds much greater risk than previously believed. The implications of this for EAP, as universities consider future economic options, are multifarious. It is likely that there will be a further growth of in-situ EAP – whether that be under the umbrella of English as a Medium of Instruction (EMI); from transnational agreements between universities and 'off-shore' campuses; College English programmes in, for example Hong Kong, or broader approaches to EAP that encompass Academic Literacies and support learning development for all students rather than for those labelled 'international'.

Such potential changes in the future will make it likely that EAP centres and individual practitioners will need to become even more reactive and adaptive to change. Work for practitioners wishing to move out of precarity is increasingly likely to be advertised globally, with individuals needing to be willing and able to relocate to work in different countries. This shift is also likely to reduce the current, highly problematic reliance on 'native speakers' as experts in EAP.

Centres will also need to become more flexible and also work harder to position themselves as an integral part of the university. The BALEAP commissioned report on the impact of Covid-19 on UK EAP (Bruce and Stakounis, 2021) suggests that some centres in the UK felt that they gained greater visibility and strengthened their position through their flexible and rapid response to moving teaching online during the pandemic in 2020. It will be necessary to maintain and expand this position if competition for international student fees increases. The risk of privatization will also grow as the lure of private companies' marketing power becomes more powerful. Centres, practitioners and EAP as a profession will need to focus more on the academic benefits they can bring in contrast to this private, market-driven provision.

Limitations of Our Volume

Finally, as editors we are aware that this volume is highly contextual. It provides reflections, examples and evidence from research conducted only within inner-circle, anglophone countries (with the majority of chapter contributors based in the UK), where EAP is, more or less, established as a field of study and area of practice. Within this context, as outlined above, there remains much to be explored. However, EAP or related practices (e.g. Writing across the Curriculum, College English teaching, EMI) are taught globally. The politics, policies and practices of each country and each institution in which EAP is offered will interact with the position, delivery, identity and status of EAP and EAP practitioners and their students working or studying within that context. While we hope that readers from any context will find that they can relate to and draw ideas from the chapters of this volume, we also acknowledge that voices from outside of the (UK) anglosphere are missing. This lacuna in examining the policies, politics and practices of EAP is one that still needs to be addressed in future by researchers and writers from those contexts.

References

Baker-Bell, A. (2020), *Linguistic Justice: Black Language, Literacy, Identity, and Pedagogy*, New York: Routledge.

Bruce, E., and H. Stakounis (2021), *The Impact of Covid-19 on the UK EAP Sector: An Examination of How Organisations Delivering EAP Were Affected and Responded in Terms of Academic Delivery and Operational Procedures*. BALEAP. Available online: https://www.baleap.org/wp-content/uploads/2021/06/BALEAP-Report-Covid-and-EAP-May-2021.pdf (accessed 24 November 2021).

Canagarajah, S. (2011), Codemeshing in Academic Writing: Identifying Teachable Strategies of Translanguaging Source', *Modern Language Journal*, 95 (3), Special Issue: Toward a Multilingual Approach in the Study of Multilingualism in School Contexts: 401–17.

Cushing, I. (2020), '"Say It Like the Queen": The Standard Language Ideology and Language Policy Making in English Primary Schools', *Language, Culture and Curriculum*, 34 (3): 321–36.

Ding, A., and I. Bruce (2017), *The English for Academic Purposes Practitioner: Operating on the Edge of Academia*, London: Palgrave Macmillan.

García, O. (2009), 'Education, Multilingualism and Translanguaging in the 21st Century', in T. Skutnabb-Kangas, R. Phillipson, A. K. Mohanty and M. Panda (eds), *Social Justice through Multilingual Education*, 140–58, Bristol Multilingual Matters.

Li, W. (2018), 'Translanguaging as a Practical Theory of Language', *Applied Linguistics*, 39 (1): 9–30. https://0-doi-org.wam.leeds.ac.uk/10.1093/applin/amx039.

McNamara, T. (2001), 'Language Assessment as Social Practice: Challenges for Research', *Language Testing*, 18 (4); 333–49. https://doi.org/10.1177/026553220101800402.

Ramjattan, V. A. (2020), 'Engineered Accents: International Teaching Assistants and Their Microaggression Learning in Engineering Departments, *Teaching in Higher Education*. doi: 10.1080/13562517.2020.1863353.

Swales, J. (1997), 'English as Tyrannosaurus Rex', *World Englishes*, 16 (3): 373–82.

Turner, J. (2004), 'Language as Academic Purpose', *Journal of English for Academic Purposes*, 3 (2): 95–109.

Index

academic literacies 22, 59, 73, 74–8, 111, 118, 123, 212
academic performance management (APM) 20
agents (recruitment) 46–7, 54–57, 60, 156–7

BALEAP (as association; jiscmail; PIMS) 154, 159, 166, 167, 169–71, 187, 188–189, 191, 192, 194–6, 212
Bourdieu, Pierre 74, 109, 112, 123, 170, 196
Brexit 53, 152
BRICS countries (*see also* MINT countries) 9

cash cow (international students as) 33, 48–50, 61, 143
casualization of labour 20, 166, 167, 177
casualized labour 166-7
CEFR (Common European Framework of Reference for Languages) 22, 140, 153
colonialism/ coloniality 46, 59, 134, 208
commercialization (of higher education) 28, 36
commodification 28, 36, 39, 142
Competency Framework for Teachers of English for Academic Purposes (CFTEAP) 10
competing logics (in higher education) 17
consultations (with writing tutors) 88, 90–5, 97, 97, 99–102
continuing professional development (CPD) 102, 169, 175, 186
corporatized (university) 16, 17, 19, 21, 22, 193
cost centre(s) 15, 16
Covid-19 33, 45, 51–2, 54, 59, 124, 149, 150, 154, 160–1, 166, 212
cultural capital 59, 74, 141, 185, 186
curriculum (university) 12, 29, 30, 45, 59, 60, 72, 75–8, 83, 109–12, 114, 116, 118, 120, 121, 124, 125, 132, 134, 138, 158–60, 192, 193, 209
curriculum policies 109, 114

deficit discourses 35, 59, 61, 62
deficit narrative(s) 38, 39, 53, 59
discourse itineraries 132, 136
diversity (linguistic and cultural) 34, 39, 48, 52, 53, 61, 74, 77, 120, 122, 134, 138, 141, 143, 158

EAP as a pharmakon 113, 114, 120, 121
EAP as a pipeline 115, 142, 205, 211
EAP associations 183, 186–9, 191, 194, 205
EAP centres 10, 35, 61, 78, 111, 120, 132–134, 138–144, 149, 152, 155, 159, 161, 186, 192, 193, 195, 205, 206, 207, 210, 212
EAP practitioners 10, 111, 120, 122–5, 144, 150, 160, 169, 183–5, 187, 191, 193, 194, 203–5, 208, 210, 213
education agents 47, 54, 55–7
embedding (academic literacies instruction) 74–8, 125, 159, 208
EMI (English as a medium of instruction) 9, 28, 30, 31, 32, 34, 35, 37, 38, 114, 212, 213
emotional impact (of working in EAP) 54, 113, 170–6, 185
employability 16, 57
ESAP (English for specific academic purposes) 72, 73, 75, 78, 79, 158
hub-and-spoke model 78, 79, 81, 83
ethical issues 57, 99, 104
ethics 45, 55, 92, 120, 190, 191, 194, 208, 210

financialization 14, 204

gatekeeping tests (English language) 713
global citizenship 141, 143

Global North 27, 29, 30, 37, 38
Global South 27, 29, 37, 38
globalization 30, 47, 48, 71, 133, 134

IELTS (International English Language Testing Scheme) 56, 71, 94, 151, 153–4, 157, 206
identity (of English for Academic purposes practitioners) 133, 172, 184–5, 189, 192, 193, 208, 213
insessional 124, 132, 150, 158–60, 174, 205, 207, 208, 211
instrumental approaches to EAP 134, 138–44, 210
intercultural communication/ exchange/ learning 27, 28, 39, 53, 142, 143, 204, 209
internationalization 3, 27–32, 34–9, 45, 46, 48, 49, 60, 111, 122, 132, 133–6, 138, 139, 141–4, 171, 204, 205

Journal of English for Academic Purposes (JEAP) 183, 184, 186–7, 188, 189

Kerr, Clark 12, 13

language as a pharmakon 120, 121
language centres (*see* EAP Centres)
language as a rhizome 120, 121
language policy 114, 131, 132, 135, 138, 209
language proficiency 132, 135, 138, 151, 152, 206, 211

management 9, 10, 14, 16, 17, 19, 30, 77, 78, 125, 149, 153–6, 161, 166, 173, 174
managerialism 14, 16, 17, 21, 192
marginalization of EAP 59, 61, 114, 120, 131, 159, 160, 165, 169, 177, 184–5, 186, 209
marketing 16, 35, 46, 47, 54, 82, 133, 134, 140, 141, 143, 156, 157, 207, 210, 212
marketization 3, 5, 14–16, 17, 21, 33, 36, 39, 46–8, 56, 60, 134, 150, 176, 192
massification 5
MINT countries (*see also* BRICS countries) 9
mission statement(s) 17, 52

monolingualism 131, 133, 134, 140, 141, 143, 144
multiversity 12

native speaker(ism) 104, 131, 165, 208, 212
neoliberal 13, 14, 33, 109, 117, 118, 120, 132–4, 166, 168, 169, 173, 174, 176, 177, 186, 188, 192
neoliberal capitalism 169, 173, 174
neoliberalism 34, 47, 132–5, 138, 140, 144, 168, 177, 184, 185
New Public Management (NPM) 15
Newman, Cardinal John 12

OECD (Organisation for Economic Cooperation and Development) 13, 19, 27, 30, 36
Office for Students (OfS) 155, 158
outsourcing 5, 189, 193

pathways 61, 110, 150, 155–8, 205, 211
Pennycook, A. 2, 158
performance appraisal 20
performativity 188
pharmakon (EAP as a pharmakon) 113, 114, 120, 121
precarious employment 165–7, 171, 205, 211
precarity 152, 161, 165–77, 191, 210–12
pre-sessional 37, 45, 53, 60, 61, 110, 124, 132, 137, 138, 150–4, 157, 160, 167, 172, 173–5, 206, 211
principled pragmatism 115
private providers 161, 184, 195, 196
privatization 5, 185, 189, 193, 196, 212
Professional Interests Meetings (PIMS) (*see* BALEAP) 159, 189, 192
professional networks (informal) 149, 154, 165, 171, 196
proofreading 4, 87–104

rankings (of universities) 15, 16, 17, 27, 33, 55, 61, 165
rankings organizations 15
recruitment (of international students) 10, 30, 33, 35, 45–57, 60, 62, 133, 139–43, 150, 152, 157, 173, 193, 204, 205, 210

responsibility-center management (US) 15

scholarship 10, 22, 51, 111, 119, 120, 122, 123, 124, 169, 185, 186, 189, 193, 194, 197, 203, 206, 207, 208, 210, 211
scholarship of teaching and learning (SoTL) 10
social justice 109, 110, 166, 177, 193, 195, 208
special interest groups (SIGs) 110, 193
student consumerism 19
student experience 18, 45, 134, 144
student mobility 30, 33, 46
student satisfaction 47
student voice 18

students as clients 14, 18, 204
students as consumers 15, 18, 19, 47, 56
students as customers 36

translanguaging 209

UNESCO 13
university rankings 15

visa regulations 30, 52, 54, 56, 60, 61, 109–10, 152–3, 154, 175
Von Humboldt, Wilhelm 11, 12

Williams, J. 18
workload allocation models 20
World Bank 13, 19
writing tutors 87–90, 93–100

www.ingramcontent.com/pod-product-compliance
Lightning Source LLC
Chambersburg PA
CBHW062219300426
44115CB00012BA/2127